URBAN CRIME PREVENTION, SURVEILLANCE, AND RESTORATIVE JUSTICE

Effects of Social Technologies

URBAN
CRIME
PREVENTION,
SURVEILLANCE,
AND
RESTORATIVE
JUSTICE

Effects of Social Technologies

EDITED BY

Paul Knepper   Jonathan Doak   Joanna Shapland

CRC Press
Taylor & Francis Group
Boca Raton   London   New York

CRC Press is an imprint of the
Taylor & Francis Group, an **informa** business

CRC Press
Taylor & Francis Group
6000 Broken Sound Parkway NW, Suite 300
Boca Raton, FL 33487-2742

© 2009 by Taylor & Francis Group, LLC
CRC Press is an imprint of Taylor & Francis Group, an Informa business

---

Library of Congress Cataloging-in-Publication Data

Urban crime prevention, surveillance, and restorative justice : effects of social technologies / author/editor(s), Paul Knepper, Jonathan Doak, and Joanna Shapland.
    p. cm.
Includes bibliographical references and index.
ISBN 978-1-4200-8437-5
  1. Crime prevention. 2. Restorative justice. 3. Electronics in crime prevention. 4. Electronic surveillance--Social aspects. 5. Social control. 6. Criminology. I. Knepper, Paul. II. Doak, Jonathan. III. Shapland, Joanna, 1950-

HV7431.U73 2009
364.4--dc22   2008030572

Visit the Taylor & Francis Web site at
http://www.taylorandfrancis.com

and the CRC Press Web site at
http://www.crcpress.com

Table of Contents

Preface

The chapters in this volume began as papers presented at the conference "Celebrating 30 Years of Criminology at the University of Sheffield," which took place in September 2006. The occasion brought together current staff and students, former staff, alumni, and friends of the Centre for Criminological Research (CCR). The 30-year period in the conference title marked the establishment of the Centre, but the tradition of criminology at Sheffield actually began a decade or so earlier.

Criminology emerged from within the Faculty of Law, which was organized shortly after the formation of the university. As constituted under the Royal Charter of 1905, the University of Sheffield had four faculties (applied science, arts, pure science, and medicine). The Faculty of Law was added in 1909 when the Privy Council approved the establishment of a professor and two lecturers in law. For many years, the character of the law faculty remained local, consistent with the prewar pattern of the university and other provincial law departments. The number of law students remained small, as did the number of full-time staff; the course in law included a number of staff who combined law teaching with the practice of law. In the decades after the war, the Department of Law expanded under the administration of Roy Marshall. Marshall recruited several members of staff, including John Wood and David McClean, who took an interest in criminology. John Wood had practiced criminal law and was interested in the working of courts and criminal procedures. He coauthored with David McClean a book about the practice of criminal law entitled *Criminal Justice and the Treatment of the Offender* (1969).

In the 1960s, within the context of university expansion across the United Kingdom generally, the University of Sheffield outlined a strategy for "growth point" subjects. Wood suggested criminology and the university agreed; the administration created a lectureship and research assistantship in criminology. In 1968, Anthony Bottoms was appointed to the lectureship, making him the first specialist lecturer in criminology at Sheffield, and John Baldwin received the assistantship. Bottoms initiated what would become an established practice, that of using the city as a site for research. The Sheffield Study on Urban Social Structure and Crime represented the first study of urban crime in a British city to include all the major council estates and it was probably the largest study of urban crime patterns since the Chicago studies. This study became *The Urban Criminal*, by Baldwin and Bottoms. Rob Mawby, who succeeded Baldwin in the assistantship in 1972, worked on a crime survey in the city, one of the first of such surveys conducted in the United Kingdom. His book, *Policing the City* (1979)—the second to appear from the Sheffield crime survey—became one of the most important studies in the debate about police-generated crime statistics. Mawby also produced an early evaluation of situational crime prevention involving vandalism of telephone kiosks in Sheffield's city center.

Criminology remained a growth point for most of the 1970s. Two new lectureships were approved, and these were filled by Ian Taylor and Paul Wiles. Ian Taylor was one of the "anarchist, irreverent" sociologists interested in the study of social deviance. Although *The New Criminology* (1973), co authored with Paul Walton and Jock Young, was written over the course of more than 2 years, and much of it before Taylor arrived in Sheffield, the preface suggests the book "would never have emerged" without meetings among the authors at Sheffield's Broomhill Tavern. Taylor also completed a PhD at Sheffield, some of the material of which became *Law and Order: Arguments for Socialism* (1981). In 1971, the Criminology Unit initiated a graduate course in criminology within the LLM curriculum, and a year later, established the MA in criminological studies. Colin Sumner was one of the first students to complete the course.

The opening of the Centre for Criminological Studies in 1976 signified the status of criminology within the university. When the Centre opened, it represented the third such center for research and teaching in criminology at British universities. The first, the Institute of Criminology at the University of Cambridge, opened in 1959, and the second, the Department of Criminology at the University of Edinburgh, opened in 1974. To mark the occasion of the inauguration of the Sheffield Centre, the criminologists at Sheffield welcomed Nils Christie from the University of Oslo. He received an honorary degree of doctor of laws and gave the foundation lecture entitled "Conflicts as Property: Societies Described through Their Types of Crime Control." Stan Cohen celebrates this event as an important moment in the rejection of "correctionalism" within British criminology. In the first chapter of *Against Criminology*, Cohen writes: "When the Norwegian sociologist Nils Christie, a leading criminologist and abolitionist, was invited to receive an honorary degree from the University of Sheffield and open its Centre of Criminology, he began his speech by saying that our proper role should be to close, not to open, such centres." Christie's lecture, published in the *British Journal of Criminology* (1977), has become one of the most widely cited in criminology.

Four years later, the Centre became the Centre for Criminological and Socio-Legal Studies, directed by Norman Lewis. The staff established an MA in sociolegal studies as a parallel to the MA in criminological studies, and the MA in criminological studies was (a few years later) discontinued in favor of the MA in sociolegal studies. This configuration was meant to support research by specialists in criminology as well as encourage empirical research into the legal system on the part of the law faculty. The center brought together "criminologists, penologists, public lawyers, sociologists of law and experts in research methodology." In 1983, Sheffield had a chair in criminology and some nine lecturers, research fellows, and other full-time staff conducting criminological research. In an article describing "Criminological Research in Great Britain" to appear in *Crime and Justice* that year, John Croft explained the "identifiable concentration is to be found in institutes, centers, or departments in…Cambridge, Edinburgh, London, Oxford and Sheffield."

Funded research projects in the early 1980s included studies of policing and gender. Tony Jefferson, who arrived from the University of Birmingham's Centre for Contemporary Cultural Studies, directed a project with Roger Grimshaw, funded by the Home Office and Cobden Trust, dealing with policing. Jefferson also directed a study with Monica Walker looking at ethnic minorities and the criminal justice system; it was funded by the Social Science Research Council (SSRC), forerunner of the Economic and Social Research Council (ESRC). These research projects led to *Interpreting Policework* (1987) and *Controlling the Constable* (1984), both co-written with Roger Grimshaw, and *The Case Against Paramilitary Policing* (1990). Carol Smart received SSRC funding for her study of sex differences and the law, a feminist analysis of the development of family law and regulation of sexual behavior in postwar Britain. Her book, *Women, Crime and Criminology* (1976), was the first feminist critique of criminology to appear in British criminology. She submitted her research on law and reproduction of patriarchal relations for the PhD in 1983. Paul Wiles and Sue Edwards received SSRC funding for a study of the routine management of discretion in the sentencing of female offenders. Jacqueline Dunn and Paul Wiles undertook a study, with ESRC support, dealing with the transition of young women from school to the crime.

In the 1980s, the Centre welcomed American criminologist Hal Pepinsky as a visiting researcher. Pepinsky spent 6 months in 1982 gathering data about policing and crime in Sheffield and published his work in *Contemporary Crises*. A number of organizational changes occurred, leading to a new course offering and some new synergy in research. In 1984, Tony Bottoms left to become Wolfson Professor of Criminology and director of the Institute of Criminology at Cambridge. Michael Cavadino and James Dignan inherited Bottoms's teaching on penal policy and a seminar entitled "the penal crisis." They subsequently created an undergraduate offering along similar lines, and to compensate for the lack of a suitable text, produced *The Penal System* (1992). International sales of the book prompted their most recent work on comparative penal legal systems. The joint center, amalgamating criminology and sociolegal studies, continued until 1985 when it split into the Centre for Criminological and Legal Research, directed by Paul Wiles, and the Centre for

Socio-Legal Studies, directed by Norman Lewis. The Centre for Criminological and Legal Research developed a BA (later LLB) in law and criminology.

Two years later, Sheffield hosted the first British Criminology Conference, which has now become the annual conference of the British Society of Criminology. Beginning in 1964, the Cambridge Institute of Criminology had hosted national conferences in criminology on a biennial basis. These conferences took place in Cambridge and served as a national catalyst for criminology. However, by the late 1970s, they had become less popular, and by the 1980s, had ceased altogether. Part of this reflected growing divisions within criminology. At the third Cambridge criminology conference in 1968, a group of sociologists broke away to form the National Deviancy Conference. Originally convened several times a year in cities across the United Kingdom (including Sheffield), NDC symposia attracted wide support. However, before the end of the 1970s, the original framework had disintegrated and NDC members had stopped meeting at well. It was suggested by Paul Wiles and Joanna Shapland that a new initiative was necessary to have a national meeting. Tony Bottoms was appointed to chair a working group of representatives from all the then existing criminology centers to provide an initial framework for the conferences; and Roger Hood, then president of the British Society of Criminology, was highly supportive. Sheffield agreed to host the first meeting, and the effort attracted funding from the Home Office and Scottish Office.

The British Criminology Conference took place at Tapton Hall in July 1987. Given the division of loyalties that had characterized British criminology, it was far from clear who, or whether anyone, would participate. However, the conference proved to be a great success with some 250 participants. It brought together, for the first time in a number of years, people from institutes of criminology, government research departments, and departments of sociology, law, psychology, social policy, and psychiatry. Subsequent conferences at the University of the West of England (1989), followed by York University (1991), and Cardiff University (1993), attracted even greater numbers of papers and participants; and it was recognized that the conferences needed a firmer structural footing. The conferences were adopted by the British Society of Criminology and have continued, now on an annual footing.

About this time, Paul Wiles and Tony Bottoms received Home Office funding for their study of communities and crime. This research examined the relationship between housing and crime in Sheffield and furthered research first started by Bottoms in the 1970s. It became the basis for their chapter on "environmental criminology" to appear in the *Oxford Handbook of Criminology*. Wiles later developed an interest in geographical information systems-based crime analysis and, with colleagues from Sheffield University's Department of Town and Regional Planning, published a study comparing crime patterns in Sheffield over a 30-year period from 1965. Wiles became professor of criminology and dean of the Faculty of Law at Sheffield, before leaving (in 1999) to become chief scientific advisor to the Home Office and director of research, development and statistics.

During the 1990s, several new staff joined the Centre. Iain Crow had previously headed research at NACRO, the national organization for offender rehabilitation and crime prevention. He has pursued research on drug use, "race" and criminal justice, offenders and unemployment, and community safety. One of his evaluation research projects, completed with Tamsin Stubbing, examined Sheffield Youth Court's fast-tracking scheme for persistent offenders. Joanna Shapland moved to Sheffield after several years at the Centre of Criminological Research at Oxford and became professor of criminal justice in 1983. She is the current director of the CCR. Shapland brought the editorship of the *British Journal of Criminology* to Sheffield and, subsequently, the *International Review of Victimology*. During the 1990s, she worked on policing, crime prevention, drugs prevention, and business and crime, many of the projects involving funding from the Home Office and other sources and many being done with Paul Wiles. More recently, she has directed, beginning in 2001, an evaluation of restorative justice schemes, funded by the Home Office (now Ministry of Justice). The project evaluates three restorative justice schemes in England and Wales involving adult and juvenile offenders in the criminal justice process. Gwen Robinson came to Sheffield to work on the restorative justice research project and has since then been appointed to a senior lectureship. She has carried out research into probation, community sentences, and risk assessment.

Jason Ditton, also appointed to a chair during the 1990s, carried out one of the first empirical studies of the effect of open-street CCTV systems Britain. His research compared Glasgow and Airdrie. Ditton directed the Scottish Centre for Criminology in Glasgow and a series of research projects in conjunction with the University of the West Indies in Trinidad. Ditton's research into "fear of crime" involved a Trinidad-based, three-wave longitudinal panel survey and British-based projects focused on enabling the fear of crime questions on the British Crime Survey to measure local concerns with greater precision. Natasha Semmens, who came to Sheffield in 1998, completed postgraduate research supervised by Ditton concerning fear of crime. She joined the Faculty of Law as a lecturer and continued research in this area, specifically, into plastic card fraud and identity theft. One of the studies carried out by Semmens and Ditton assessed the seasonality of the fear of crime using street interviews conducted in Glasgow and Sheffield.

By 1999, criminologists within the law faculty initiated the MA in international criminology, reflective of Sheffield's position as an international site for research and teaching in criminology. Joanna Shapland became the UK representative on the governing council of GERN, the Groupe Européen de Recherches sur les Normativités, the leading European research network on criminology and criminal justice. International links with the University of Leuven, the University of Ghent, and the University of Oslo produced agreements for exchange of staff and students. More recently, postgraduates at Sheffield founded the first European network for postgraduates in criminology. Jamie Waters and Matthew Hall, in conjunction with researchers at the Scottish Centre for Crime and Justice Research, University of Glasgow, organized the European Postgraduate and Early Stage Researchers Working Group within the European Society of Criminology. The group met for the first time at the ESC conference in Tübingen, Germany.

In 2002, Tony Bottoms and Joanna Shapland brought Sheffield into the ESRC network for research into the Social Context of Pathways in Crime. The network has undertaken research into early years factors in delinquency (London), adolescent factors (Cambridge), and young adults (Sheffield) as well as bringing together longitudinal studies under way in Chicago, Pittsburgh, Montreal, Zürich, and Tübingen. Bottoms maintained strong ties with Sheffield, and beginning in 2002, has held a visiting professorship. The Sheffield-based research involves interviews over a period of years with 113 young adult recidivist offenders.

During that same year, the Centre for Criminological and Legal Research became the CCR. As a designated research center within the university's framework, CCR coordinates research rather than teaching in criminology. Members are drawn from various disciplines, including sociology, history, psychology, geography, forensic pathology, and health. Simon Holdaway, who had come to Sheffield as a lecturer in the Department of Sociological Studies, became the CCR's first director. During the 1980s, he directed research projects concerning the occupational culture of British police, recruitment of Black and Asian officers, race relations policy in the probation service, and resignation of Black and Asian officers from the police service. He published *Inside the British Police* (1984), *Recruiting a Multiracial Police Force* (1991), and *The Racialisation of British Policing* (1996). Holdaway also contributed to development of the BA in social policy and criminology, taught by staff from law and sociology, and establishment of a lectureship in social policy and criminology within the Department of Sociological Studies to support the course. In 2003, Clive Norris received a chair in sociology and criminology and became a deputy director of the Centre. Norris, who began his research career carrying out ethnographic study of police, has developed the sociology of surveillance. He has contributed to studies of CCTV control rooms and the "Urban Eye" project, a comparison of CCTV use in seven European cities. The *Maximum Surveillance Society*, coauthored with Gary Armstrong, appeared in 1999. Norris's work in this area brought to Sheffield a series of international conferences concerning surveillance and society. The first of these, on CCTV and Social Control, convened in 2004; it attracted

80 delegates from 16 countries, and at subsequent events in 2006 and 2008, the size of the conference continued to grow.

The Department of Sociological Studies has contributed additional expertise to Sheffield criminology. Richard Jenkins has brought his anthropological research into witchcraft prosecutions and working-class youth in the transition to adulthood to the study of crime and deviance. Alan France, a founder of Sheffield University's Centre for the Study of Youth of Youth and Childhood, codirected the ESRC-funded Longitudinal Research Network: Pathways Into and Out of Crime. Paul Knepper has written about the theory of crime prevention and carried out historical research into racialization of crime. Together with colleagues at the Institute of Forensic Studies, University of Malta, he received funding from the British Academy to study the role of the British Empire in the internationalization of crime.

Criminology at Sheffield has benefited from links with other departments as well, including the Department of History. In 2005, the CCR acquired a second deputy director: Robert Shoemaker. Shoemaker, professor of 18th-century history, specializes in the history of crime. He has directed a project, funded by the Arts and Humanities Research Council, with Clive Emsley (Open University) and Tim Hitchcock (University of Hertfordshire) to create on online edition of all trials at the Old Bailey from 1674 to 1913.

In 2008, the CCR has more than 30 members of academic staff, engaged in a wide variety of criminological and criminal justice research across eight departments of the University of Sheffield. It is very much an interdisciplinary research center, welcoming researchers taking different perspectives on crime, deviance, and justice. It looks forward to its next 30 years.

We would like to thank the contributors to this volume; all of us have agreed that royalties from this book are to be received by the CCR to support postgraduates in criminology. Finally we would like to thank Taylor & Francis Group. Carolyn Spence believed in our project from the beginning and Jay Margolis has seen this book through to completion.

Introduction

Social Technology in Criminology:
The Relationship between Criminology and Social Policy

Contents

Social Technology and Criminology

Crime prevention, surveillance, and restorative justice have transformed the response to crime in recent years. Each offers a means of responding to crime, which does not entirely rely on the traditional modes of operation of criminal justice agencies such as police and prisons. Each has brought in new kinds of workers with new skills. Each has had a significant impact in thinking about crime policy, introducing new conceptual languages and reassessing traditional aims and priorities.

Although such efforts have attracted a great deal of criminological interest, they have been discussed in separate literatures rather than as instances of a social enterprise with common features. In this chapter, we explore these three alternatives within the framework of social technology. By *social technology*, we mean coordinated action, derived from an organized field of knowledge, to achieve particular results. In bringing these three areas together, alongside further examples, within a discussion of social technology, this volume seeks to develop an understanding of the interaction between knowledge, planning, and social repercussions. This understanding provides a valuable basis for assessing proposals for social improvements related to crime.

To put the matter in a different way, the study of social technology in criminology has to do with the ethics of criminology. All of the major academic societies of criminology have adopted codes of ethics for researchers, but these refer to the production of knowledge rather than its use in society. There is a difference, as Shapland (2000) explained in her keynote address to the British Society of Criminology, between ethics in criminology and the ethics of criminology. Ethics *in* criminology has to do with adhering to protocols for the conduct of research; the relationship to research subjects, means of gathering data, and so on. The ethics *of* criminology has to do with the use of this knowledge in society; the relationship between criminologists and policymakers and the use of research as a basis for policymaking. Our discussion contributes to ongoing debates about the relationship between Anglo-American criminology and public policy concerning crime (Brownstein, 2007; Chancer & McLaughlin, 2007; Greenberg, 2006; LaFree, 2007; Tonry, 2004; Walters, 2004; Zedner & Ashworth, 2003).

In this introductory chapter, we will pursue the meaning of social technology. Specifically, we will explore each aspect: the knowledge base of criminology, the users of criminological knowledge, and the purpose to which this knowledge is put. We discuss the ethics of criminology from a combined discussion of crime prevention, surveillance, and restorative justice; and particularly, from drawing on the chapters in this book.

The Knowledge Base of Criminology

Criminology has traditionally drawn upon many disciplines, including law, sociology, and psychology. Many have argued about whether it can be taken to comprise a field of study separate from other social sciences (Newburn, 2007; Rock, 2007). However, there is clearly now a set of accepted discourses, findings, and theories that is intended primarily to bear upon crime, criminalization, deviance, and criminal justice. In this sense, criminology is an "organized field of knowledge." Within that field, the most important themes have been science—in its broadest sense of organized knowledge—and social—that crime, and so on, cannot be understood without taking on board not just elements at the individual level but also those of groups and of society. Dedication to the idea of systematic acquisition of knowledge, rather than ideology or a retreat to armchair philosophy, has characterized criminology—or at least academic criminology.

Media-Based Criminology

Academic criminology, however, is not the only source, or even sometimes the most highly regarded source, of knowledge about crime. Garland and Sparks (2000) propose that there are three sources of knowledge about crime, or three sites for the production of criminology. These are (1) the university, with social science and scholarly language; (2) the government and practice of control and criminal justice; and (3) popular culture, filtered through the media and including political rhetoric. This conception of three criminologies—academic, media-based, and governmental—provides a useful way of thinking about the current state of affairs.

After the Second World War, academic criminology enjoyed preeminence. National governments and international organizations solicited the advice of social science researchers and established institutes of criminology. The Cambridge Institute of Criminology opened in the 1950s, along with institutes at the University of California at Berkeley (1950), Melbourne University (1951), the University of Oslo (1954), and the Hebrew University of Jerusalem (1959). However, in recent years, the balance of power has shifted. Beginning in about 1970 or so, academic criminology lost ground to media-based criminology. As television became a central institution of modern life, popular knowledge replaced academic advice in the policy imagination. During the past 30 years, the presentation of crime across media formats, including television news, drama series, reality television, and feature films, has reinforced a curiously singular message: crime is a feature of modern life, for reasons that cannot be grasped; and government by itself cannot protect the public (Cavender, 2004).

It has become common for criminologists to lament the gap between what academic criminology feels it knows and what politicians do. As Garland and Sparks (2001) put it: "in the 1990s, as criminology flourishes in the academy, its influence in national penal policy appears to be diminishing." Radzinowicz (1999) pointed to this problem in his reflections on the growth of criminology as an academic field during the past half century. Beginning from its base at Cambridge, London School of Economics, and Oxford in the 1950s and 1960s, academic criminology expanded from the 1970s to the extent that virtually all British universities today offer some sort of course. Despite the success of criminology at universities, and the production of criminological knowledge through research, politicians and policymakers seem increasingly to rely on media-based imagery and politicized vocabularies in fashioning the government's response. "What I find particularly disturbing is the gap between 'criminology' and 'criminal policy', between the study of crime and punishment and the actual mode of controlling crime" (Radzinowicz, 1999). Similar comments have been made about the situation in the United States and in the Nordic countries, as well as in Australia and New Zealand. Alfred Blumstein argues that the overt and irrational politicization of crime in the United States has replaced criminological research in policy making. "The role of research findings in the public policy arena," he says, "does seem largely to have been put aside, though only temporarily one would hope" (1994).

Perhaps we overestimate the novelty of our situation. Media-based criminology has always been a powerful rival. Extending our historical view further back than the past 50 years, we can see that media-based criminology preceded the organization of academic criminology. Shoemaker (in this book) demonstrates that crime was a recurring topic in almost every form of 18th-century print. As print became more available, for the first time in English history, popular understandings of the nature of crime as a social problem were shaped more by what people read than by personal experience and reports of friends and acquaintances. Pamphlets by social reformers, such as Patrick Colquhoun and Henry Fielding, tended to exaggerate the extent of crime to justify their projects. Newspapers overemphasized violence, not only in the frequency of their reports but also in the tone and substance of reporting. Printed reports of trial proceedings shaped understandings of crime and justice, by what was left out as much as what was said. Edited versions of trials portrayed English justice as a coherent and efficient system. Shoemaker concludes that 18th-century readers approached this surfeit of information with a skeptical eye; they knew the crime problem was more complicated than reformers like Fielding made it appear. Perhaps the difference today is that criminologists are less confident of the acuity and knowledge base of the general public: they worry that media presentation is taken as reality; criminological nuance disregarded in the age of sound bites.

Critcher's analysis (in this book) concerns the moral regulation of media, rather than media portrayals of crime as such, but also contributes to an understanding of media power in relation to criminology. He reviews the rise of the film industry, comics, and videos in 20th-century Britain and America. Cinematographs rose to popularity in the 1930s and became even more popular after the war. Reaction to dramatic content was nervous and centered on the impact on youth: boys, it was felt, would be incited to commit crime and girls to indulge in illicit romance. Comic books, which included crime as well as horror, cowboy, and war genres, attracted similar concerns. The early emphasis on comics as a potential cause of criminal behavior gave way to concern about the inherent depravity of the content and its impact on children's minds. Fears about the decline of British civilization (reflecting the decline in prestige from old imperial days) and the corrupting influence of American culture surrounded comics, as they did films. After the "panic" about "video nasties" in the 1980s, however, concern over the role of media in prompting deviant behavior has waned although never entirely died; it was concluded that viewers interpreted themes metaphorically rather than literally.

Seeing the balance of power among university, media, and governmental criminologies in historic perspective suggests that explanations for the decline of academic criminology in government policymaking need to look beyond the rise of media-based criminology. Academic criminology managed to emerge despite the head start enjoyed by media-based criminology, and it thrived at a time when the cinema was already very influential. It also suggests that we ought not to underestimate, nor discount, "the public." Shoemaker and Critcher point to a British public that was, as early as the 18th century, capable of sifting and evaluating media portrayals of crime and justice. The assumption that popular views of crime represent collective ideology or false consciousness underestimates what the masses are capable of and exaggerates the role of intellectuals in promoting truth.

Preoccupation with Science and Policy

There is a difference between criminologists seeking to have a voice in policymaking and criminologists wanting to be *the* voice in policymaking. Criminologists' concern about the gap between what criminologists know and what policymakers do derives in large part from the belief that organized knowledge (science) and research present a superior form of knowledge (Blumstein, 1994; Brownstein, 2007). Conclusions made by academic criminologists, because they are drawn from scientific research, should trump those of the other criminologies, media-based and governmental. Hood (2002) urges criminologists to speak from a firm base of "scientifically rigorous" research as "this is what distinguishes criminology from other types of discourse about crime. Unless legitimacy can be claimed for this view, the 'criminologist' will be treated as just another person with an 'opinion' on the subject."

In the 1960s, the heyday of criminologists' claimed influence on policymaking, it is interesting that, despite sociological criminology's growing interest in power within criminal justice, there was little insight into criminology's own power within criminal justice policymaking. The power of the state and of the criminal justice system over individuals, both directly and through labeling, was being recognized. The power of (some) criminologists, both within and outside government, to influence those processes was not blazoned.

Thirty years ago, Christie (1977) explained what is lost when "experts" in criminal justice exercise a claim to priority based on scientific knowledge. Ordinary citizens should have a voice because of the knowledge they possess about how to resolve their own conflicts. He described how the professionals, lawyers and social workers, steal the management of conflict by convincing us we do not really know how to go about it. "Conflict thieves" promote the idea that they possess the sole, or legitimate, means of conflict resolution. Christie (in this book) returns to this theme. The success of restorative justice in recent years has seen a push (driven by those undertaking the activity) toward the professionalization of mediation and a new category of conflict thieves in the person of mediation specialists:

> I warned against lawyers here in Sheffield 30 years ago, and called them professional thieves (Christie, 1977). They still are, but are now followed by a flock of well-educated generalists on the outlook for challenging tasks that it may be possible to convert into paid work.

The intrusion of educated specialists into conflict resolution carries the danger that it will estrange ordinary citizens from the means of settling their own disputes, particularly poorer residents of cities with little formal education. This is regrettable, Christie explains, because residents of poor neighborhoods possess "nonauthorized knowledge" or "life knowledge"—the experiences of everyday life, acquired and exchanged, in homes, pubs, and shops. The gains made by the new conflict thieves result in a loss of this sort of knowledge.

These processes of professionalization are common when new fields of social activity open up (Dietrich & Roberts, 1997). Lawyers and doctors have, in the past decades, been joined by many other professionals within criminal justice. In such a newly becoming professionalized area, those workers initially in the field are keen to protect their hard-won expertise and may also seek to protect their economic activity by "drawing up the ladder" behind them and erecting new barriers to first-time entrants, involving training requirements and educational/practice tests to belong to the new professional bodies (Allaker & Shapland, 1994). If they also create knowledge that they seek to protect and not to give out to those who receive their services, then they create and perpetuate both power and knowledge asymmetries, which disempower ordinary people. Criminologists are not necessary accelerators of these processes. They could choose to empower ordinary people by making knowledge more available and facilitating discussion. However, if they choose to facilitate processes of professionalization in fields previously occupied by ordinary people, or solely to empower government knowledge through government evaluation and research, they are in effect choosing to empower particular parties in these emerging fields of the reaction to crime.

Various social thinkers have made similar distinctions between kinds of knowledge. Christie mentions Bourdieu's "practical knowledge," but there is also Oakeshott's (1962) "traditional knowledge" and Polanyi's (1958) "tacit knowledge." In Polanyi's terms, explicit knowledge can be written out in words, graphed, or expressed in mathematical formulas; the knowledge contained in a cookery book, for example. Explicit knowledge appears superior because it lends itself to precise formulation. It can be written down, stored, distributed, and accessed by various means, from books to computers. Tacit knowledge cannot be expressed directly because it exists only in use. It is an inarticulate, or prearticulate form of knowing, such as the knowledge of how to ride a bicycle. For Polanyi (1958), "we know more than we can tell." Polanyi argues for the validity of personal knowledge within the moral order: "As we know order from disorder, health from sickness, the ingenious from the trivial, we may distinguish with equal authority good from evil, charity from cruelty, justice from injustice" (quoted in Scott and Moleski, 2005). People already know important things about crime.

Curiously, criminologists approve of triangulation in the context of research methodology but seem less interested in pursuing it in relation to policymaking. Good empirical research seeks to make sense of data from various sources; conclusions are to be taken from reflection of a comprehensive range of the best available data. Similarly, good policymaking should include "data" from all sources—from scientific criminology as well as from ordinary life. It may be that in claiming a more modest role for ourselves, as one voice in a larger conversation, we have a more appropriate basis for affirming our importance in the policymaking process. It may also be that we could support different parties through the skills we possess. What we know may become more valuable, not so much by acknowledging what we do not know but by acknowledging what others know. However, triangulation of knowledge for policymaking is about more, or something other than, reclaiming the prominence criminology enjoyed in the 1950s and 1960s. It is an essential contribution to the ethics of criminology: assessment of crime policies is not solely the province of criminologists (or of politicians or civil servants) but also a matter for all those whose lives are affected by the policies.

The reaction to the belated realization of the power of knowledge and of the different weights given to different knowledge producers could result in a "bunker mentality." Criminologists might say, "Well, government and the media don't seem to want to listen to us whenever we want to speak today. They're happy to ignore us. So we'll go away and do our own thing, remain within our own academic circles, keep our knowledge to ourselves." This seems to us to be a self-devaluing of criminological knowledge. Others may not always listen; criminology's power may have diminished—but surely this does not negate criminology's results and insights. Radzinowicz (1994) also pointed out the need for criminologists to go public and keep public. If we know that certain types of initiatives in criminal justice tend to lead to certain results (e.g., talking "tough" on crime to more punitive sentences), then others may need to know this as well.

Knowledge for Crime Reduction

Do academic criminologists really know enough to justify a role in policy-making about crime? More precisely, given that crime reduction has become the major goal of policy both in North America and in Europe, do criminologists know enough about how to reduce crime? Mystery writer Dashiell Hammett rejected science as a means of understanding crime because, as he put it: "criminals are so damned unscientific." There is a lively debate among criminologists. Some criminologists insist that some research is of sufficient quality to serve as a reliable guide to policymaking (Hood, 2002; Farrington, 2000); others believe that we still have some way to go (Currie, 2007; Greenberg, 2006; Wiles, 2002).

To be sure, we do not know as much as we would like. There is much to be accomplished, but we lack certain knowledge of how to realize our ambitions. And, in a sense, our dilemma is even more serious than acknowledging the incompleteness of our knowledge base because there are ethical limits to the use of what we do know. There are good theoretical and empirical reasons for believing that those most likely to engage in crime (property crime, violent crime) will come from the most disadvantaged areas. However, using this knowledge for prevention is problematic. Using social policy for crime reduction can lead to "criminalization of social policy," the cynical view of the welfare state as justified only to the extent that it reduces crime. Rather than promoting universal welfare provision because it is a good thing to do so, using social welfare as a matter of crime prevention assumes programs are justifiable because those in disadvantaged areas are criminal or potentially criminal. It reduces the welfare state to an aspect of crime policy (Crawford, 1998).

The idea of research-driven policy has appeal because it holds the promise of making the most of crime-reduction resources and of not making costly errors or creating unfortunate side effects. Government resources can be targeted to those populations where they will be most effective. By identifying potential criminality, we can engage in crime prevention and achieve the promise of criminology itself. However, whether or not we know enough to target interventions properly, we also need to appreciate that all crime reduction efforts have societal and ethical implications—and to realize that we need to raise and to discuss those implications. One well-known example is targeted interventions aimed at "early intervention": schemes that intervene in the lives of those young people and their parents with clusters of disadvantage, that is, from societal groups who have been shown to be most likely to produce criminality in adolescence and adulthood (Farrington et al., 2006). This has been driven by meta-evaluations of research to identify "what works" in crime prevention (Sherman et al., 1998). Such interventions may "work"; early intervention into the lives of individuals judged at-risk may keep them out of criminal court. However, as Shapland (2000) points out, such measures can also be extremely intrusive. They reach into schools, houses, and neighborhoods, engaging the state in parenting, friendships, and relationships. They bring the public into the private lives of individuals and their families. Early interventions represent "interventions into people's lives, ones that can support and enrich, but ones which can also stigma-tise and control." Because they tend to be forced upon the minority by the majority, they are more like to "confine than empower." Criminologists may need to persuade others that there is a need to engage with these social and ethical issues.

Rather than focus on those thought to have the greatest likelihood of becoming criminals, would there be similar results if crime prevention could be directed toward those with the greatest likelihood of becoming victims? Research along the lines pursued by Bottoms and Costello (in this book) sug-gests that focusing on potential victims is also possible because the most likely to become future victims are prior victims. Criminological research in the past two decades has uncovered the phenomenon of "repeat victimization," the same person or property being revictimized within a specific time frame. Analyses of this phenomenon have drawn from victimization surveys and recorded crime information but have tended to examine short-term patterns (between 12 and 15 months). Using a unique data set from Sheffield incor-porating information about victims and offenders, they examined long-term trends in repeat victimization. Specifically, they examine patterns of domestic burglary repeat victimization over a period of approximately 9 years, distin-guishing between short-term and long-term risk.

Victim-centered crime prevention, however, also contains ethical and distributional power debates. Wiles and Pease (2001) point out that crime reduction policy informed by the knowledge of repeat victimization repre-sents the most elegant application of distributive justice. However, this only represents a "fair" policy if the costs of such crime reduction policies do not fall upon more disadvantaged groups. Rawls' (1971) "difference principle" insists that inequalities are justified only if they are designed to bring the greatest benefit to the least advantaged social groups. Although philosophers of distributive justice have tended not to include crime (or the currently hyped buzz-word "security") in the inventory of social goods (but have focused on education, employment, etc.), it is possible to think through this principle for crime policy. By directing crime prevention initiatives toward repeat victims, targeted crime prevention works to the benefits of the most disadvantaged, those with the greatest likelihood of becoming future victims—providing the costs of such crime prevention are provided by public funds. The difficulty is that victim-centered crime prevention measures have tended to focus upon property-based situational crime prevention measures, with costs falling on owners or tenants. Again, this is a debate that could be informed considerably by criminological knowledge but that needs to encompass in addition government, media, and ordinary people's knowledge.

Users of Criminological Knowledge

Much of the discussion about the use of criminological knowledge has centered on the state. Given the role of the state in the delivery of criminal justice, this is understandable. However, in our definition of social technology, we refer to "coordinated action" in reference to the use of criminological knowledge. Although national government remains the most significant user, or potential user, a comprehensive understanding cannot be acquired by focusing only on the relationship between criminological knowledge and government policymaking.

Rethinking the State

Rethinking the state, or national government, as the most important maker of crime policies is underway. Aas (2007), Jones and Newburn (2004), and Lilly and Knepper (1992) have outlined the parameters of "policy transfer" across national boundaries. The export and import of crime policies takes place on a global scale. In their analysis of electronic tagging, Lilly and Knepper (1992) describe an international policymaking environment that involves more than the export of policies from the United States to the United Kingdom. The environment involves a network of multinational corporations selling the technology and national governments buying into the policy.

The emerging field of "surveillance studies" seeks to make sense of the transnational context of surveillance in a global society. Computer and telecommunications technology and international political developments have made national borders less relevant. Foucault's (1977) vision of panopticism has supplied a prominent conceptual understanding. Informed by 19th-century models of the prison, he described how a few individuals watch many; the mechanisms of surveillance allowing for the observed to be watched without their knowledge and preventing the masses from returning the gaze on the few. Surveillance encapsulates hierarchical authority, the authority to enact a discipline throughout society with a coherent interior logic. The extent to which this model offers a useful representation of surveillance in contemporary society has been questioned. The British government certainly seems to want it to be so. Since 1996, there has been large-scale government investment in developing IT infrastructure of the police and criminal justice system. Previously, information technology was left to individual forces and agencies. However, in the last decade, the government has sought to place IT strategy and infrastructure under direct control by central government. This has included creation of a national digital radio system, many databases from the sex offenders' register to a DNA register, and nationally coordinated software programs for exchange and integration of information across the criminal justice system (Norris, 2007).

However, even as intense and extensive as this effort continues to be, it is only part of the vast "surveillant assemblage" (Haggerty & Ericson, 2000). There is no centralized, efficient, logical system hardwired for social control but rather "scattered systems of calculation" ranging from police agencies to banks and financial institutions, hospitals, schools, and so on. The "hard surveillance" of governments—electronic monitoring of offenders and intercepts of suspects communication—occurs alongside the "soft surveillance" of corporations and businesses, usually with cooperation if not consent. Although the information gained by such means is kept for marketing, consumer profiling, and the like, this can be accessed by governments. Institutions outside the formal criminal justice system are being drawn into the identification and apprehension of lawbreakers, and the regulating and monitoring of behavior consistent with government interests. However, this may not be the most important point. In contemporary society, the hierarchy of surveillance has been democratized. Whereas poor people continue to be subject to the surveillance systems exercised by social welfare and criminal justice, the middle and upper classes are increasingly subject to routine forms of observation. Technologies of observation allow for the scrutiny of the powerful by the institutions and the general population (Haggerty & Ericson, 2000). The extension of state control has also widened the scope of state surveillance.

Knepper and Norris (in this book) offer a review of knowledge transfer in the British Empire. Fingerprint technology emerged in the context of British India. Faced with the daunting prospect of administering a vast continent of diverse peoples, colonial administrators relied on scientific knowledge. Knowledge became particularly important after the Sepoy Mutiny when colonial authorities saw how the very little they understood about the peoples of India engendered violence and political aspirations. The inspector of police in Bengal, Edward Henry, worked out the basis of fingerprint classification, and the colonial system of administration in which administrators crisscrossed the planet brought him back to London. Once the knowledge of verifying personal identity was in hand, the Colonial Office sought to use it throughout the colonies. Consultants were sent to the small colony of Malta. Unlike India, it was tiny, it had a European population, and crime was not thought to be a problem. What did worry British authorities in Malta was that of foreigners and foreign criminality, a nonspecific fear of "the other" as inscrutable and dangerous. In this way, the attempt to introduce fingerprints occurred for similar reasons as fingerprints first emerged in India.

Criminology and Business Trade

If government officials no longer value criminologists' advice, some business managers do. Commercial organizations that seek to provide services to criminal justice or crime reduction agencies are quite interested in criminological knowledge, or more accurately, in those aspects that can be used to increase profit from trade. A substantial body of work within criminology has sought to identify one or another aspect of crime, or the response to crime, with market forces (e.g., Crawford's chapter in this book). However, criminologists have only rarely been interested in research-driven business practice and the use of criminology by business remains underresearched.

Clarke (2004) insists that criminologists should renounce the traditional reluctance to include business and industry within our remit. Many criminologists view crime prevention on behalf of business and industry as unworthy and ignoble, but this, he thinks, should change. Business and industry are the main vehicles for bringing scientific technology to everyday life, and technology represents a primary medium for criminal activity. In this sense, business has a primary role in "creating crime." As it is part of the problem, it should be part of the solution. Furthermore, businesses are the victims of a tremendous amount of crimes. Unreported crimes, from shoplifting to employee theft, consume significant resources. For the most part, businesses rely on private security to minimize their losses rather than the police (Shapland, 1995).

Crime science, essentially a partnership between business and government, has taken shape in recent years to deliver situational crime prevention. It has tended to receive a skeptical reception from academic criminology. Hope and Karstedt (2003) place the emergence of crime science within recent political history. The departure from the democratic welfare contract has brought about the demise of "the social," together with a new focus on governance issues invoking the new technologies of control. Because the crime science lacks this social element, they doubt that it will succeed. Hence, they see a social policy vacuum existing within current crime prevention discourse, such that crime prevention issues are discussed exclusively within the framework of criminal justice. Among other things, the emphasis on technological solutions to crime prevention has led, indirectly, to a decline in tolerance for minor forms of deviance (by youth and neighbors). The depletion of tolerance has, in turn, created greater demand for technological solutions. They call for rethinking crime prevention along the lines of remedying the disintegration of the moral and social fabric of society, brought about by the dismantling of the welfare state. Crime prevention policies should aim to strengthen and restore the types of social cohesion and bonds associated with crime control in modern society.

Ethical concerns surrounding the use of criminology by business are not unlike those concerning use of this knowledge by government in one very important sense. Social scientists bear a particular moral responsibility, Popper (1994) said, because social science investigations "concern the use and misuse of power pure and simple." He was thinking about the relationship between social science knowledge and government intervention, but this insight applies to the use of criminological knowledge by business as well. One of the moral obligations of the social scientist ought to be that if one discovers a social technology that endangers human freedom, the social scientist incurs the duty to not only warn people of the danger but also to pursue "effective countermeasures." Surveillance technology affords a useful example. It is one thing to criticize government interventions that impinge on individual privacy and another thing to empower individuals to maintain surveillance of government.

Of course, business and industry are already engaged in society's response to crime. Business might be considered the "fourth criminology," alongside Garland and Sparks' (2000) university-based, media-based, and governmental criminologies. Nellis (in this book) explains the way in which electronic monitoring constitutes not simply a technology but rather an "automated sociotechnical system," a technology sustained by a range of human activities, including a range of commercial enterprises. These include equipment manufacturers; staff trained to fit tags, monitor control rooms, and liaise with government; social workers (in some countries) to counsel offenders; and legal specialists and government officials concerned with gaining compliance in community supervision. Nellis examines the way in which the managerial state has empowered the private sector to pursue innovation in crime policy and how the "electronic monitoring industry" has organized itself in response: first in the United States, then in Europe. There are three types of commercial enterprises in the electronic monitoring field: technology-producing companies, operational service-providing companies, and combined technology and service-providing companies. This relationship has led to state simulation of technological innovation, transnational showcasing, and customizing new developments in telecommunications technology. These activities have brought about what can be described as "e-topian correctionalism," a mentality that envisages an expanding role for electronic/digital technology in offender management. This mentality is most evident in the relationship between the business enterprise and the managerial state, "who each simulate the other to imagine and realise new ways of regulating offenders' behaviour."

The Aims of Criminology

Finally, our definition of social technology includes reference to the aims or goals of criminology. The most important concept in this connection is that of unintended consequences, a familiar theme in sociology, emphasized by Elias (1978), among others.

Working within or against Criminal Justice: Unintended Consequences

Elias pointed out that planned change entails unintended effects. Development, in the sense of "developing societies," he explained, refers to an activity, something people do with aims in mind and an amount of planning. It is carried out by people in government posts and their associates, experts working through aid agencies and nongovernmental organizations. They tend to see economic problems, or needs, and pursue economic solutions, in the form of power-generating plants, roadways, bridges, and the like. However, "purely economic plans may fail because other non-economic but functionally interdependent aspects of a society act as a brake by pulling in the opposite direction." The development that was consciously planned may set in motion development of a quite different kind not intended by the government or others making the plans. "Planned actions in the form of government decisions may have unanticipated, unintended consequences" (Elias, 1978).

Unintended consequences can be seen in the relationship of restorative justice to criminal justice. In the 1970s, what came to be understood as restorative justice movements appeared in more than one country, initiated by groups outside the criminal justice system. In North America, Mennonites started projects aimed at bringing about "victim-offender reconciliation" and the movement later spread to United Kingdom. The process pursued the unconventional goal of "reconciliation" between victim and offender; offenders would accept responsibility for their actions and take steps to repair the hurt to their victims and community. In the process of becoming institutionalized, voluntary and church-led initiatives became dependent on working relationships with agencies of criminal justice; they could become easily distorted into offender-oriented programs. What was intended as a means of responding to conflict outside the formal system gave rise to a new category of professional conflict managers, and careerism within the new class of mediators altered the role from community representatives to individuals with personal agendas. By 1990, even as Zehr (1990) outlined his vision of a response to promote reconciliation, he warned about the subversion of visions. "As reforming visions are made operational, they tend to be diverted (or subverted) from their original intents." However, here the unintended consequences stemmed from the original aim to divert the resolution of conflicts from criminal justice—which closer ties to criminal justice then subverted. If the power of criminal justice is recognized from the outset and it is appreciated that it does have a role to play in responding to crime (Christie, this volume), then there may even be positive unintended effects.

Restorative justice also yields an example where results have been positive to the extent of bringing about reconciliation beyond criminal justice as such. Doak and O'Mahony (in this book) explore how restorative became a means of legitimizing conventional criminal justice in a divided society, Northern Ireland. The statutory youth conferencing scheme implemented in Northern Ireland followed the New Zealand model, although it placed more emphasis on the role of victims. Northern Ireland was emerging from three decades of political conflict that had brought out deep suspicion of the police, criminal justice, and political institutions generally. The Justice (Northern Ireland) Act 2002 placed family conferencing within the criminal justice system, and it became the primary means of responding to youth crime. Based on analyses from 185 conferences held between 2003 and 2005, Doak and O'Mahony found generally positive results from the standpoint of victims, offenders, and the community. They attribute this positive impact to the fact that restorative justice had become mainstream, with a statutory and institutional footing placing it at the center of criminal justice. Conferences were mandatory, not discretionary, with regard to the Public Prosecution Service and the judiciary. Restorative justice in Northern Ireland also had the added effect of contributing to the transition process from conflict to stability and normalization. Ironically, restorative justice may succeed in bringing about some reconciliation of wider social conflicts where it represents the official criminal justice response rather than a private response on the margins of the official criminal justice system.

Similarly, Shapland (in this book) documents positive outcomes of restorative justice for adult offenders in the criminal justice context. Restorative justice projects represent one of the key new policy initiatives for dealing with young offenders engaged in less serious offenses; such projects can also contribute to improving the response to serious offending by adults. Drawing on evaluation research concerning restorative justice schemes involving adults in five areas of England and Wales, she identifies three major themes: ensuring procedural justice so that communication can occur between the participants; future-oriented problem solving taking into account the problems leading to the offender's conduct and as symbolic reparation for victims; and the potential of restorative justice for restoring the victims' sense of security. The extent to which restorative justice contributes to the sense of security represents an unintended outcome. "Security" has become a primary goal of crime policy in the decades since the restorative justice projects initiated by Zehr (1990) and others in the 1970s. However, in providing a medium for offenders and victims to consider the future, restorative justice may help meet ordinary people's security needs.

How should criminologists respond to the reality of spontaneous change and unintended consequences? If criminology is to take seriously that whatever our intentions, the results of crime reduction programs will have social outcomes outside our control, then we ought to think about how best to respond. Shapland (2000) suggests that something along the lines of "informed consent" needs to emerge. The concept is a familiar step in the course of doing research aimed at gathering knowledge but less clear when applied to the recipients of policies resulting from that knowledge. Nevertheless, the principle merits consideration. Becoming the target of government crime reduction efforts should be as voluntary as becoming a subject in the research that contributed to formation of the intervention.

Spontaneous and Planned Change

A sociological process related to unintended consequences, and one that is even less understood, concerns spontaneous change within society. Government policies in the area of crime prevention, as well as movements along the lines of restorative justice, imply planned society activities. There is the sense that "reforms" or "improvements" in the response to crime result from planned, purposeful efforts. Furthermore, positive social change is invariably understood to be planned change. To overcome the failings of criminal justice at present, it is necessary to pursue different goals by a plan of action. However, as Elias recognized, some of the most positive social developments that have occurred in the past two centuries are not the result of planning. "Though there has been a progressive reduction in inequality between and within countries since the end of the 18th century, it is absolutely certain that no one consciously planned it or intentionally brought it about" (1978).

Crawford (in this book) offers an example of spontaneous change in his analysis of youth offender panels in England and Wales, intended to be a mainstream means of responding to offending by young people, which have substituted a panel drawn from the community, plus a professional youth worker, for traditional youth court sentencing. It was envisaged to involve elements of restorative justice, both in (sometimes) inviting victims to be present and in including community members in the decision panel. He attributes the rise of restorative justice in this context not to deliberate humanist reform of criminal justice but as a consequence of an emergent culture of control described as "contractualisation." Contractual governance introduced a new language of contracts to social regulation. It introduced a distinct image of human association and a discrete communication system between individuals and the state that is deeply rooted in modes of consumption. He analyzes youth offender panels in England and Wales to reveal restorative justice as an expression of contractual governance consistent with a consumption-oriented model of compliance comparable to technologies initiated to tackle antisocial behavior. Not only does this youth panel form of restorative justice present a movement outside criminal justice, it also extends from the larger and unplanned shift toward contractual governance within new modes of consumption and commerce. To understand the rapid diffusion of "restorative justice" projects, initiatives need to be framed against larger structural changes occurring within civil society and the business sector.

Conclusions

Crime prevention, surveillance, and restorative justice can been seen as social technologies with common characteristics. Understanding these characteristics contributes to an ethics of criminology, to a grasp of the use of criminological knowledge in society. Although each of these projects has its own aims and methods, involving particular histories and social contexts, they can all be analyzed as coordinated action, derived from an organized field of knowledge, to achieve particular results. Criminology has always engaged with social policy. More recently, a growing appreciation of its powerlessness and of others' occasional lack of appreciation of criminology's knowledge has tended to result in criminological navel-gazing and, for some, quiet despair. Instead, however, it may be that criminology needs to appreciate its own role and deficiencies in moderating or initiating social action. The call may be for criminology and criminologists to realize the ways in which their knowledge can sharpen and deepen the debates already being engaged in by the media, government, and business with their own knowledge. Engaging in such debates may enable the social and ethical implications of social action to come to the fore and create a new model for the bonding of science and social within criminology.

Paul Knepper
University of Sheffield

Jonathan Doak
Nottingham Trent University

Joanna Shapland
University of Sheffield

References

Aas, K. (2007). Analysing a world in motion: Global flows meet "criminology of the other." *Theoretical Criminology, 11,* 283–303.

Allaker, J., & Shapland, J. (1994). *Organising UK professions: Continuing and change* (The Law Society Research and Planning Unit Research Study 16). London: Law Society.

Blumstein, A. (1994). Interaction of criminological research and public policy. *Journal of Quantitative Criminology, 12,* 349–361.

Brownstein, H. (2007). How criminologists as researchers can contribute to social policy and practice. *Criminal Justice Policy Review, 18,* 119–131.

Cavender, G. (2004). Media and crime policy: A reconsideration of David Garland's *The Culture of Control. Punishment and Society, 6,* 335–348.

Chancer, L., & McLaughlin E. (2007). Public criminologies: Diverse perspectives on academia and policy. *Theoretical Criminology, 11,* 155–173.

Christie, N. (1977). Conflicts as property. *British Journal of Criminology, 17,* 1–15.

Clarke, R. (2004). Technology, criminology and crime science. *European Journal on Criminal Policy and Research, 10,* 55–63.

Crawford, A. (1998). *Crime prevention and community safety: Politics, policies and practices.* Harlow: Longman.

Currie, E. (2007). Against marginality: Arguments for a public criminology. *Theoretical Criminology, 11,* 175–190.

Dietrich, M., & Roberts J. (1997). Beyond the economics of professionalism. In J. Broadbent, M. Dietrich, & J. Roberts (Eds.), *The end of the professions? The restructuring of professional work* (pp. 14–33). London: Routledge.

Elias, N. (1978). *What is sociology?* London: Hutchinson.

Farrington, D. (2000). Explaining and preventing crime: The globalization of knowledge. *Criminology, 38,* 1–24.

Farrington, D., Coid, J., Harnett, L., Jolliffe, D., Soteriou, N., Turner, R., & West, D. (2006). *Criminal careers up to age 50 and life success up to age 48: New findings from the Cambridge Study in Delinquent Development* (Home Office Research Study 299). London: Home Office. Available at the Home Office Web site, http://www.homeoffice.gov.uk/rds/pdfs06/hors299.pdf

Foucault, M. (1977). *Discipline and punish.* London: Allen Lane.

Garland, D., & Sparks, R. (2000). Criminology, social theory, and the challenge of our times. *British Journal of Criminology, 40,* 189–204.

Greenberg, D. (2006). Criminological research and crime control policy: Not a marriage made in heaven. *Criminology and Public Policy, 5,* 203–212.

Haggerty, K., & Ericson, R. (2000). The surveillant assemblage. *British Journal of Sociology, 51,* 605–622.

Hood, R. (2002). Criminology and penal policy: The vital role of empirical research. In A. E. Bottoms & M. Tonry (Eds.), *Ideology, crime and criminal justice: A symposium in honour of Sir Leon Radzinowicz* (pp. 153–172). Cullompton: Willan.

Hope, T., & Karstedt, S. (2003). Towards a new social crime prevention. In H. Kury & J. Obergfell-Fuchs (Eds.), *Crime prevention: New approaches* (pp. 461–489). Mainz: Weisser Ring.

Jones, T., & Newburn, T. (2004). The convergence of US and UK crime control policy: Exploring substance and process. In T. Newburn & R. Sparks (Eds.), *Criminal Justice and Political Cultures* (pp. 123–151). Cullompton: Willan.

LaFree, G. (2007). Expanding criminology's domain: The American Society of Criminology 2006 Presidential Address. *Criminology, 45,* 1–31.

Lilly, J. R., & Knepper, P. (1992). An international perspective on the privatisation of corrections. *The Howard Journal of Criminal Justice, 31,* 174–191.

Newburn, T. (2007). Understanding crime and criminology. In *Criminology* (pp. 2–19). Cullompton: Willan.

Norris, C. (2007). The intensification and bifurcation of surveillance in criminal justice policy. *European Journal of Criminal Policy and Research, 13,* 139–158.

Oakeshott, M. (1962). *Rationalism in politics.* New York: Basic Books.

Polanyi, M. (1958). *The logic of liberty: Reflections and rejoinders.* Chicago: University of Chicago Press.

Popper, K. (1994). *The myth of the framework.* London: Routledge.

Radzinowicz, L. (1999). *Adventures in criminology.* London: Routledge.

Radzinowicz, L. 1994. Reflections on the state of criminology. *British Journal of Criminology, 34,* 99–104.

Rawls, J. (1971). *A theory of justice.* Cambridge: Harvard University Press.

Rock, P. (2007). Sociological theories of crime. In M. Maguire, R. Morgan, & R. Reiner (Eds.), *The Oxford handbook of criminology* (4th ed., pp. 3–42). Oxford: Oxford University Press.

Scott, W., & Moleski, M. (2005). *Michael Polanyi: Scientist and philosopher.* Oxford: Oxford University Press.

Shapland, J. (1995). Preventing retail-sector crimes. In *Crime and justice: A review of research* (Vol. 19, pp. 263–342). Chicago: University of Chicago Press.

Shapland, J. (2000). Reducing crime: Implications for criminology present and criminology's futures. In G. Mair & R. Tarling (Eds.), *The British Criminology Conference: Selected Proceedings.* Liverpool: British Society of Criminology, 1–15.

Sherman, L., Gottfredson, D., MacKenzie, D., Eck, J., Reuter, P., & Bushway, S. (1998). *What works, what doesn't, what's promising.* Washington, DC: National Institute of Justice.

Walters, R. (2004). *Deviant knowledge: Criminology, politics and policy.* Cullompton: Willan.

Wiles, P. (2002). Criminology in the 21st century: Public good or private interest? *Australian and New Zealand Journal of Criminology, 35,* 238–252.

Wiles, P., & Pease, K. (2001). Distributive justice and crime. In R. Matthews & J. Pitts (Eds.), *Crime, disorder and community safety* (pp. 219–240). London: Routledge.

Zedner, L., & Ashworth, A. (Eds.). (2003). *The criminological foundations of penal policy: Essays in honour of Roger Hood.* Oxford: Oxford University Press.

Zehr, H. (1990). *Changing lenses: A new focus for crime and justice.* Scottsdale, PA: Herald Press.

Print Culture and the Creation of Public Knowledge about Crime in 18th-Century London

1

ROBERT SHOEMAKER

Contents

Introduction

Eighteenth-century London was the first modern city. At the start of the century, it already had a population of more than half a million people; it experienced high levels of immigration; and there were significant possibilities for social mobility, both upward and downward. It had an emerging nonofficial "public sphere" of debate, stimulated by the development of a multifaceted print culture. Encouraged by the end of prepublication censorship in 1695 and growing levels of literacy among both men and women, early 18th-century London witnessed an explosion of printed literature, not just in the traditional forms of the book, pamphlet, broadside, and ballad, but also in new genres such as the newspaper, periodical, and novel, and crime was a recurring theme in almost every form of 18th-century print.

This explosion of printed literature shaped public attitudes toward crime. For the first time in English history, popular understandings of the nature of crime as a social problem were shaped more by what people read than by personal experience and oral reports. As the Reverend Robert Kirk observed in 1689 or 1690, "Few in [London] know the fourth parts of its streets, far

1

less can they get intelligence of the hundredth part of the special affairs and remarkable passages in it, unless by public printed papers" (Brett-James, 1935). The references to crime in Londoners' diaries and correspondence from this period are relatively rare and based only to a limited extent on their personal experiences of crime or of crimes committed on their neighbors and acquaintances. Of the few crimes they did record, burglaries and street fights, not the robberies and unprovoked assaults that were the subject of so much public concern, were the most common. A similar conclusion emerges from analyzing the geographical location of the crimes prosecuted at the Old Bailey, London's court for trying felony indictments. Even a notorious crime hot spot like Drury Lane, with its disorderly houses and brothels, was the location of, on average, only two crimes a year tried at the Old Bailey during the 18th century—and some neighboring streets and alleys had none. Similar low levels of prosecutions occurred in three streets known as centers of receiving stolen goods, vice, and theft on the northeastern border of the city, just outside its jurisdiction, and in a cluster of five notorious streets and alleys in the former ecclesiastical sanctuary of Whitefriars, known as Alsatia.* Although many crimes went unreported (and in many more cases, the culprits were never identified), it is significant that so few crimes in these neighborhoods led to publicly reported prosecutions. Instead of through personal experience or local knowledge, 18th-century residents of the metropolis learned about crime predominantly through printed literature, either directly through reading or indirectly through hearing reports from other readers.

What some learned from this literature was that crime, particularly violent crime, was a serious and growing problem. Consequently, diarists and correspondents recorded their and others' fears of travelling. Georg Lichtenberg, a German visitor, wrote to a bookseller and publisher back home in 1770 that "not an evening passes when not only one, but three, four, or five robberies are committed by footpads" (Mare & Quarrell, 1938). Similarly, the author and politician Horace Walpole reported in a letter to Horace Mann in 1782 that "we are in a state of war...I mean from the enormous profusion of housebreakers, highwaymen, and footpads—and what is worse, from the savage barbarities of the two latter, who commit the most wanton cruelties....The grievance is so crying, that one dare not stir out after dinner, but well armed" (Walpole, 1937–1938). These statements may be exaggerated, but they are important because, in the context of the unusually inclusive local governments of the City of London and the suburban parishes, Londoners

---

* Calculations based on the "place and map search" function of the Old Bailey Proceedings Online (www.oldbaileyonline.org; hereafter OBP). The three streets on the northeastern border of the city referred to are Houndsditch, Petticoat Lane, and Rosemary Lane; the five streets in Alsatia are Mitre Lane, Fetter Lane, Ram Alley, Mitford Lane, and Hanging Sword Alley.

holding such views provided support and pressure for important innovations in policing and punishment in this period, notably reforms to the night watch, the creation of the Bow Street Runners, and the introduction of transportation on a systematic basis (Beattie, 2001; Reynolds, 1998). However, not everyone came to the same conclusion. The French visitor Pierre-Jean Grosley, who visited London during a postwar crime wave in 1763, reported back to his compatriots that although the English police system was weak and low-level offenses such as prostitution and riots were common, serious crime was *not* a problem: "London is the only great city in Europe where neither murders nor assassinations happen" (1772). We need to investigate how observers came to such disparate conclusions and particularly to ask how discussions of crime in print contributed to the construction of public attitudes toward crime. In considering this issue, it is important to be aware of the wide range of print genres in which crime was discussed and to pay attention to evidence of reader response, where such evidence survives. Before 1772, no statistics on the number of crimes prosecuted were available, so it was the *qualitative* descriptions of crime, and the accumulated impact of large numbers of individual crime reports, that were important. This chapter will focus on four genres: social policy pamphlets, newspapers, printed trial reports, and criminal biographies. A more comprehensive study of the literature about crime would also need to consider fictional representations including ballads, novels, and satirical prints, but these would present different problems of interpretation.

Social Policy Pamphlets and Newspapers

The most dramatic, but perhaps least influential (in part owing to the small number published), accounts in print of the crime problem were the social policy pamphlets that attempted to influence government policy. As Ruth Paley (1989) argued, in this literature, "the printed word was all too often the instrument of the propagandist." Exaggerated statements, frequently unfavorably comparing London's unsafe streets with foreign places perceived to be less civilized, were used to back calls for government action. At the start of the century, *Hanging Not Punishment Enough for Murtherers, High-Way Men, and House Breakers*, which outlined several penal reforms for "the perusal of the two Houses of Parliament," complained about "the lamentable increase of high-way-men, and house-breakers among us" and claimed that "if some remedy [is] not found to stop this growing evil, we shall shortly not dare to travel in England, unless, as in the desarts [sic] of Arabia, it be in large companies, and arm'd" (1701). In 1751, the author and magistrate Henry Fielding, whose reputation in government circles had suffered a setback two years earlier owing to his mishandling of the Bosavern

Penlez case (when, with Fielding's support, a young man was probably wrongly convicted and hanged for participation in a riot), sought (with limited success) to influence the newly formed parliamentary committee investigating ways of reducing violent crime by publishing his *An Enquiry into the Causes of the Late Increase of Robbers* (Paley, 1989). In justifying his case for various moral, judicial, and penal reforms, Fielding wrote that the "streets of this town, and the roads leading to it, will shortly be impassable without the utmost hazard" and said London was threatened with "gangs of rogues" at least as dangerous as "those which the Italians call the Banditi" (Fielding, 1751). Late in the century, Patrick Colquhoun, a stipendiary magistrate whose ambitious plans for police reform were rebuffed by the Home Office (Paley, 2004), chose to publish these instead in his *Treatise on the Police of the Metropolis* (1796). Like Fielding, to justify his proposed reforms, he described the crime problem in apocalyptic terms: "All ranks must bear testimony to the insecurity...which arises from the phalanx of criminal people, who are suffered...to deprive us of the privilege of travelling upon the highways, or of approaching the capital, in any direction, after dark, without danger of being assaulted, and robbed; and perhaps wounded or murdered" (Colquhoun, 1796). Such exaggerated statements were published to justify their authors' pet projects, and their impact on public opinion is questionable. Although these pamphlets sold well, references to them rarely appear in diaries and correspondence.

In contrast, the daily reports of crime in the newspapers were almost certainly far more influential in shaping public understandings of crime. The modern newspaper was invented in 18th-century London. The first successful daily paper, the *Daily Courant*, began publication in 1702, and the number of newspapers published, and their circulation, increased dramatically during the century. In 1712, there were around a dozen titles published with a circulation of around 44,000 per week, and it has been estimated that by the 1780s, one third of the capital's residents read a paper (or heard one read, e.g., in coffeehouses and alehouses) (Barker, 2000). In 1782, Walpole described newspapers as "oracles of the times, and what everybody reads and cites" (1937–1983). Although foreign news often dominated, crime was a recurrent feature of domestic news reporting, perhaps because crime reports were a cheap and reliably constant source of news: Victim reports, committals to Newgate, preliminary hearings, and trials took place on a regular basis, and reports were easy to obtain. These formed a major part of newspaper content—10% of the news reporting in the late 18th century, according to Peter King (2007)—and they were influential. At the start of the century, *Hanging Not Punishment Enough* (1701) cited the "the publick news daily full of so many relations of robberies and murthers" as part of its evidence that the roads had become "so dangerous and unsafe."

As today, newspapers presented a distorted picture by paying dispropor-tionate attention to violent crime, perhaps reinforcing what readers encoun-tered in pamphlets such as Fielding's *Enquiry*. Occasionally, the papers reported general observations on the state of crime in London, as when the *Whitehall Evening Post* commented in 1749, during a postwar crime wave, on "the frequency of audacious street robberies repeated in this great metropolis...there is no possibility of stirring from our habitations after dark, without the hazard of a fractured skull" (Rogers, 1992). However, it was the daily reporting of individual crimes that probably had a bigger impact on public perceptions. These reports exaggerated levels of violence: Almost three quarters (73%) of 128 issues of London papers sampled between 1723 and 1763 included reports of at least one violent crime, and a quarter of all the crimes reported involved violence (robberies, assaults, murders). Almost every time Londoners opened a newspaper, they encountered a report of a violent crime. In contrast, thefts involving violence and murders account for only 7% of the crimes tried at the Old Bailey—as a proportion of all serious crimes tried, newspapers were almost four times more likely to report violent crimes than any other type of offense. In comparison, only 9% of newspaper crime reports concerned burglary and 6% concerned pickpocketing despite the fact these were the two crimes most frequently mentioned from personal experience in private diaries. The papers also exaggerated the extent of violent crime through repetition. Horace Walpole was robbed by the highwayman James Maclaine in 1749, when Walpole was slightly injured when Maclaine's pistol accidentally fired, but Walpole said "the frequent repetition" of the story in the newspapers was "much worse than the robbery" (1937–1983). Similarly, he noted that riots in the city in 1771 "possibly...make less impression on the spot than by a collection of them crowded into a newspaper" (1937–1983).

Newspapers not only overemphasized violence by the frequency of their reports but also with the tone and substance of their reporting. This was due in part to practical constraints: Until the 1760s, pressures of space meant that reports tended to be very brief. As Esther Snell has argued, such reports inevitably tended to privilege action over motivation, which made crimes seem difficult to understand and therefore more threaten-ing (2007). Moreover, in concise reports, the use of shorthand labels such as "highwaymen" and "footpads" had the effect of representing criminals as habitual and therefore more threatening criminals. However, the negative language went further. Reports tended to adopt a pejorative tone, with robbers frequently labeled as rogues, ruffians, and villains and often described as working in gangs, and evocative language was used to describe any violence they used. When Martin Bellamy, an associate of the street robber James Dalton, was apprehended in 1728, the *Weekly Journal; or British Gazetteer* reported that "Martin Bellamy, a sturdy and desperate villain, supposed to belong to the gangs of street robbers, was taken at Hockley in the Hole, a case of loaded pistols and 70 guineas being found in his pockets." Not only was the language negative, but, according to a rival paper, the reporting was also exaggerated: 2 days later, the *Daily Journal* claimed that Bellamy, now labeled a taylor, had been taken unarmed, with only 9 pence in his pocket, when he was trying to sell some stolen silk. Nonetheless, the *Daily Journal* also claimed that he belonged to two gangs: "a gang of street robbers" and "a gang of housebreakers."* Although there is evidence that there were *some* networks of criminals operating in 18th-century London, including one centered around James Dalton (which involved Bellamy), historians agree that, by using the language of "gangs," newspapers and other commentators wildly exaggerated the organization, extent, and durability of criminal networks at the time (Beattie, 1986; Shore, 2003).

Comparison of newspaper reports with other accounts of the same crimes provides further evidence of how newspapers subtly tended to exaggerate the violence. Compare the accounts of the robbery of Thomas Cane by Christopher Rawlins in Holborn around midnight on February 6, 1728. Cane testified at the Old Bailey that "the coach in which he was in was stopp'd...by two persons, one of them putting a pistol into the coach, took his watch and money." A newspaper report of the actual crime, however, stated that he was "set upon by two robbers, who holding each a pistol to his breast, demanded his money, watch and rings." Not only did the newspaper report two pistols rather than one, but it used the terms *set upon* and *demanded* to highlight the egregiousness of the crime.† Similarly, when John Delaport testified at the Old Bailey about how he was robbed on April 4, 1749, his description of the crime was far less colorful than the report that appeared in the *London Evening Post* just after the crime. Delaport testified that, as he was traveling on his horse through Islington at about 8 o'clock in the evening, he was approached by three armed men who told him to stop and "snapped" [fired] a pistol. According to Delaport, this startled "my horse [who] went from under me, and I fell into a ditch; they pulled me out, one of them demanded my money." The *London Evening Post*, however, reported that Delaport "was *attacked* by three footpads and a fellow on horseback...who *knocked* [italics added] him off his horse into a ditch"—subtle changes in the story that accentuated the violence.‡

As King (2007) and Snell (2007) recently suggested, newspapers also spread fear owing to the fact many of the crime reports were told from the victim's point of view and involved unsolved and unprosecuted crimes (to

---

* *Weekly Journal; or British Gazetteer*, February 24, 1728; *Daily Journal*, February 26, 1728.
† OBP, May 1728, Christopher Rawlings (t17280501-31); *London Journal*, February 10, 1728.
‡ OBP, Apr 1749, Lawrence Lee and Peter Murphy (t17490411-5); *London Evening Post*, April 4, 1749.

this can be added the numerous advertisements offering rewards for the return of stolen goods; Styles, 1989). However, the exaggerated reporting of violent crime in newspapers was not just inadvertent; it was in some ways intentional. King (2000) has argued that in a kind of vicious circle, the papers exacerbated the violence in crime because readers expected them to report it. Thus, he argues, "reports of 'gangs infesting' a particular neighbourhood may have been grounded more in the local community's fears and stereotypes or in newspapers' needs to increase their circulation that in observed reality."

Readers responded to newspaper crime reports in a number of ways. The papers were consumed both directly through reading and indirectly through discussion of their content at coffeehouses and other venues. In repeating stories to their acquaintances, some readers exaggerated the violence further. When the papers reported in 1793 that the body of a Frenchman had been discovered in the Thames, by the time Mary Berry repeated the story to Horace Walpole, it had been transformed into a crime: murder by drowning (Walpole, 1937–1983). Similarly, in his report of the coal heavers' riotous attack on the house of John Green in April 1768 in a letter to Horace Mann, Walpole wrote that Green, who was heavily armed, "killed 18 or 20, but you will see the trial at large in the papers." In fact, the papers had reported that only three coal heavers were killed, and Green was tried for the murder of only one of them (Walpole, 1937–1983).* Some readers were so convinced by the newspapers' reports of the threat posed by violent crime that they responded by arming themselves, banding together to form prosecution societies and offer rewards for apprehending criminals, and, when they became witnesses or victims of crime, prosecuting the culprits formally (King, 1987). King has suggested that the selective reporting of the most threatening aspects of crime in the newspapers could so successfully stimulate fears of crime that at certain times (such as at the conclusions of wars when England faced the prospect of an influx of unemployed and possibly violent demobilized soldiers) they could create "moral panics," leading to increased prosecutions even when crime itself was not increasing. Thus, he found that following newspaper reports of impending demobilization after successful peace negotiations in January 1783, prosecutions for violent thefts increased *before* the soldiers had even returned home (King, 2000).

However, other readers, aware that newspapers often spread scandal to increase their readership, read the papers more critically. Because newspaper reporting emerged in the context of political crises and party conflict in the late seventeenth and early eighteenth centuries, Londoners treated

* OBP, May 1768, Thomas Gilberthorp and John Green (t17680518-38).

newspapers with cynicism from the very start of this genre (Faller, 1988). Walpole repeatedly told his correspondents that the newspapers could not be trusted. He wrote to one that half of the reports of robberies and murders in the papers were "lies" (though he recognized that they nonetheless "fill the imagination"), and he wrote to another that "if a paragraph in a newspaper contains a word of truth, it is sure to be accompanied with two or three blunders…[the] papers published in the face of the whole town [are] nothing but lies, every one of which fifty persons could contradict and disprove"— although elsewhere he acknowledged that reports "seldom fail to reach the outlines at least of incidents" (Walpole, 1937–1983). Walpole exaggerated for effect, but the point is important—readers did not necessarily trust what they read in the papers.

It should also be recognized that the messages about crime found in the papers were not entirely negative—reports of detections, arrests, convictions, and punishments, King (2000) suggests, provided a more "reassuring tone" and "may have provided a significant counterbalance" to the repeated stories of unsolved violent crimes. Thus, newspaper reports of Old Bailey trials focused primarily on the cases that resulted in convictions, with the greatest attention given to those sentenced to death, demonstrating that crime would be punished. Acquittals were typically not reported at all, or only the number of not guilty verdicts was given. Similarly, in the 1750s, Henry and John Fielding used the *Covent Garden Journal* and the *Public Advertiser* to advertise the services—and the successes—of their Bow Street rotation office and its "runners" in detecting thieves (Beattie, 2007; Shoemaker, 2004).

In addition, newspaper reports occasionally presented certain types of crime in a relatively positive light. Descriptions of highway robberies "regularly reported" instances of polite or chivalrous conduct, including examples of robbers returning items of sentimental value to their victims or giving them money to enable them to return home (McKenzie, 2007). Particularly when they were safely behind bars, highwaymen could be represented in unthreatening terms. John Hawkins and William Simpson, whose gang was accused in 1722 in the *Weekly Journal; or British Gazetteer*, of having cut out the tongue of a woman who had witnessed one of their robberies so she could not testify against them, received sympathetic treatment in the same paper only a week later after their arrest for robbing the Bristol mail. Here they were described as "persons of a genteel and extraordinary behaviour, of good countenance and address," who had been betrayed by another member of the gang, Ralph Wilson, who had turned King's evidence. The two had therefore become "the objects of much pity and concern."*

---

* *Weekly Journal; or British Gazetteer*, April 28 and May 5, 1722.

Overall, as King (2007) argues, the papers provided "a kaleidoscope of different and often contradictory messages" about crime. However, the common theme running through virtually all newspaper reports was that crime was a frequent occurrence—and it demanded, and sometimes received, decisive action from law enforcement officials (such as the Bow Street Runners) and the courts.

Old Bailey Proceedings

This message was also found in the *Old Bailey Proceedings*, another new genre that had a significant impact on public perceptions, in this case particularly of criminal justice. First published in 1674, the *Proceedings* quickly became an established periodical, published after every session of the court until 1913. They were initially remarkably popular: The Swiss visitor Béat Louis de Muralt (1726) reported that around 1700, the *Proceedings* were "in the opinion of many people, one of the most diverting things a man can read in London." Although early editions were inexpensive and targeted at a popular audience, they quickly acquired the appearance of an official publication. Owing to demands by the City of London that they provide more systematic coverage, over the course of the 18th century they expanded considerably and became more expensive, with a corresponding narrowing of the readership.

The *Proceedings*, also known as the "sessions papers," sought to present an image of impartiality and authority. Licensed by the city, which kept an occasional eye on their content, the publishers had to report trials in a way that would keep the authorities happy and hold on to their essentially middle-class audience. Given severe constraints on space, reports had to be selective: One typical edition at midcentury reported a total of 60 trials held over 4 days in only 19 double-columned pages—not much more than half a column for each trial, which probably lasted around 20 to 30 minutes.* The trial of the poet and playwright Richard Savage for murder in 1727 unusually lasted 8 hours, but the account in the *Proceedings*, partly presented in the first person as verbatim testimony, is only 2,447 words, which could easily have been spoken in under an hour. What is significant is what got left out: The trials were edited to present a particular image of crime and public justice to their readers. There is not much evidence of the *Proceedings* actually *misreporting* what went on in the Old Bailey courtroom (although there is some)—as a public space, there were too many witnesses to the events for the *Proceedings* to be able to tell outright lies (Langbein, 2003). However, the

* OBP, January 1750.

story of a trial could be distinctively "spun" by the decisions about what to include and what to leave out (Shoemaker, 2008).

In terms of the representation of crime, unsurprisingly the *Proceedings*, like the newspapers, focused more attention on violent crimes, while relatively mundane thefts were very briefly reported. This contributed to the popular impression that crime was a serious problem—in addition to the newspapers, the "sessions papers monthly" were cited by *Hanging Not Punishment Enough* (1701) as evidence that robbery and murder had become so widespread. However, the *Proceedings* also sought to entertain its readers, as can be seen in the extensive reports of sexual offenses, including thefts committed by prostitutes on their clients with their titillating circumstantial details.

More importantly, the *Proceedings* reassured readers that the courts could cope with the problem of violent crime. Trial reports were constructed to present a positive image of justice, in which criminals (who were sometimes portrayed as habitual, by the use of references to their appearances in earlier trials) were shown as receiving their just desserts. Comparison with other available accounts of the same trials indicates that several aspects of the criminal trial were often either omitted or severely pruned in the published *Proceedings* so that they could make this point. The omissions include procedural matters such as the participation of lawyers, evidence of jury decision making, the judges' summing up, and evidence concerning the case for the defense and acquittals. For example, pretrial pleading and most evidence of participation by lawyers were excluded. Lawyers participated in a minority of trials in this period, but the *Proceedings* rarely reported what they said, including their opening statements, arguments with the judge, and cross-examinations. The omission of legal arguments had the effect of presenting trials as a direct confrontation between the victim and the accused, with no distracting interventions by lawyers to muddy the waters—and thus no suggestions that the verdict was the result of technicalities or arguments introduced by lawyers. Instead, verdicts were presented as the direct result of the facts produced by the witnesses: Justice was presented as unproblematic and in a coherent narrative form (Shoemaker, 2008).

Similarly, the judges' summing up was rarely reported. Although, after the constitutional struggles of the late 17th century, judges were no longer allowed to coerce juries into arriving at specific verdicts, their summing up could be partial, giving the jury a clear steer as to the expected verdict. By leaving these out, once again the *Proceedings* presented an image that verdicts were arrived at solely as a result of the confrontation between victim and defense evidence, free of any outside interference. The *Proceedings* also do not tell us anything about the jury's decision-making process: how long it took them to reach a verdict, whether they returned to ask the judge any questions, and whether they tried to present a verdict in an unconventional form (Shoemaker, 2008). For example, at the conclusion of the trial of the highwaymen Hawkins and Simpson in 1722, the jury was uncertain about whether it could credit some evidence, a receipt, introduced by one defense witness in support of an alibi, which the prosecution had attempted to discredit by pointing out that some of the writing was in a different color of ink. We learn from a nonofficial account of the trial that "After staying out about an hour, the jury returned into court without agreeing on a verdict, saying they could not be convinced that [the] receipt was not genuine, merely on account of the different colours of the ink." In response, the judge suggested that the weight of all the prosecution witnesses was greater than that of a single defendant witness. Consequently, the jury returned a guilty verdict (*Malefactor's Register*, 1779). Compare this evidence of how the verdict was arrived at with the brief account of the conclusion of the trial in the *Proceedings*: "The prisoners insisted on their innocence; but the evidence being positive, and fortified by many concurrent circumstances, the jury found them guilty of the indictment."* Given that both defendants were sentenced to death, it is perhaps not surprising that the *Proceedings* suppressed the jury's difficulties in arriving at its verdict.

The *Proceedings* thus focused on the confrontation between the victim and the accused, but even here, much was left out. Although both prosecution and defense evidence was summarized, the case for the defense was more brutally pruned, sometimes to the extent of leaving it out altogether, thereby emphasizing the culpability of the accused (Shoemaker, 2008). The report of Richard Savage's defense in his trial for murder in 1727, after a late-night spontaneous barroom swordfight that led to the death of James Sinclair, provides a good example of this limited reporting. His defense, which reportedly took an hour, was summarized in the *Proceedings* in 574 words. What was left out included Savage's testimony that the affair was totally unpremeditated and that he had acted in self-defense and the character evidence presented by what an alternative account called "several persons of distinction" (Johnson, 1744). What *was* reported in the *Proceedings* was presented in disbelieving tones: In one passage, for example, it was reported that "Savage…made some observations on the depositions of [the prosecution witnesses], in which he *presumed* [italics added], there were some incoherencies…"† Savage was convicted of murder and sentenced to death, although later pardoned; by weighting the evidence significantly in favor of the prosecution, the *Proceedings* served to justify that verdict and sentence.

Savage was far too respectable to protest at his treatment by the court, but other defendants expressed defiance in the courtroom, behavior that once again was not reported in the *Proceedings*. Thus, when William Fairall was tried for breaking into a customs house with about 30 others and stealing

---

* OBP, May 1722, John Hawkins and George Simpson (t17220510-3).
† OBP, December 1717, Richard Savage et al. (t17271206-24).

£500 worth of tea, according to the *Proceedings*, he offered no defense at his trial.* According to another account, however, although he offered no testimony, he nonetheless made his views known in the courtroom: "Fairall at his Trial seem'd to shew the utmost Daringness, and Unconcern, even shewing Tokens of Threats to a Witness, as he was giving his Evidence to the Court, and standing all the while in the Barr with a Smile or rather a Sneer upon his Countenance" (Taylor, 1749). Needless to say, this was not reported in the *Proceedings*, and the image presented was by implication that Fairall accepted his conviction and later death sentence without protest. Similarly, the *Proceedings* rarely reported the speeches defendants made to the court before their sentencing. Given that these pleas for mercy rarely succeeded and that defendants were frequently sentenced to death (although many were later pardoned), it is not surprising that these speeches were usually omitted—the publisher did not want to present the convicts in a more sympathetic light than it did the judges who tried them (Shoemaker, 2008).

In addition, the *Proceedings* paid much less attention to acquittals than it did to convictions: Between 1720 and 1770, reports of trials that led to a verdict of not guilty were 40% shorter than those which led to convictions (Shoemaker, 2008). Unsurprisingly, given the clear message the *Proceedings* intended to convey to the public that crime did not pay, there was little desire to report criminals being let off without punishment nor did the *Proceedings* wish to inform readers of the arguments and tricks defendants used to avoid conviction. In fact, for one short period in the early 1790s, the city even went so far as to ban reporting of trials that resulted in not-guilty verdicts because they were thought to provide criminals with methods of "fabricating defences, especially alibis." Significantly, however, this policy only lasted two years (Devereaux, 1996). Demand for the *Proceedings* decreased once their coverage was reduced and the image of public justice had become so obviously biased. One of the most important messages the *Proceedings* intended to convey was the impartiality of justice at the Old Bailey, hardly a message that was conveyed by only reproducing guilty verdicts.

This additional message—that trials at the Old Bailey were conducted fairly—meant that the *Proceedings* did normally present both sides of the story: The defense case was usually reported, however briefly. This means that the *Proceedings* provided a rare opportunity for the voices of accused criminals to be presented in print, in however attenuated and edited a form that might be (in contrast to the newspapers' almost exclusive focus on reports by victims and the authorities). For example, female thieves, whose voices were rarely reported in any other form of print, had their defense testimonies reported in the *Proceedings*, providing reading audiences with

---

* OBP, April 1749, Thomas Kingsmill et al. (t17490405-36).

a set of representations of female criminality found in few other publications (one notable exception is Daniel Defoe's novel *Moll Flanders* [1722], itself arguably influenced by the stories told in the *Proceedings*). Thus, women accused of theft explained in the *Proceedings*, in terms which were often quite plausible, how they stole out of economic "necessity" and how they happened to be found in possession of stolen goods in ways that rendered their guilt questionable because they had been given, or borrowed, the goods or, more often, because the goods were given in payment for sexual services rendered or, alternatively, that the prosecution was maliciously motivated because the accused had refused to have sex with the prosecutor (Shoemaker, in press). Because the *Proceedings* had to present both sides of the story, however much the publisher wanted to send a message that crime did not pay, these trial reports possessed what one literary critic has described as a "resistance to closure" (Gladfelder, 2001).

It also important to note that the *Proceedings*, like newspapers, were sometimes read critically. Although there is evidence that many readers accepted the *Proceedings* as authoritative, others published pamphlets complaining about the partial or distorted nature of trial reports in the *Proceedings*, and such complaints were also occasionally published in the *Gentleman's Magazine* and newspapers. At the conclusion of his term of office as Lord Mayor in November 1775, John Wilkes complained bitterly of inadequate reporting in the *Proceedings*, which, he said, "had been long and universally complained of" (Shoemaker, 2008). At least some readers will have been aware of these complaints, and of competing publications which provided alternative accounts of some trials, and they will have read the picture of justice presented in the *Proceedings* with some skepticism.

Ordinary's Accounts

The point of view of the accused was even more apparent in the *Proceedings'* sister publication, known as the *Ordinary's Accounts*, which provided biographies and the "last dying speeches" of executed felons. The Ordinary was the chaplain of Newgate prison, and his job was to counsel the prisoners awaiting their punishment and, by encouraging them to reflect on their sins, prepare them to meet their maker. As a profitable sideline, he was allowed to publish accounts of these criminals' lives and their last days and minutes before their executions. The Ordinaries had an ideological agenda: Their accounts of the lives and behavior of those condemned to hang were moulded to show prisoners, with the help of the Ordinary, coming to terms with their sinful past, confessing their crimes, and preparing for a Christian death. The message to the reading public was clearly to demonstrate the wages of sin: If you engage in vice, you will be stepping onto a slippery slope that could well land you eventually at the gallows. Lincoln Faller (1987) identified the common narrative patterns found in criminal biographies such as these and he argued that the approaches adopted allowed respectable society both to come to terms with the behavior of its most threatening criminals and to justify the use of capital punishment for those convicted (see also, for the 17th century, Rosenberg, 2004; Sharpe, 1985). However, others have pointed out that 18th-century criminal biographies, including the *Ordinary's Accounts*, gave a "certain freedom of expression" and even extended "generosity" to convicted felons who were given opportunities to shape their life stories in ways that often subverted the expected posttrial script of confession and repentance (Linebaugh, 1977; McKenzie, 2007). What is remarkable about the *Accounts* is that they gave a voice to the condemned, in the sense that they indirectly allowed convicts to tell their own life stories in print and present their versions of the events surrounding their crimes. Although the Ordinaries sometimes criticized and sarcastically commented on these stories, they nonetheless included them because, as Andrea McKenzie has argued, the views of men and women facing imminent death were thought to be particularly truthful at this time. In telling their stories, convicts were able introduce mitigating factors in justification of their crimes, while always acknowledging their general sinfulness and sincere repentance (MacKenzie, 2007).

This was even true in the case of Catherine Hayes, who was convicted with two men in 1726 of the gruesome murder of her husband, followed by cutting up the body and secretly disposing of the pieces. Unsurprisingly, this sensational case was the subject of several publications, many of which portrayed Hayes as the typical female villain who had an ungovernable temper and loose morals and who had not only instigated the crime (and the cover-up) but had committed adultery with one of her husband's killers, Thomas Billings (who, to make the story even worse, was her illegitimate son according to some reports). Despite the horrific crime and the allegations about her character, the Ordinary reported Hayes's side of the story, which was that her husband had mistreated her by not allowing her to conduct religious worship and had beat her, sometimes breaking her ribs and bones, and that he had killed two newborn children of hers and buried them under some fruit trees. In modern language, she was a battered wife. She claimed she had been unaware of the two men's plans for the murder and that she had been in the next room when the crime took place, and she justified her participation in the cover-up by his mistreatment of her. The Ordinary treated all these claims skeptically, comparing them to the contradictory testimonies of her accomplices, yet he reported them, and in concluding his report he said more positively that she "seemed to be a woman of good natural parts, but grossly ignorant in religious matters," and he repeated her claim that "she had been just and upright in her dealings, charitable to the poor, careful in houshold affairs, [and] faithful and dutiful to her husband" (Guthrie, 1726). These are remarkable things to say about a woman convicted of a cold-blooded murder. Ultimately, readers, who encountered a much more negative picture of Hayes in the newspapers and other printed accounts, were left to draw their own conclusions, but at least they were exposed to two sides of the story.

The *Ordinary's Accounts* ceased publication in the 1770s, by which time the middle-class reading public appears to have lost interest in the lives of ordinary criminals, and readers ceased to believe that everyone had a tendency to criminality that meant that they would benefit from such moral lessons (MacKenzie, 2007). Nonetheless, this fascinating genre demonstrates, even more than its sister publication the *Proceedings*, that representations of criminals in some print genres were far from the largely one-dimensional images found in the newspapers. By providing some accounts, however, mediated, from the point of view of the accused, readers were able to gain some understanding of why crimes were committed and why some of the accused may have actually been innocent.

Criminal Biographies

The heavy public demand for information about criminal lives led to the publication of numerous other criminal biographies. Desperate for copy, hack writers canvassed the prisoners in Newgate looking for suitable stories, which they published with advertisements that the material was "taken from the mouth of" the criminal or from "papers of his own writing" (McKenzie, 1998). Some of these biographies presented even more sympathetic images of crime to their readers, particularly in the case of highway robbery. James Maclaine, together with his partner William Plunket, was active on the roads around London in 1749 and 1750, and he used the proceeds of their crimes to live an opulent gentlemanly lifestyle in the fashionable St. James's district of the metropolis, socializing with the very types of people who were his victims. His trial excited huge public interest after his apprehension in the summer of 1750, with numerous ladies and gentlemen visiting him in Newgate prison and giving him money for his support. Unsurprisingly, the case was retailed in several publications, which adopted various perspectives. The account of his trial in the *Proceedings* suggests nothing very chivalrous or gentlemanly about his crimes (he and Plunket were reported as threatening "to blow the brains out" of a victim who had concealed some of his money),* and showing less sympathy than usual, the Ordinary of Newgate was skeptical of his claims to gentility: "Though he...in his dress and equipage very much affected the fine gentleman,...yet to a man acquainted with

* OBP, October 1750, James Macleane [sic] (t17500912-22).

good breeding, that can distinguish it from impudence and affectation, there was very little in his address or behaviour, that could entitle him to that character" (Taylor, 1750).

On the other hand, some of the other biographies presented a more positive view of Maclaine, such as "The Gentleman Highwayman." One reported that robbers such as Maclaine had "some claim, to what we call in this country a gentleman...they have gained more honour, by going to the gallows...than they could have attained by an age of industry." In the accounts of Maclaine and Plunket's crimes, their activities were presented as involving polite and chivalrous behavior. In one robbery, Plunket supposedly put his pistol in his pocket "for fear of frightening the ladies, [and] without forcing [a lady] out of the coach, [took] what small matter she offered without further search." Before riding off with their loot, they bid "a polite adieu to the passengers" (*Complete History*, 1750). Concurrently, four print etchings and engravings were sold, depicting Maclaine in genteel clothing (O'Connell, 2003). Another biography provided justification for their crimes by reporting Plunket's statement to a victim "that they did not rob thro' wantonness, as the great ones did, who daily rob 'em of millions, for the support of luxury and corruption, but that they were forced to it for their immediate subsistence" (*Genuine Account*, 1750).

These positive (if by no means entirely uncritical) representations of highway robbery were no doubt read skeptically. After the arrest of Maclaine in 1750, Walpole noted that "there are as many prints and pamphlets about [Maclaine] as the earthquake," which had recently occurred in London. He purchased three of these pamphlets, but, perhaps as a result of his own experience as one of Maclaine's victims the previous year, he was not seduced by the fashion of celebrating Maclaine as a gentleman highwayman. As he commented, "his profession is no joke" (Walpole, 1937–1983). Nonetheless, it is remarkable that such pamphlets were published at all in 1750, at a time of considerable public concern about crime after the demobilization of military forces at the end of the War of the Austrian Succession, and only a year later, Fielding would publish his *Enquiry*, with its no-holds barred account of the threat robbers posed to the safety of the nation, not least by those (like Maclaine) who were motivated by the pursuit of "luxury." Despite the unpromising context, Maclaine the highway robber emerged in some biographies as a heroic figure, and some Londoners responded positively to such representations, treating men like Maclaine as celebrities. Maclaine was visited in Newgate and given financial assistance and was even the subject of petitions to the King demanding a pardon (Shoemaker, 2006). John Boswell was similarly impressed by the highwayman John Lewis in 1763. After a visit to Newgate, he described him as "a genteel, spirited young fellow." Having read the stories of "roguery and wickedness" in the "*Lives of the Convicts*, and other such books," Boswell's curiosity was aroused by this case and he went the next day to Tyburn to see him hanged (Boswell, 1950).

Highwaymen like Maclaine and Lewis, and also Jack Rann, known as "Sixteen String Jack," and William Hawke, known as "the Flying Highwayman," clearly knew how to manipulate the opportunities provided by print culture to represent themselves in a positive light (Shoemaker, 2006). We should not think of criminal biographies as being simply "about" criminals; these publications were also to some extent created by them, through the stories they supplied to compilers including the Ordinaries and the hack writers and artists who waited around Newgate looking for content.

Conclusion

In the 18th century, Londoners came to rely more than ever before on the medium of print for their understandings of the nature and extent of crime in the metropolis, and in their readings, they encountered remarkably diverse representations of serious crime. Although the predominant tone, found in the genres published most frequently (newspapers and the *Proceedings*), represented crime as violent and threatening, while supporting the work of the courts in addressing the problem, the papers sometimes reported highway robbers in sympathetic terms and trial reports presented two sides of the story, however briefly. Because this was a time when the public was keen to know more about the lives of individual criminals, whether for purposes of entertainment or instruction, other printed publications provided more detailed accounts from the point of view of the criminal. In the end, it is likely that 18th-century readers, faced with competing and sometimes contradictory accounts of crime, read all of this literature, including the official accounts, with a skeptical eye. This forms a vital, and underappreciated, context for understanding 18th-century debates about crime and penal and judicial reform, and it helps explain why, despite widespread worries about the extent of crime and doubts about the merits of the death penalty as the primary means of dealing with it, support for both policing and penal reforms in the period was limited. In short, the reading public knew the crime problem was more complicated than reformers like Henry Fielding made it appear. Print culture did not disseminate a single, negative image of crime, although through frequent coverage, it repeatedly called attention to the problem and by doing so exaggerated its significance. The contradictory images found in printed representations of crime facilitated a debate, at least implicitly. What readers actually concluded from reading these representations is of course a different (and difficult) question, and one that cries out for further investigation, despite the limited sources available on this topic.

The multivocal representation of criminality in 18th-century print culture, however, did not last. From the 1750s, there was increasing skepticism in print of highwaymen's claims to the status of a gentleman as readers found the repeated stories of violence and theft in the newspapers and *Old Bailey Proceedings* more compelling (Shoemaker, 2006). In the 1770s, the character of printed literature about crime changed significantly, due to both new financial and official constraints on publication and the shifting cultural preoccupations of readers, as respectable society lost interest in the life experiences of members of the deviant lower classes. The *Ordinary's Accounts* ceased publication, and as the *Proceedings* came under increasing control of the City of London, they lost much of their audience because of their growing comprehensiveness and increased cost (Devereaux, 2002; McKenzie, 2007). Consequently, newspapers became even more than before the dominant source of public knowledge about crime. Although their coverage of crime expanded in the late 18th century, it also became more selective, focusing primarily on crimes committed by apparently respectable men and women (Devereaux, 2007). Although some forms of cheap print, such as ballads and execution broadsides, continued to disseminate relatively sympathetic images of the common criminal (Gatrell, 1994), these had largely disappeared from the literature consumed by middle- and upper-class readers. Thus, the period covered in this chapter, roughly between the 1690s and the 1770s, was somewhat a golden age of writing about crime, in which crime was a key theme in print culture, even among that consumed by elite readers, and the voices of criminals and their victims could clearly be heard. This sympathetic treatment would reappear in some 19th-century fictional accounts, such as in the depiction of highway robbery in William Harrison Ainsworth's novel *Rookwood* in 1834. However, in terms of the forms of print that influenced opinion makers, representations of crime became more uniformly negative in the 19th century, thereby providing support for the establishment of the Metropolitan Police and other judicial and penal reforms.

References

Barker, H. (2000). *Newspapers, politics and English society, 1689–1855*. Harlow: Longman.

Beattie, J. M. (1986). *Crime and the courts in England 1660–1800*. Princeton, NJ: Princeton University Press.

Beattie, J. M. (2001). *Policing and punishment in London 1660–1750: Urban crime and the limits of terror*. Oxford: Oxford University Press.

Beattie, J. M. (2007). Sir John Fielding and public justice: The Bow Street Magistrates' Court, 1754–1780. *Law and History Review, 25*(1), 61–100.

Boswell, J. (1950). In F. A. Pottle (Ed.), *Boswell's London journal 1762–63*. New York: McGraw-Hill.

Brett-James, N. G. (1935). *The growth of Stuart London*. London: George Allen and Unwin.

Colquhoun, P. (1796). *A treatise on the police of the metropolis*. London: H. Fry for C. Dilly.

A complete history of James Maclean, the gentleman highwayman, who was executed at Tyburn, on Wednesday, October 3, 1750, for a robbery on the highway. (1750). London: Charles Corbett.

Devereaux, S. (1996). The City and the sessions paper: "Public justice" in London, 1770–1800. *Journal of British Studies, 35*, 466–503.

Devereaux, S. (2002). The fall of the sessions paper: Criminal trial and the popular press in late eighteenth-century London. *Criminal Justice History, 18*, 57–88.

Devereaux, S. (2007). From sessions to newspaper? Criminal trial reporting, the nature of crime, and the London press, 1770–1800. *London Journal, 32*, 1–27.

Faller, L. (1987). *Turned to account: The forms and functions of criminal biography in late seventeenth- and early eighteenth-century England*. Cambridge: Cambridge University Press.

Faller, L. (1988). King William, "K. J.", and James Whitney: The several lives and affiliations of a Jacobite robber. *Eighteenth-Century Life, 12*, 88–104.

Fielding, H. (1751). *An enquiry into the causes of the late increase of robbers*. London: A. Millar.

Gatrell, V. A. C. (1994). *The hanging tree: Execution and the English people 1770–1868*. Oxford: Oxford University Press.

A genuine account of the life and actions of James Maclean, highwayman, to the time of his trial and receiving sentence at the Old Bailey. (1750). London: W. Falstaff.

Gladfelder, H. (2001). *Criminality and narrative in eighteenth-century England*. London: Johns Hopkins University Press.

Grosley, P.-J. (1772). *A tour to London: Or new observations on England and its inhabitants* (T. Nugent & L. Davis, Trans.). London: Royal Society.

Guthrie, J. (1726). *The ordinary of Newgate and his account, of the behaviour, confession, and last dying words of the malefactors, who were executed…May, 1726 at Tyburn*. London: John Applebee.

Hanging not punishment enough for murtherers, high-way men, and house breakers. (1701). London: A. Baldwin.

Johnson, S. (1744). *An account of the life of Mr Richard Savage*. London: J. Roberts.

King, P. (1987). Newspaper reporting, prosecution practice and perceptions of urban crime: The Colchester crime wave of 1765. *Continuity and Change, 2*, 423–454.

King, P. (2000). *Crime, justice and discretion in England, 1740–1820*. Oxford: Oxford University Press.

King, P. (2007). Newspaper reporting and attitudes to crime and justice in late eighteenth- and early-nineteenth-century London. *Continuity and Change, 22*, 73–112.

Langbein, J. H. (2003). *The origins of adversary criminal trial*. Oxford: Oxford University Press.

Linebaugh, P. (1977). "The ordinary of Newgate and his account." In J. S. Cockburn (Ed.), *Crime in England 1550–1800* (pp. 246–269). London: Methuen.

The malefactor's register; or, the Newgate and Tyburn calendar (5 vols.) (1779). London: Alexander Hogg.

Mare, M. H., & Quarrell, W. H. (Eds.) (1938). *Lichtenberg's visits to England.* Oxford: Clarendon Press.

McKenzie, A. (1998). Making crime pay: Motives, marketing strategies, and the printed literature of crime in England 1670–1770. In G. T. Smith, A. N. May, & S. Devereaux (Eds.), *Criminal justice in the old world and the new: Essays in honour of J. M. Beattie* (pp. 235–269). Toronto: Centre of Criminology, University of Toronto.

McKenzie, A. (2007). *Tyburn's martyrs: Execution in England, 1675–1775.* London: Hambledon Continuum.

de Muralt, B.-L. (1726). *Letters describing the character and customs of the English and French nations* [translated from French]. London: T. Edlin.

O'Connell, S. (Ed.) (2003). *London 1753.* London: British Museum Press.

Paley, R. (1989). An imperfect, inadequate and wretched system? Policing London before Peel. *Criminal Justice History, 10,* 95–130.

Paley, R. (2004). *Colquhoun, Patrick, Oxford Dictionary of National Biography.* Retrieved from www.oxforddnb.com, December 2, 2007.

Reynolds, E. A. (1998). *Before the bobbies: The night watch and police reform in metropolitan London, 1720–1830.* Basingstoke: Macmillan.

Rogers, N. (1992). Confronting the crime wave: The debate over social reform and regulation, 1749–53. In L. Davison, T. Hitchcock, T. Keirn, & R. Shoemaker (Eds.), *Stilling the grumbling hive: The response to social and economic problems in England, 1689–1750* (pp. 77–98). Stroud: Alan Sutton.

Rosenberg, P. (2004). Sanctifying the robe: Punitive violence and the English press, 1650–1700. In S. Devereaux & P. Griffiths (Eds.), *Penal practice and culture, 1500–1900: Punishing the English* (pp. 157–182). Basingstoke: Palgrave Macmillan.

Sharpe, J. A. (1985). "Last dying speeches": Religion, ideology and public execution in seventeenth-century England. *Past and Present, 107,* 144–167.

Shoemaker, R. (2004). *The London mob: Violence and disorder in eighteenth-century England.* London: Hambledon & London.

Shoemaker, R. (2006). The street robber and the gentleman highwayman: Changing representations and perceptions of robbery in London, 1690–1800. *Cultural and Social History, 3,* 1–25.

Shoemaker, R. (2008). The Old Bailey proceedings and the representation of crime and criminal justice in eighteenth-century London. *Journal of British Studies, 47,* 559–580.

Shoemaker, R. (in press), Print and the female voice: representations of women's crime in London, 1690–1735.

Shore, H. (2003). Crime, criminal networks, and the survival strategies of the poor in early eighteenth-century London. In S. King & A. Tomkins (Eds.), *The poor in England 1700–1850: An economy of makeshifts* (pp. 137–165). Manchester: Manchester University Press.

Snell, E. (2007). Discourses of criminality in the eighteenth-century press: The presentation of crime in *The Kentish Post,* 1717–1768. *Continuity and Change, 22,* 13–47.

Styles, J. (1989). Print and policing: Crime advertising in eighteenth-century provincial England. In D. Hay & F. Snyder (Eds.), *Policing and prosecution in Britain 1750–1850* (pp. 55–111). Oxford: Clarendon Press.

Taylor, J. (1749). *The ordinary of Newgate's account of the behaviour, confession, and dying words of the nine malefactors who were executed at Tyburn on Wednesday the 26th of April 1749.* London: T. Parker and C. Corbett.

Taylor, J. (1750). *The ordinary of Newgate's account of the behaviour, confession, and dying words, of the twelve malefactors who were executed at Tyburn on Wednesday the 3d of October, 1750.* London: T. Parker and C. Corbett.

Walpole, H. (1937–1983). In W. S. Lewis (Ed.), *Horace Walpole's correspondence* (48 vols.). London: Oxford University Press.

Crime Prevention and the Understanding of Repeat Victimization: A Longitudinal Study

2

ANTHONY BOTTOMS
ANDREW COSTELLO

Contents

Introduction

As the title of this book indicates, crime prevention is one of its central themes. Crime prevention is, of course, at least as old as the first door bolt; and in England, it was famously proclaimed as the primary purpose of policing at the time of the creation of the Metropolitan Police in the first half of the 19th century. However, in the last 30 years, we have seen in many countries, including Britain, the more systematic development of a set of planned and coordinated governmental activities designed to promote crime prevention activities (see, e.g., Hughes, 1998). In England and Wales, one of the central aspects of this recent policy focus on crime prevention has been a special interest in the prevention of repeat victimization, a story that has been lucidly told by Laycock (2001). Among other things, these developments

23

resulted in the creation, in 1995, of a "police performance indicator" on repeat victimization as one of the criteria by which the Home Office could measure the effectiveness of local police forces in the prevention of crime (see Farrell, Edmunds, Hobbs, & Laycock, 2000).

In what Laycock (2001) has called the British "repeat victimization story," two strands have run side by side—a research strand and an organizational strand. The research strand has provided a growing body of research into repeat victimization, while the organizational strand has sought to translate these research findings into appropriate crime prevention activities. By common consent, the research leaders in this process have been Ken Pease and Graham Farrell. Ken Pease's interest in repeat victimization first became apparent to the wider criminological community through the Kirkholt Burglary Prevention Project in Greater Manchester (Forrester, Chatterton, & Pease, 1988a; Forrester, Frenz, O'Connell, & Pease, 1990). The subsequent recruitment of Graham Farrell has produced a formidable research double-act that has, for nearly two decades, consistently kept repeat victimization high on the agendas of criminologists and those responsible organizationally for crime prevention (see, e.g., Farrell, 1995; Farrell and Pease, 1993, 2001, 2006, 2007; Pease, 1998, 2008). Undoubtedly, this influential string of publications has become the standard way of understanding repeat victimization—in Kuhn's (1996) terminology, the "normal science" of the topic for most researchers.

As Kuhn makes clear, when a particular way of viewing a scientific topic has become widely accepted (normal science), those who seek to challenge it face, at least initially, an uphill task. In this chapter, one of our principal aims is to examine such a challenge to the "normal science" of repeat victimization— namely, an important article by Hope and Trickett (2004), which has been largely neglected by Anglophone researchers because it has so far been published only in French.* We attempt this task in part by means of theoretical discussion; but more important, we seek to test both some of Hope and Trickett's hypotheses and some arising from the more well-established (Pease–Farrell) understandings of repeat victimization, against a data set containing information on 8 years of recorded crime in the city of Sheffield, United Kingdom.

We believe that such an analysis is particularly appropriate for this volume. The first empirical criminological research to be conducted at the University of Sheffield was a general analysis of recorded crime in Sheffield (Baldwin & Bottoms, 1976); and from this baseline study, various other criminological analyses of a sociospatial character were subsequently developed (e.g., Bottoms, Mawby, & Walker, 1987; Bottoms, Mawby, & Xanthos, 1989;

---

* An English version of the article is to appear in the *International Review of Victimology*, volume 15. In the present chapter, when giving quotations from Hope and Trickett's article, we have used the original English version (kindly supplied to us by Professor Hope), but the page numbers refer to the pagination of the published French version.

Bottoms & Wiles, 1986; Mawby, 1979; Wiles & Costello, 2000). Arising from this research background, and a history of excellent relations between the University and the South Yorkshire Police, we are fortunate to have access to a longitudinal data set which, we hope to demonstrate, can shed some new light on the controversy described above.*

Explaining Repeat Victimization

Historically, the first research study in Britain to draw attention to the frequency of repeat victimization was the pilot victimization survey conducted by Richard F. Sparks, Hazel Genn, and David Dodd (1977) in three London boroughs in the early 1970s. In a subsequent article, Richard Sparks (1981) raised, as a hypothesis, the possibility that "being a victim on one occasion… increases one's future probability of victimization," only to dismiss this in the following terms:

> In some social situations such [statistical] models may be intuitively reasonable, but criminal victimization does not seem to be one of them. For example, perhaps a burglar breaks into a house or store and finds many things worth stealing and few precautions against theft. He tells other burglars about this or plans to go back himself, thus increasing the probability of second and subsequent burglaries. Perhaps a man who has been assaulted may become paranoid and belligerent…thereby increasing his probability of being assaulted in the future. These examples are pretty far-fetched, and not many more suggest themselves (p. 767).

A decade later, however, Polvi, Looman, Humphries, and Pease (1990, 1991) published the first evidence that much repeat victimization occur very swiftly—often within a month of the first victimization. Their study was of residential burglary, but replications for other offenses rapidly established the "fast repeat" as an apparently general phenomenon in repeat victimization (see, e.g., Farrell, 1995). These results produced two significant consequences. First, on an analytical level, the burglary example given by Sparks in 1981 no longer seemed so "far-fetched." If the normal time pattern for repeats were that they occur at random intervals over time, that would be one thing; but the strong "bunching" pattern of repeats immediately after the first victimization suggested inferentially that the two incidents might be causally linked. Second, and more practically, if repeats often occur swiftly, then there would

* We wish to express our deep thanks to South Yorkshire Police for their kindness over many years in making data of this kind available, initially to Professor Paul Wiles and subsequently to Andrew Costello. The present chapter is published with the permission of South Yorkshire Police, but any views expressed are those of the authors and do not necessarily represent the views of South Yorkshire Police.

seem to be some obvious implications for crime prevention—in burglary, for example, there would be some definite point in improving domestic security immediately after a victimization (or, as Forrester, Chatterton, & Pease, 1988b, put it in a memorable title for a magazine article, contrary to proverbial wisdom, it would indeed seem to be "best to lock the door after the horse has bolted"). This logic was quickly disseminated to crime prevention teams.

In the late 1990s, Ken Pease was asked by the Police Research Group in the Home Office to produce a "stocktaking report," summarizing the then-current research knowledge on repeat victimization for the benefit of police officers and other practitioners (Laycock, 2001). In this report, unoriginally entitled *Taking Stock*, Pease offered the following as a very short précis of some of the main findings of repeat victimization research up to that date (Pease, 1998):

> victimization is the best single predictor of victimization;…when victimization recurs it tends to do so quickly;…a major reason for repetition is that offenders take later advantage of opportunities which the first offence throws up.

As will be apparent, the main emphasis in this summary is—in radical contrast to Sparks (1981)—on victimization as a boost to further victimization, with the assumption that the same offenders are often responsible for the revictimization. This "boost" explanation is one of what have become the two-standard explanatory approaches to the repeat victimization phenomenon, the other being usually described as "flag."* This latter term is derived from the idea that certain features of the person or address tend to "flag" it as a desirable target. To take a simple example, there is research evidence that better-off households within deprived areas are disproportionately the targets for thefts involving cars (see Mayhew, Maung, & Mirrlees-Black, 1993). A "flag" explanation of this finding would be that the relatively attractive criminal opportunity offered by these households, and their vehicles, is readily apparent to various potential offenders, without the need for any communication between offenders on the matter.

Although Pease's (1998) brief summary of the key results of repeat victimization research (above) seems to emphasize "boost" explanations, it is important to point out that later in the same publication he states explicitly that "everyone will recognise flag accounts as making sense." Hence, he indicated, his concern was "to spell out the evidence for boost explanations of repeat victimization, without ever losing sight of the pertinence of flag accounts." In essence, this has remained Pease's position for the last decade, and it has recently been restated (Pease, 2008).

---

* An alternative terminology is sometimes used in the RV literature, derived from standard terms in statistics. This contrasts "risk heterogeneity" (flag) with "state dependency" or "event-dependency" (boost); readers will find this terminology used in some quotations given later in this chapter.

We will draw attention to two further matters raised by Ken Pease and Graham Farrell before moving on to the Hope–Trickett challenge. First, both Pease and Farrell have frequently been at pains to point out that for various technical reasons repeat victimization is often undercounted, both in victimization surveys and in recorded crime data (see, e.g., Farrell and Pease, 1993, 2007). They have also recently argued that when such matters are taken fully into account, "victimization is even more concentrated on particular people and households" than the previous evidence had indicated (Farrell & Pease, 2007). In drawing attention to such matters, Pease and Farrell are clearly motivated by a wish to make transparent what might reasonably be described as the misery of repeated victimization, and by a practical wish to alleviate that misery.

Second, Pease and Farrell are well aware of the skepticism regarding boost accounts of repeat victimization that were offered in the early 1980s by Richard Sparks (1981; see above) and separately by James Nelson (1980). In an interesting comment on these authors in his 1998 monograph, Pease did not, as might have been expected, emphasize especially the subsequently discovered time-course issue (see above) but rather the possibility of seeing "crime sequences as the unfolding of a relationship." In more detail:

> What has changed since Sparks and Nelson were so scathing has been attention to crimes like domestic violence, embezzlement, sexual abuse of children and bullying. These offences are typically perpetrated as series of events, with a dynamic in which the consequences of offences early in the series may speed or slow the rate of offending, or halt it altogether. Having considered such offences, the notion that crime events against the same victim are dependent upon each other now seems less "far fetched." We are now much more likely to see crime sequences as the unfolding of a relationship. Being prepared to look at matters in this way through the example of domestic violence, we are now readier to recognise links between apparently one-off events like burglary and robbery (1998, p. 14).

What is fascinating about these two further topics is that—as we shall shortly see—both the "concentration [of victimization] on particular people and households," and the possibility of "seeing crime sequences as the unfolding of a relationship" constitute important issues within Hope and Trickett's (2004) critique of orthodox repeat victimization scholarship. It is to that critique that we must now turn.

In 2004, Tim Hope and Alan Trickett did not come fresh to the study of repeat victimization; both had contributed valuably to the developing literature on victimization, including repeat victimization (see, e.g., Hope, Bryan, Trickett, & Osborn, 2001; Osborn, Ellingworth, Hope, and Trickett, 1996). However, they had become convinced that a different approach to some of the issues was necessary, and their article spells out reasons for this view.

First, Hope and Trickett (2004) consider that too little attention has been paid in the literature to the relative rarity of victimization: "there are many more non-victims than victims, and respondents reporting higher victimization frequencies are even rarer." Second, and linked to the first point, they produce evidence that many victims are not long-term victims, but, having been victimized, revert to their previous status of nonvictim; thus, as they put it, there might be a "differential and decremental tendency towards *immunity from crime risk* [italics added]" in the general population.* Third, the authors are very interested in the results reported by those who have investigated what they describe as the "double-hurdle" model of crime victimization; that is to say, what if anything distinguishes victims from nonvictims (first hurdle) and repeat victims from single victims (second hurdle)? In particular, the article by Osborn et al. (1996) (for which both Hope and Trickett were coauthors) was seen to be of special interest; the analysis in that article found "little evidence that repeat victims have distinctive characteristics compared with single victims." Fourth and more technically, for statistical reasons Hope and Trickett were critical of the use of the Poisson distribution by some repeat victimization researchers and found themselves returning, for that and other statistical reasons, to Nelson's (1980) and Sparks' (1981) early analyses, noting for example that Nelson (1980) had found the negative binomial model "to be a very promising tool for understanding and analyzing multiple victimization."†

After a complex argument, Hope and Trickett ultimately describe their "general solution" to the many puzzles presented by the data on crime victimization as being "to posit two polar risk groups in the general population." More fully:

> the general tendency over time in the population is towards immunity from crime victimization....[T]here is a sizeable subgroup...that is more or less permanently immune from victimization, and...the most likely outcome from crime victimization is no further victimization over the longer term. Nevertheless, there is a non-negligible group in the population that would appear to suffer chronic victimization (p. 399).

Comparing these conclusions with those of the orthodox account of repeat victimization, it would seem—at least at first sight—that for Pease and Farrell, victimization begets victimization; but for Hope and Trickett, it

---

* For an earlier reference to "immunization" (or "once bitten, twice shy") in the context of victimization, see Biderman (1980).

† As Hope and Trickett (2004) put it: "the Poisson model is regarded as appropriate for the statistical analysis of data that consist of a number of discrete events occurring over a fixed time interval, which reports of crime victimization incidents...would appear superficially to resemble. *The simple Poisson model assumes that successive events occur independently of each other over time at a constant rate* [italics added]....Yet neither Nelson (1980)...nor Sparks et al. (1977)...could describe the observed distribution of crime victimization frequencies using the simple Poisson model."

does not. Moreover, for Pease and Farrell, fast repeats are central, but Hope and Trickett place little emphasis on fast repeats. Finally and perhaps most important, Hope and Trickett explicitly challenge the focus on "boost" explanations that has been central to the crime prevention policies arising from the orthodox research tradition. They say instead that "while victimization may flag (indicate) differential risk, it would seem less likely, following the immunity model, that it serves to boost (cause) the likelihood of further victimization."

That this debate has practical consequences for crime prevention policy is clear. For example, after a study of repeat burglaries in The Netherlands (discussed more fully later in this chapter), Edward Kleemans (2001) concluded—in accordance with the understandings of much orthodox repeat victimization scholarship—that "prevention measures should be implemented as soon as possible after the event" to forestall fast repeats. More controversially, he added that "there's no need for permanent crime prevention," because the threat is short term and temporary. Pease and Farrell would of course support the first part of this advice, but the second part goes against their "victimization begets victimization" thesis. For Hope and Trickett, by contrast, the first part of Kleemans' statement would seem to be doubtful (because of the "tendency toward immunity" and their skepticism about "boost" explanations), and while the second part is true for most victims, Hope and Trickett would argue that it damagingly understates the potential for chronic victimization of a minority of victims.

In a recent seminar presentation at the Centre for Criminological Research, University of Sheffield, Hope (2007a, see also 2007c) interestingly stated that an implication of his analyses with Alan Trickett is that criminologists and persons concerned with crime prevention should alter their preconceptions about repeat victimization. For many, he believes, the fast burglary repeat has become the perceived "standard case" of an repeat victimization incident. However, in reality, he suggests, the standard case of repeat victimization is a continuing victimization, exemplified by a woman trapped in a relationship with a man who regularly practices violence within the home—and, he argues, some property crime revictimizations are exactly like this. Intriguingly, however—and unnoticed by Hope—something rather similar was already suggested by Ken Pease (1998) in *Taking Stock* a decade ago (see above). Perhaps, therefore, there is greater scope for reconciliation between the two viewpoints than might at first be apparent.

Disentangling "Boost" and "Flag"

If we are to address seriously the controversy between the orthodox account of repeat victimization and the Hope–Trickett challenge, we will need a sound method of providing valid evidence for the existence of "boost" or "flag" effects.

According to Pease (2008), there are currently four main scholarly papers that have attempted to disentangle boost and flag effects in relation to offenses against individuals and households: these are articles by Lauritsen and Davis-Quinet (1995), Osborn and Tseloni (1998), Tseloni and Pease (2003), and Wittebrood and Nieuwbeerta (2000). There are technical differences in statistical method as between these articles, but the general approach adopted is a sophisticated modeling of the probability of initial victimization of individuals or households, and then a process of testing whether the chances of a subsequent victimization are statistically affected by an initial victimization. The focus, throughout these studies, is on the victim, with virtually no reference to the offender. As Pease notes, the conclusion of all but one of the relevant papers is that "both boost and flag accounts contribute materially to the phenomenon of repeat victimization" (2008), although methodologically the studies are "bedevilled by the fact that one can't measure everything about a person or place, so that 'unmeasured heterogeneity', that is, the existence of enduring differences that haven't been measured, makes conclusions difficult" (ibid.).

A further important article in a similar vein examined a different kind of crime, namely, offenses (and other calls for police service) occurring in and around fast-food restaurants over a 3-year period (Spelman, 1995). Such establishments have a substantially greater crime incidence rate than do individuals or households, but the rate also varies considerably by establishment—some habitually have very high rates, some much lower. Spelman treated this "long term" rate as a flag effect, but he was also able to identify some short-term boost effects. In this particular context, however, his analysis suggested that, in explaining repeat victimization, the longer term incidence rate was five times more important than were the boost events. Hence, in crime-preventive terms, "for this sample at least, long-term problem-solving" (or dealing with the reasons for high recurrent incidence rates at some locations) was argued to be "an appropriate response" (1995). Spelman's article is important not only because it provides further evidence for the existence of a "mixed economy" of boost and flag effects, but also perhaps because it provides an instructive contrast to Ken Pease's approach to repeat victimization issues. It will be recalled that Pease's (1998) self-described concern is to "spell out the evidence for boost explanations of repeat victimization, without ever losing sight of flag," while Spelman's article could not unreasonably be described as the obverse of this (i.e., providing strong evidence for flag, without losing sight of boost). How far Spelman's results are generalizable to noncommercial contexts remains, however, a problematic issue.

Undeniably, the tradition of work summarized in the preceding paragraphs is very important. Nevertheless, it seems to us to omit a vital dimension. Hedström (2005) has in recent years usefully reemphasized the importance, when one develops social science explanations, of focusing on the mechanism by which the studied effect is produced. In the present instance, the studied effect is repeated victimization of a person or address, so what are the possible mechanisms? The flag approach to explanation essentially postulates that something about the victim or address is similarly attractive to different offenders, who need have no contact with one another, and who are not themselves influenced by their own previous offenses in choosing the next victim or target. By contrast, boost accounts explicitly postulate that something relating to Victimization 1 helps to trigger Victimization 2—for example, the realization by a burglar that entry was easy and that he left some stealable goods behind, or a tip-off by one offender to another that a particular household will by now have replaced the stolen goods. Thus, when viewed from within a "mechanism" perspective, the difference between boost and flag explanations lies centrally in the perceptions of offenders. This is, regrettably, a topic that has been researched only to a limited extent in the general context of repeat victimization,* and it is very rarely mentioned in the technical boost/flag literature. An exception to this is, however, to be found in the 1998 overview by Ken Pease (1998), who suggested that "the most persuasive and self-explanatory evidence [for 'boost' effects] is to be found in offender accounts. Offenders who repeatedly target the same place or person can at least articulate why" (see also Pease, 2008). In our view, this is a wholly correct observation. What it does not do, however, is to quantify the extent to which "boost" effects occur; it merely confirms that they do sometimes occur.

An implication of this line of argument is that, in using any particular data set to test for apparent "flag" or "boost" effects, we always need to consider carefully how far the available data will provide evidence of, or a valid inference relating to, the key mechanisms of offenders' perceptions. We must also be cautious in dealing with any data set that does not directly include information on such perceptions—as most data sets do not.

The centrality of offenders' perceptions to the boost/flag debate does not, however, mean that victims' reactions to their victimizations are irrelevant in the explanation of repeat victimization. The clearest example of this point is perhaps seen in domestic violence situations, where the victim's reaction (e.g., passive submission, assertion of her rights and dignity, leaving home) is obviously of potential relevance to the likelihood of subsequent offending. This dimension of what he calls "victim's agency" has recently been valuably emphasized by Hope (2007c), and it is easy to see that in a given repeat victimization explanatory context one might need to be aware of offenders' perceptions, victims' agency, and the interaction between them.

---

* For a summary of offender accounts to 1998, see Pease (1998). In his various writings, including Pease (2008), Ken Pease especially emphasizes the value of the offender-based research by Ashton, Brown, Senior, and Pease (1998).

Repeat Victimization: The Longitudinal Dimension

It seems obvious that, when studying repeat victimization, the inclusion of a significant longitudinal dimension is important, a point that was made nearly 30 years ago by James Nelson (1980). The need for longitudinal analysis has more recently been brought into sharp focus by Hope and Trickett's arguments about "trends toward immunity" and the possible existence of a small group of long-term, chronically victimized people and households.

Yet most empirical studies of repeat victimization have used relatively short time frames. In the United Kingdom, a particular reason for this has been that most repeat victimization analyses are based on the British Crime Survey (BCS), which—for the most part—asks its respondents to recall offenses of which they have been the victims only over a 12-month period.* Moreover, there is no "panel" dimension within the BCS, so each "sweep" of the BCS recruits a different sample; and it is not possible to cumulate results from several sweeps for the same individual respondent. The National Crime Victimization Survey in the United States does embed a panel within its sampling strategy, but its approach to repeat victimization has been heavily criticized on other grounds (for a discussion, see Planty and Strom, 2007).

In principle, police-recorded crime data can be cumulated into a longitudinal data set and, in fact, most of the repeat victimization research with a study period of more than a year is based on police-recorded data—as indeed is our own research, reported in the rest of this chapter. Nevertheless, there have been surprisingly few really long-term studies of victimization, and not all of these have fully exploited the longitudinal dimensions of their data. For example, despite the generally strong attention paid by the repeat victimization literature to the offense of residential burglary, we have been able to discover only three English-language analyses† of repeat victimization for residential burglary that (a) cover a period of 4 years or more and (b) are based on repeated data collections.‡ In order of publication, these are:

---

* There are two exceptions to this. First, some sweeps of the BCS have asked respondents who reported specific victimizations within the 12-month reference period "were any of these very similar incidents, when the same thing was done under the same circumstances and probably by the same people?" (see Chenery, Ellingworth, Tseloni, & Pease, 1996). In principle, respondents could, in answering this question, be referring also to some offenses outside the reference period. Second and more significantly, the 1992 BCS asked questions not only about the reference year but about prior victimizations in the 4 years preceding the reference year. For an analysis of repeat victimization based on these questions, see Hope, Bryan, Trickett, and Osborn (2001).

† Recently, Dutch researchers have examined various aspects of victimization and revictimization using a 9-year data set on recorded crime for The Hague (see Bernasco, 2008), but so far no general repeat victimization results have been published in English for the whole period.

‡ Bernasco (2008) reached a similar conclusion about burglaries that were close to one another "in space." This raises the issue of so-called "near-repeats," an important topic that has recently attracted significant research attention, but which is beyond the scope of this chapter.

1. Polvi et al. (1991). A 4-year study of residential burglaries in Saskatoon, Canada, based on a full police data set of such offenses for the final year of the study (1987), supplemented by a trawl back through police data for the three preceding years (1984–1986 inclusive) for those addresses victimized in 1987 only.
2. Kleemans (2001). A 6-year study of residential burglary in Enschede, The Netherlands, based on full police data sets. However, the detailed analyses of repeat victimization are mostly restricted to the relationship between successive pairs of offenses, so that, for example, we are not told what proportions of dwellings that were victimized in the first 2 years were victims or nonvictims in the last 2 years.
3. F. Morgan (2001). A 5-year study of police-recorded residential burglary in a suburb in Perth, Western Australia, focusing especially on contrasts between two subareas with different crime rates. This study more fully exploits the longitudinal nature of the data but is possibly limited in its generalizability because of the small area studied (the suburb comprised only 1,000 dwelling units).

The nature of the available data in the study by Polvi et al. (1991) precludes examination of Hope and Trickett's "tendency to immunity" hypothesis. The other two studies will be referred to as the discussion proceeds.

The Present Study: Explaining the Data Set

The present study is based on a large data set of nearly 120,000 recorded crimes against households in the city of Sheffield, United Kingdom, for the period April 1998 to August 2006 inclusive, a period of 101 months. Thus, it spans a much longer period than most repeat victimization research; and it does so using data for the whole of a large British city.

In more detail, the data set comprises a total of 118,558 offenses, in four offense categories:

1. Burglary or attempted burglary in a dwelling (52,267 offenses).
2. Burglary or attempted burglary in a garage, shed, or outhouse, where a residential address was listed as the offense location (i.e., excluding garages housing commercial vehicles, etc.) (22,066 offenses).
3. Theft or attempted theft in a dwelling (3,981 offenses).*

---

* In English law, "theft in a dwelling" differs from "burglary in a dwelling" because in burglary offenses the offender is required to be a trespasser, while in theft offenses that is not the case. Hence, "theft in a dwelling" refers to offenses where the offender was in the dwelling with the householder's permission—for example, theft by a visitor or by a tradesman.

    4. Criminal damage relating to a dwelling, excluding arson (primarily damage to the structure of the dwelling itself) (40,244 offenses).

The BCS also uses a category of "household offenses," but this includes offenses against vehicles, which we have deliberately omitted to concentrate the analysis. It is also worth noting that our definition of criminal damage to the home is relatively restricted and excludes damage to garages and sheds unless they were on the same plot of land as the dwelling.

    It is well established in the criminological literature (see, e.g., Maguire, 2007) that considerable care must be taken in interpreting police-recorded crime data, because of the potential biases created by (a) the nonreporting of offenses by the public to the police (including differential reporting of different offenses) and (b) the nonrecording by the police of offenses reported to them by the public (including differential recording of different offenses). In the present instance, we have little relevant data on police recording practices (though see below), but we have extracted information from the 2005–2006 BCS data set on the national rates of reporting of different offenses to the police by the public. For the offenses in our study, these reporting rates are as follows: residential burglary, 67%; garage/shed burglary, 51%; criminal damage to the home, 38%; theft in a dwelling, 36%. Thus, the reporting of an incident of residential burglary is nearly twice as probable as the reporting of criminal damage or theft in a dwelling, and these differences need to be borne in mind in interpreting the data.

    Figure 2.1 shows graphically the counts for the four offenses over the 101 months of the study. The offense count for all four offenses taken together was broadly stable. Within this total, however, residential burglary decreased (reflecting national trends in both recorded crime and BCS data), while criminal damage increased from about 2002, very possibly as a result of changes to the national police recording standards, which from 2002 required a more inclusive approach to the recording of more minor offenses (see Maguire, 2007).

    It is important to note that researching repeat victimization using a recorded crime data set is a very different undertaking than if one uses a crime survey such as the BCS. The principal difference is that crime survey researchers can collect full demographic and social data on respondents and their households, but a recorded crime data set contains no information at all about nonvictimized households and minimal social information about victimized households. To partially overcome these deficiencies, in the present study we have used relevant small-area data from the 2001 National Census so that we can link crime data to some social information about the communities where victims live. On a more positive note, when using recorded

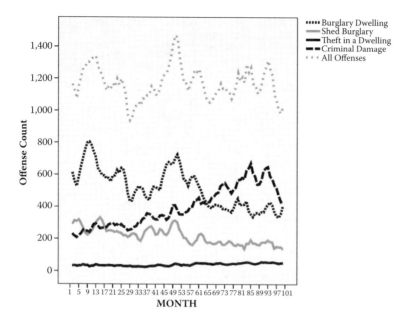

Figure 2.1 Counts of recorded offenses across the study period.

crime data, one has access to some information that is not available in crime surveys, and hence, for example, in the final part of this chapter we are able to utilize data on detected offenders to test whether the same offenders are involved in successive victimizations.

Repeat Victimization: Basic Data

Table 2.1 provides basic data on victimization and repeat victimization for the offenses in this study over the whole 101-month research period. As regards repeat victimization, the raw data are sufficiently detailed for us to be able to identify repeats to specific households over the whole research period, although not whether the residents in that household have changed during this period.

Table 2.1a includes data for all four offenses combined, while Table 2.1b and Tables 2.1c provide specific data for the two most common offenses (residential burglary and damage to the home). As noted above, there are some important technical differences between these two offenses (a differential reporting rate by the public to the police, different time trends in crime incidence over the study period, a likely difference in relation to the 2002 change in recording standards); hence, if on a specific matter a similar result is obtained for both offenses, other things being equal this increases one's confidence in the validity of the result.

Table 2.1 Repeat Victimization for Household Offenses in Sheffield, April 1998–August 2006 (%)

No. of occasions household was victimized	Whether household victimized	Percentages for victimized households only	Percentage of offenses
	(a) All household offenses		
0	67	—	—
1	22	67	41
2	6	19	24
3	2	7	13
4+	2	6	22
	100	100	100
	(n = 217,618)	(n = 72,871)	(n = 118,206)
	(b) Residential burglary		
0	82	—	—
1	14	79	60
2	3	15	23
3	1	4	9
4+	0.4	2	8
	100	100	100
	(n = 217,618)	(n = 39,779)	(n = 52,172)
	(c) Damage to home		
0	88	—	—
1	9	73	47
2	2	16	20
3	0.7	6	11
4+	0.7	6	21
	100	100	100
	(n = 217,618)	(n = 26,054)	(n = 40,111)

Those conversant with the literature on repeat victimization will recognize that the data in Table 2.1 show a familiar picture of marked disparity between households in the extent of their victimization (see, e.g., Farrell, 1995; Pease, 1998). For example, taking all offenses together (Table 2.1a), two thirds of Sheffield households had no household offenses at all recorded by the police during this period of eight and a half years—a large degree of immunity. On the other hand, 2% of the households suffered 22% of all the offenses recorded in the study—a large degree of misery. Among specific offenses, this bipolar pattern was particularly marked in the case of damage to the home (Table 2.1c).

Criminologists working in sociospatial criminology have developed an analytically very useful set of concepts for distinguishing different aspects of crime in a given geographical area over a given period. These are:

- *incidence*, or the total crime rate in the area per 1,000 population or per 1,000 households;
- *prevalence*, or the proportion of persons or households victimized for a given crime or crimes, regardless of whether they are once-only victims or repeat victims during the study period;
- *concentration*, or the average number of victimizations suffered by each victim during the study period.

When studying repeat victimization, it is particularly valuable to consider the concentration rate and the prevalence rate for areas. The concentration rate is of course a direct measure of repeat victimization, while the prevalence rate is statistically independent of concentration (while incidence = prevalence × concentration). Previous repeat victimization studies (beginning with Trickett, Osborn, Seymour, & Pease, 1992) have found that areal prevalence and concentration rates are positively correlated, that is, as the crime prevalence rate for an area increases, so does the average number of victimizations per victim. In the present study, this result was strongly replicated when all household crimes were considered together (the correlation between prevalence and concentration was .80, $p < .001$), and also for the two most numerous offenses in the study, residential burglary and damage to the home ($r = .78$ and .84, respectively; both $p < .001$). Interestingly, however, the other two offenses showed less strongly correlated patterns (shed/garage burglary $r = .22$, $p < .001$; theft in a dwelling $r = .01$, nonsignificant). In the case of shed and garage burglaries, it was also found that the geographical patterning of the victimizations was very different from the other offenses. While for all other offenses in this study there was a strong negative correlation between the income level of the area and the incidence of household offenses (ranging from .50 in the case of residential burglary to .88 for damage to the home), such a correlation was completely absent for shed and garage burglaries. This is a finding that would merit fuller investigation on another occasion.

Finally, in assessing the basic features of repeat victimization for household offenses in this data set, we considered how prevalence and concentration rates varied over the 8 years of the study period. As Table 2.2 shows, for all crimes taken together, the prevalence rate declined slightly, while the concentration rate rose slightly, during the period. Residential burglary showed a particularly interesting pattern, with a steep decline in prevalence but virtually no change in concentration (a pattern similar to that shown in the BCS during this period: see Hope, 2007b). Criminal damage, by contrast, showed a doubling in the prevalence rate but a more modest change in concentration.

Having thus set out some of the basic features of repeat victimization in this data set, we can turn more directly to the issues raised in Hope and Trickett's (2004) article.

Table 2.2 Prevalence and Concentration Indices, Years 1–8 (Year 1 = 100)

Year	All household crime		Residential burglary		Damage to home	
	Preva-lence	Concen-tration	Preva-lence	Concen-tration	Preva-lence	Concen-tration
1	100	100	100	100	100	100
2	97	100	89	99	114	102
3	86	100	77	98	115	102
4	94	101	82	99	136	103
5	101	103	90	99	153	107
6	87	105	63	100	177	108
7	89	107	60	98	207	112
8	91	107	56	98	220	112

Replicating the Hope–Trickett Analysis

Empirically, the most important section of Hope and Trickett's article is their reanalysis of the victimization data from an earlier research report coauthored by Foster and Hope (1993). Among the data collected for this earlier project were before-and-after household crime surveys with a panel element (conducted in 1987 and 1990), where the main original purpose of the data collection was to measure changes in victimization between the two study years in an experimental area and a control area. The purpose of the reanalysis was to compare the 1987 and 1990 victimization data for these areas to test three hypotheses arising from Hope and Trickett's postulated "immunity model." These hypotheses were (a) that there is a general trend toward immunity over time, regardless of initial victim state; (b) that a significant subgroup in the population appears to be immune from victimization, in that they are not victimized either in 1987 or 1990; and (c) that there is nevertheless a chronic group in the population who are repeatedly victimized over time. Using the Foster and Hope data, all three hypotheses were supported (see Hope and Trickett, 2004).

Using recorded crime data (rather than crime survey data as in the Foster-Hope study), we are able to retest these hypotheses in the present analysis, but with two improvements, namely, (a) a substantially longer follow-up period than the 3 years available in the Foster–Hope data set and (b) a substantially larger numerical sample. We tested the hypotheses by comparing victimizations in the first 3 years (1998–2001) and the last 3 years (2003–2006) of our study period, using two-way tables (see Table 2.3) similar to those developed in Hope and Trickett's (2004) analysis. In brief, all three of the Hope–Trickett hypotheses were again supported both for all household offenses (Table 2.3a) and for residential burglaries and damage to the home (Tables 2.3b and 2.3c). Taking all household offenses together, for example:

Table 2.3   Comparison of Households' Victimization in the First 3 Years (1998–2001) and Final 3 Years (2003–2006) of the Study Period

Period 1	Period 2			
	Not victimized	Single victim	Repeat victim	Total
	(a) All household offenses			
Not victimized	160,799 (87.2%)	19,031 (10.3%)	4,511 (2.4%)	184,341 (100.0%)
Single victim	22,016 (82.2%)	3,468 (13.0%)	1,303 (4.9%)	26,797 (100.0%)
Repeat victim	4,430 (68.4%)	1,409 (21.7%)	641 (9.9%)	6,480 (100.0%)
Total	187,177 (86.0%)	23,918 (11.0%)	6,455 (3.0%)	217,618 (100.0%)
$\chi^2 = 2{,}705.4$ $(df = 4)$, $p < .001$.				
	(b) Residential burglary			
Not victimized	188,455 (94.7%)	9,517 (4.8%)	1,035 (0.5%)	198,997 (100.0%)
Single victim	14,665 (90.8%)	1,300 (8.0%)	191 (1.2%)	16,156 (100.0%)
Repeat victim	2,117 (85.9%)	259 (10.5%)	89 (3.6%)	2,465 (100.0%)
Total	205,227 (94.3%)	11,076 (5.1%)	1,315 (0.6%)	217,618 (100.0%)
$\chi^2 = 981.1$ $(df = 4)$, $p < .001$.				
	(c) Damage to the home			
Not victimized	197,245 (94.1%)	9,807 (4.7%)	2,563 (1.2%)	209,615 (100.0%)
Single victim	5,720 (84.0%)	697 (10.2%)	391 (5.7%)	6,808 (100.0%)
Repeat victim	804 (71.3%)	179 (15.9%)	144 (12.8%)	1,127 (100.0%)
Total	203,769 (93.6%)	10,683 (4.9%)	3,098 (1.4%)	217,618 (100.0%)
$\chi^2 = 2{,}797.1$ $(df = 4)$, $p < .001$.				

1. Concerning Hypothesis (a): 82% of singly victimized households at Period 1 were not victimized at Period 2; and this was even true of two thirds of those households that had been repeatedly victimized at Period 1.
2. Concerning Hypothesis (b): A total of 160,800 households—nearly three quarters of all the households in Sheffield—had no recorded victimizations for any household crime in any of the 6 years comprising Period 1 (1998–2001) or Period 2 (2003–2006).*
3. Concerning Hypothesis (c): Nevertheless, victimization at Period 2 was very significantly more probable for those who were victimized at Period 1 ($p < .001$). There is even a small group of 641 households (0.3% of all households in Sheffield) that were *repeat* victims *both* within Period 1 and within Period 2. This tiny group of households suffered 3.8% of all the offenses on the police register throughout the 101 months of the study period, and they averaged over seven victimizations per address in this period. Clearly, therefore, they may reasonably be described as "chronic" victims, in the language of Hope and Trickett.

---

* In addition, as Table 2.1 shows, the great majority of these households (67% of all households, rather than 74%) also had no household crimes in the intervening 29 months (2001–2003).

Thus, this empirical analysis strongly supports all the key features of the Hope–Trickett analysis, using a different kind of data than theirs (recorded crime rather than a household survey) and with one of the longest follow-up periods yet used in repeat victimization research. These results clearly suggest that Hope and Trickett's immunity thesis should be taken very seriously by all researchers interested in repeat victimization.

We turn now to another facet of the Hope–Trickett analysis, namely, some questions raised by what they describe as the "double hurdle approach" (see above). In his small Australian longitudinal study, Frank Morgan (2001) drew attention to some intriguing results when he compared the data for two subareas, with differing overall burglary rates, within the Perth suburb that he was researching. Morgan noted, first, the apparently greater "importance of repeat burglary to victims in low-burglary rate areas relative to their expected risk" and, second, the fact that "burglary victims from high- and low-risk areas appear to converge in their likelihood of future burglary when compared with their burglary-free neighbours." He further noted that these results were consistent with some earlier findings by Osborn et al. (1996), which appeared to suggest that "protection against subsequent victimization is reduced in low-risk households, and that differences in overall or initial risk shrank for repeat victimization" (Morgan, 2001). Hope and Trickett regarded these data as constituting an important, if somewhat puzzling, element within the overall framework of results available to criminological researchers on repeat victimization.

The Sheffield data allow for the first examination of these issues with a large sample of recorded crimes, so we will consider the empirical findings before commenting on this aspect of Hope and Trickett's overall argument. Relevant data are given in Table 2.4, where for analytical purposes we have divided the areas of the city into quintiles based on the incidence of the relevant crime(s) being considered—that is, the incidence of all household offenses in Table 2.4a, residential burglary in Table 2.4b, and so on. The first column shows, for the various different offenses, the probability of a given household being victimized for the relevant offense(s) within the first 2 years of the study period (i.e., the prevalence rate, or "Hurdle 1"). The second column shows the probability of such a victimized household becoming a repeat victim, at any time during the 101-month study period after the initial victimization ("Hurdle 2").

Naturally, the data for Hurdle 1 show a declining prevalence rate as one moves from the highest crime rate quintile (Quintile 1) to the lowest (Quintile 5). Less obviously, the same pattern is repeated for Hurdle 2, although here the proportionate gap between Quintiles 1 and 5 is, as in the previous studies, consistently smaller than in the equivalent data for Hurdle 1. It follows that, as column 3 of the table shows, the ratio of the revictimization rate to the

Table 2.4   The "Double-Hurdle" Model Applied to Area Quintiles for the Relevant Offences

Quintile	Hurdle 1: nonvictim to victim	Hurdle 2: victim to repeat victim	Hurdle 2/hurdle 1 ratio
(a) All household offenses			
1 (High)	0.190	0.576	3.037
2	0.141	0.478	3.391
3	0.098	0.402	4.111
4	0.075	0.328	4.373
5 (Low)	0.014	0.256	17.964
(b) Residential burglary			
1 (High)	0.131	0.421	3.205
2	0.081	0.331	4.091
3	0.049	0.236	4.808
4	0.036	0.161	4.470
5 (Low)	0.022	0.128	5.710
(c) Damage to home			
1 (High)	0.063	0.473	7.555
2	0.030	0.320	10.849
3	0.015	0.201	13.070
4	0.010	0.160	16.250
5 (Low)	0.005	0.090	19.228

Note: "Hurdle 1" refers to a victimization for the relevant offense at some point in the first two years of the study period. "Hurdle 2" refers to an initial victim in the first 24 months subsequently becoming a repeat victim (at any time in the study period).

initial victimization rate is consistently greatest in the low-crime areas; and therefore, exactly as in Morgan's Perth study, the data show the greater "importance of repeat burglary to victims in low-burglary rate areas *relative to their expected risk* [italics added]." In short, therefore, the patterns of recorded crime data in Sheffield on this issue are very similar indeed to those found by Morgan and, earlier, by Osborn et al.

In their article, Hope and Trickett reconsider the Morgan/Osborn et al. findings, after they have presented their overall thesis about immunity. In this concluding discussion, they suggest that the data for low-rate areas might be "interpreted as a hypothetical prediction of what might happen *if* victimization occurs to breach immunity and *if* no action is taken to restore it. In other words, if both of these were to happen, then the probability of victimization would be raised considerably—people who were hitherto immune would then come to resemble chronic victims." Perhaps this is so. However, Hope and Trickett also note an alternative explanation for the data, namely, that they might reflect "unmeasured event-dependency" (ibid.). In our view, this second possibility is the more likely, although to explain why, we need first to consider the Sheffield data on fast repeats.

The Time Course of Repeat Victimization

Having examined some of the main issues raised by Hope and Trickett, it is now appropriate to assess how far the Sheffield data support some of the claims of the more orthodox school of repeat victimization researchers. Here we shall concentrate especially on Pease's (1998, p. 3) summary, in which (as previously noted) he claimed that:

> Victimization is the best single predictor of victimization;...when victimization recurs it tends to do so quickly...a major reason for repetition is that offenders take later advantage of opportunities which the first offence throws up.

A central issue raised by this statement is, clearly, the time course of repeat victimization, and in particular the extent of "fast repeats." Unfortunately, however, there are technical problems in presenting valid data on the time course of repeat victimization, especially when using data sets covering a short overall time-span. (This is because, with time-limited data sets, it is often difficult to secure uniform follow-up periods for all the victimizations—early victimizations can receive a longish follow-up, but later victimizations often require truncated follow-ups.) To avoid these difficulties, we have measured the repeat victimization time course for the Sheffield sample by including only households that were first victimized in the first 4 years of the study, and we have then followed up each victimized household for a standardized period of 4 years from the first victimization. Figure 2.2 shows the resulting distribution of the period between the first and the second victimizations. The pattern shown is rather similar to that found in many earlier studies (e.g., Farrell, 1995; Kleemans, 2001; Polvi et al., 1991)—that is, a sharp peak in the early months of the follow-up period, followed by a gently declining curve thereafter. However, in this particular graph the slope of the curve is less steep than in some other studies.

But is the apparent message given by the time-course data perhaps artifactual? Spelman (1995) has usefully pointed out that time-course graphs of the sort shown in Figure 2.2 could be generated even if "there were *no* changes in risks [of revictimization] over time and all locations ran identical risks" (emphasis in original). The reason for this is because:

> the number of victims eligible for revictimization drops steadily over time. Everyone is eligible for revictimization during month 1; some proportion

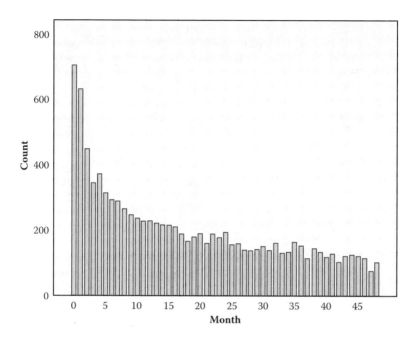

Figure 2.2 Time course of second victimizations over a standardized 4-year period (all household offenses). Data show number of complete months between the first and the second victimization for any household offense.

(say, 10 per cent) are revictimized, leaving 90 per cent of the original sample available for victimization in month 2; 10 per cent of the remainder is 9 per cent; and so on (p. 369).

However, in the present instance, the total number of households is so large (217,618)—relative to the counts shown in Figure 2.2—that the shape of the curve changes very little if one corrects each month's data to exclude previously victimized households from the denominator. Thus, for example, the revictimization rate in Month 1 is 704 of 217,618 households, or 3.2 per 1,000 households; in Month 2 it is 631 of 216,914, or 2.9 per 1,000 households; then by Month 6, the corrected rate has dropped to 1.5 per 1,000 households, and by month 12 to 1.1 per 1,000. In short, there is no doubt that there is a strong "bunching" effect of repeat victimization for household offenses in the months immediately after the first victimization.

It is at this point that the previously discussed issue of mechanisms becomes central to the discussion. As Bernasco (2008) has pointed out, it is certainly possible to construct hypothetical scenarios for "flag" explanations of fast repeats—for example, a family might go on holiday (perhaps in a blaze of local publicity), leaving their house vulnerable for a limited period, an opportunity which various offenders independently accept. Perhaps this kind of thing really does sometimes happen—criminologists have not systematically

Table 2.5   Time Patterns for Revictimizations after a First Victimization within the Initial 2 Years of Study Period, Differentiated by Total Victimizations in the Study Period (All Household Offenses)

Total victimizations in study period	% of included households revictimized within 30 days of first victimization	No. of households
2	4.8%	5,933
3	7.5%	2,940
4–5	9.3%	1,761
6+	13.8%	803
All	6.8%	10,987

$\chi^2 = 120.9 \ (df = 3), p < .001.$

investigated the matter. However, despite such examples, it is surely impossible to believe that "flag" is the dominant explanation for fast repeats, given the size of the effect, and its consistency across research projects. Given these facts, some linkage between the first and second events seems inescapably likely to be the main explanation—and "linkage" implies "boost" rather than "flag." For these reasons, it is rather disappointing that Hope and Trickett (2004), who as we have seen tend to minimize the significance of boost explanations, say so little about the time course of repeat victimization.

The overall thrust of our arguments to this point is therefore that we should take both fast repeats and the "immunity thesis" (including its emphasis on long-term chronic victimization) seriously in developing our overall understanding of repeat victimization. But how do these two phenomena relate to each other? This is an almost totally unexplored question within the repeat victimization literature. One possible hypothesis is that "chronic victims" are a separate group, continually victimized, and that the "fast repeats" tend to occur predominantly to other households, with less frequent victimizations. We tested this hypothesis on the Sheffield data, with results as shown in Table 2.5. Households with a minimum of two victimizations were first differentiated according to the total number of household offenses they had suffered during the whole 101 months. Then, only those households first victimized within the first 2 years were selected, and the proportion of such households revictimized within 30 days was calculated. (This test was deliberately designed so that the "fast repeat" data were independent of the "total number of victimizations" data.) As may be seen, a statistically significant result was obtained, but one that was in the reverse direction from the "separate phenomena" hypothesis that we had constructed. Instead, households with a large number of victimizations over the study period were statistically more likely also to suffer a fast repeat when they were first victimized: the two phenomena coincided. A possible

Table 2.6   Detected Pairs of Revictimizations: Time-Course Comparisons[*] (All Household Offenses)

	Same offender for both offenses	Different offender
Median time-lapse	2.0	19.0
Modal time-lapse	0.0	3.0
Mean time-lapse	6.8	26.7
n	668	782

Mann–Whitney test for comparison of means, $U = 100,934.0$, $p < .001$.

[a] Data were calculated as complete months of time elapsed between the two detected offenses, for example, a 2-week period is coded as 0, a 10-week period as 2.

reason for this convergence is that multiple victimized households tend to be located in high-crime and socially deprived areas and that offenders also often live in such areas (see, e.g., Craglia and Costello, 2005); hence, it is easier for them to select chronically vulnerable households because they know the area and they can also, as elsewhere, follow up with fast repeats. However, this is largely speculative, because such processes have not yet been researched.

The above discussion considers time-course issues from the point of view of the victim. What happens if we switch the focus and instead consider the viewpoint of the offender?

Pease's (1998) contention is that "a major reason for repetition is that offenders take later advantage of opportunities which the first offense throws up." His assumption, at least for household offenses, is clearly that the same offenders return to the scene; and there is indeed interview-based evidence from offenders that they sometimes do this (see reviews in, e.g., Pease, 1998; Bernasco, 2008). A recorded crime data set with the ability to link offense and offender data allows a direct statistical test of the "same offender" hypothesis; and Bernasco (2008) has recently used a 9-year data set on detected burglaries in The Hague to conduct such a test. His conclusion is that pairs of detected burglaries that are close to one another in time[*] are much more likely to involve the same offender(s) than are other burglaries.

We carried out a similar test on the Sheffield data as regard the time course of repeat victimization; although in doing so, we were, like Bernasco, aware of potential research pitfalls arising from the fact that detection rates for these offenses are low (in the case of the offenses in the Sheffield data set, overall 14%) and that this necessarily to an extent complicates the interpretation of the results. With this caveat, our results were in fact very similar to those of Bernasco

---

[*] Bernasco (2008) reached a similar conclusion about burglaries that were close to one another "in space." This raises the issue of so-called near-repeats, an important topic that has recently attracted significant research attention but which is beyond the scope of this chapter.

(see Table 2.6). There was a striking difference, for example, between the median time-lapse for pairs of detected offenses where the same offender was involved (median = 2–3 months) and for pairs that involved different offenders (median = 19–20 months). This adds to the evidence suggesting that there might well be a difference in the appropriate explanation for fast repeats and for slower repeats. It is also worth noting that, overall, less than half of the detected pairs of offenses (668 of 1450, or 46.1%) involved the same offender returning.

In light of all the evidence, from the Sheffield study and other studies, how far can Pease's (1998) now 10-year-old summary still be said to be valid? Let us break the summary down into its three component parts, but this time in reverse order from the original:

1. "A major reason for repetition is that offenders take later advantage of opportunities which the first offense throws up." This claim is partly true, but it is true very predominantly for fast repeats rather than slower repeats (Table 2.6).

2. "When victimization occurs it tends to do so quickly." As we have seen, there is substantial empirical support for this claim. On the other hand, we should not neglect the fact that there are also significant numbers of slower repeats (in Figure 2.2, e.g., 71% of all the repeats occur 6 months or more after the first victimization). Moreover, Hope and Trickett claim, and Table 2.3 shows, that there is a small group of victims who are continually victimized. Although they too suffer fast repeats (Table 2.5), an exclusive crime-preventive focus on the fast repeat would fail to capture the real misery of their situation, which is the chronic character of their victimization.

3. "Victimization is the best single predictor of victimization." Let us immediately leave aside the question whether it is "the best" predictor and concentrate on whether it is a significant predictor. From what has been said above, it is clear that it is a significant predictor for fast repeats. But what about the longer term? Given the data in support of the "immunity hypothesis," it might seem that victimization is not a continual predictor of revictimization. In fact, however, as Table 2.7 shows, with each successive victimization there is an enhanced probability of subsequent victimization, so Pease's (1998) summary is correct. The reason why the data support both Pease's claim and Hope and Trickett's immunity hypothesis lies in the relatively low proportions of revictimizations. It is only after the third victimization in the sequence that most victims are revictimized, and by then we are dealing with only 1.5% of the households in Sheffield.

In short, then, Pease's (1998) summary, in all its three aspects, is accurate for fast repeats but rather less accurate for the longer term. In this, it

Table 2.7   Cumulative Probabilities of Revictimization for Any Household Offense

	n	% of all Sheffield households[a]	% of previously victimized households[b]
A. First victimization within 24 months	24,188	11.1	—
B. Second victimization by 48 months	6,942	3.2	28.7
C. Third victimization by 72 months	3,235	1.5	46.6
D. Fourth victimization by 96 months	1,900	0.9	58.7

[a] n for all Sheffield households = 217,618.

[b] That is, the n shown in the relevant row expressed as a percentage of the n of the previous row (e.g., in row B, 6,942 ÷ 24,188 = 28.7%).

contrasts markedly with Hope and Trickett's analysis, which is strong on longer term issues but virtually ignores fast repeats. A main conclusion of the present analysis must therefore be that the criminological community needs a better synthesis between these different research approaches.

Finally, we return to the issues raised in the previous section concerning Morgan's (2001) observation about the greater "importance of repeat burglary to victims in low-burglary rate areas, relative to their expected risk." At the end of our previous discussion, we quoted Hope and Trickett's somewhat complex and conditional ("if…if…") conclusions on this matter, but we noted that they also posited a possible alternative explanation, that of "unmeasured event dependency" (or "boost"). In light of the discussion in the present section, it seems to us that this alternative explanation has substantial merit. Fast repeats, which can predominantly be attributed to "boost" explanations, do occur. Although they occur more frequently to chronically victimized households in high-crime rate areas, they also occur in low-rate areas. Given that the overall crime rate is, by definition, lower in such areas, it should not be surprising if the risks of (especially) fast repeats make the risk ratio for a further offense jump more sharply from Hurdle 1 to Hurdle 2 in low-crime areas than it does in high-crime areas.

Concluding Discussion

As previously noted, our analysis, and the exploration of the Sheffield longitudinal data set, has led to the conclusion that there are substantial merits both in "orthodox" repeat victimization scholarship (exemplified especially in the work of Pease and Farrell) and in some of the challenges to that scholarship in the work of Hope and Trickett (2004). However, both approaches also seem to have some blind spots. The obvious way forward seems to be to combine the positive merits of each approach in a creative synthesis.

Types of Repeat Victimization

We suggest that a central feature of such a synthesis should be a clear recognition that repeat victimization is not, on the available evidence, a unitary phenomenon but rather occurs in very different ways in different contexts. To help researchers and crime prevention practitioners to understand this diversity, we think it will be valuable to follow the lead of Max Weber and to construct some "ideal types" of repeat victimization, recalling that for Weber ideal types are "exaggerated or one-sided descriptions that emphasise particular aspects of what is obviously a richer and more complicated reality, but whose very unreality aids us in disentangling the different elements" that are contained in the complexity of the real world (Kronman, 1983).

On this basis, we think at least three "ideal types" of repeat victimization can usefully be distinguished. The first type can be described, in Ken Pease's (1998) words, as a crime sequence within which is embedded the unfolding of a relationship. Pease's examples of this type of repeat victimization include "domestic violence, embezzlement, sexual abuse of children and bullying." In effect agreeing with Pease on this point, Hope (2007a, 2007c) has suggested that one of Hope and Trickett's two "polar risk groups," namely, the chronic victims, can be seen as being analogous to the victims trapped in abusive domestic relationships. Researchers in fact currently know very little about households who suffer long-term victimization for household crimes (see further below), but one telling statistic from the present study is perhaps relevant to this discussion. Of the 641 households that were repeat victims both in the first 3 years and the last 3 years of the study period (see Table 2.3), no fewer than 53% also had a household member who was identified in police files—at some point in the 8 years of the study—as being an offender. This is a very high proportion; it suggests that chronic victims might often be embedded in some of the complex relational networks of friendship, resentment and retaliation that earlier studies of "offenders as victims" have noted (see Lauritson and Laub, 2007).

But by no means all repeat victimization, even of the chronic type, is necessarily relational. Earlier, we gave as an example the relatively affluent household in a deprived area suffering from vehicle crime. Similarly, such households might experience repeat victimization for household crimes, for "flag" reasons, with no necessary "relationship" between the victims and the multiple offenders who choose their house as a target. A concrete example of this type of repeat victimization is the vicarage (priest's house) in a deprived area, which is often perceived by other residents—rightly or otherwise—as being relatively affluent, and for which there is evidence of above-average victimization levels.

Both of the first two ideal types of repeat victimization are long term, but as we have seen, repeat victimization does not have to be long term. A third ideal type of repeat victimization would therefore be the fast repeat in a low-crime area. As it happens, one of us (A.E.B.) has personal experience of this kind of repeat victimization: at the time, his house was in a low-crime, semirural area, happily existing in a state akin to Hope and Trickett's permanent immunity. But a burglar took advantage of a short absence on holiday, and then within 2 weeks (and despite the family's return) tried the same modus operandi again.* Thereafter, however, the house reverted to its traditional state of immunity. There was certainly nothing "relational" about these events, although there was, obviously, what Hope (2007c) has described as "victim's agency" in response to the first victimization.

It seems clear to us that these three different ideal types of repeat victimization all exist—and there might also be other ideal types worth describing. Naturally, however, in the real world the types will sometimes overlap.

Oddly, very little attention has been given in the repeat victimization literature to differentiating different types of repeat victimization—certainly nothing like as much attention as has been given to the issues raised by "boost" and "flag" accounts. Yet arguably, the differentiation of types of repeat victimization is the more important of these topics because the different types seem to require both different explanatory accounts (an intellectual task) and different crime prevention strategies (a practical task). As we have noted, in our view, a much fuller discussion of the different types of repeat victimization is the best way to take forward the creative research synthesis that is now clearly needed.

Implications for Future Research

As regard future research, the most glaring research gap to have emerged from the analysis in this chapter is the serious lack of research into long-term repeat victimization for household offenses. The reasons for this are not difficult to uncover: orthodox repeat victimization scholarship has focused on the statistical importance of the fast repeat (see Figure 2.2) and its crime prevention implications, and the full significance of longer-term repeats has emerged from research analyses only in the recent past. Hence, we know that both of our first two ideal types of repeat victimization exist (i.e., "long-term relational" and "long-term flag"), but we currently know very little in detail about them nor do we have any way of estimating their relative size. In addition, if one adopts a "mechanism-based" approach to explanation (Hedström, 2005), then offenders' accounts of repeat victimization must be of central importance (see above); but the limited amount of research into offender accounts of

---

* AEB remains grateful to the then rather new repeat victimization literature, which had alerted him to the possibility of a fast repeat. This led to the rapid installation of additional security, which foiled the burglar's attempt to get into the house on the second occasion. It is good to know that criminological analysis can sometimes have valuable practical consequences in everyday life.

repeat victimization has hardly considered longer term repeat victimization. This topic, then, should be a serious priority for future research attention.

Implications for Crime Prevention

In a recent article, Farrell and Pease (2006) have reviewed the research evidence on programs designed to prevent repeat residential burglary. Using rigorous standards for the evaluation of research, they concluded that, on present evidence, the most successful preventive efforts are "context specific," use multiple tactics, have strong implementation, and are focused on high burglary rate situations. The authors also note ruefully that "the evidence regarding preventive effectiveness is quite sobering in light of the significant progress that has been made in the more general empirical investigation of the nature of repeat residential burglary and repeat victimization"—in other words, repeat victimization analysis has been better than repeat victimization preventive practice.

Among the other issues that are raised in this article by Farrell and Pease (2006), one is perhaps worth special mention, especially given the clear statistical evidence that repeat victimization for household crime is disproportionately concentrated in poor areas:

> It is clear that a key issue relating to implementation is: who pays for prevention equipment? The evidence suggests that victims are often unable or unwilling to invest in additional security even when warned of increased crime risks (p. 174).

However, in light of the discussion in this chapter, it seems that this issue is a little more complex than Farrell and Pease indicate in this quotation—for much may depend on the long-term victimization prospects.

If a household has very limited resources and is told, after a first burglary (a) that there is a heightened short-term risk of repeat victimization, but (b) the risk of such a second victimization is less than 30%, and that, even if they are revictimized, there is then a 53% probability of immunity over the succeeding two years (see Table 2.7), they might well decide to accept the initial risk of revictimization. If, however, on the best risk assessments (for which data are not yet available), it looks as if the household might be in serious danger of becoming a "long-term chronic" victimized household, then the cost-benefit analysis might look very different.* Thus, it would seem, in light of the analysis in this chapter, there is a strong case for some rethinking, not only of our understanding of repeat victimization but also perhaps of some of the conceptual foundations of our preventive policies.

---

* Of course, also, the fact that "long-term chronic" revictimizations are most likely to occur in the most deprived neighborhoods will be a highly relevant consideration for policy.

Acknowledgment

We are most grateful to Graham Farrell, Ken Pease, and Tim Hope for their invaluable and constructive comments on an earlier draft of this chapter.

References

Ashton, J., Brown, I., Senior, B., & Pease, K. (1998). Repeat victimisation: Offender accounts. *International Journal of Risk, Security and Crime Prevention, 3,* 269–280.

Baldwin, J., & Bottoms, A. E. (1976). *The urban criminal.* London: Tavistock.

Bernasco, W. (2008). Them again? Same-offender involvement in repeat and near repeat burglaries. *European Journal of Criminology, 5.*

Biderman, A. D. (1980). Notes on measurement by crime vicitimization surveys. In S. E. Fienberg & A. J. Reiss Jr. (Eds.), *Indicators of crime and criminal justice: Quantitative studies* (pp. 29–32). Washington, D.C.: U.S. Bureau of Statistics.

Bottoms, A. E., Mawby, R. I., & Walker, M. A. (1987). A localised crime survey in contrasting areas of a city. *British Journal of Criminology, 27,* 125–154.

Bottoms, A. E., Mawby, R. I., & Xanthos, P. (1989). A tale of two estates. In D. Downes (Ed.), *Crime and the city* (pp. 36–87). Basingstoke: Macmillan.

Bottoms, A. E., & Wiles, P. (1986). Housing tenure and community crime careers in Britain. In A.J. Reiss Jr. & M. Tonry (Eds.), *Communities and crime* (pp. 101–162). Chicago: University of Chicago Press.

Chenery, S., Ellingworth, D., Tseloni, A., & Pease, K. (1996). Crimes which repeat: Undigested evidence from the British Crime Survey 1992. *International Journal of Risk, Society and Crime Prevention, 1,* 207–216.

Craglia, M., & Costello, A. N. (2005). A model of offenders in England. In F. Toppen & M. Painho (Eds.), *AGILE 2005 (Association Geographic Information Laboratories Europe): Eighth Conference on Geographic Information Science* (pp. 489–497). Lisbon: Universidade Nova de Lisboa.

Farrell, G. (1995). Predicting and preventing revictimization. In M. Tonry & D. P. Farrington (Eds.), *Building a safer society; Strategic approaches to crime prevention* (pp. 469–534). Chicago: University of Chicago Press.

Farrell, G., Edmunds, A., Hobbs, L., & Laycock G. (2000). *RV snapshot: UK policing and repeat victimisation* (Crime Reduction Research Series Paper 5). London: Home Office.

Farrell, G., & Pease, K. (1993). *Once bitten, twice bitten: Repeat victimisation and its implications for crime prevention* (Crime Prevention Unit Series Paper 46). London: Home Office Police Department.

Farrell, G., & Pease, K. (Eds.). (2001). *Repeat victimization.* Monsey, NY: Criminal Justice Press.

Farrell, G., & Pease, K. (2006). Preventing repeat residential burglary victimization. In B. C. Welsh & D. P. Farrington (Eds.), *Preventing crime: What works for children, victims and places.* Dordrecht: Springer.

Farrell, G., & Pease, K. (2007). The sting in the tail of the British Crime Survey: Multiple victimizations. In M. Hough & M. Maxfield (Eds.), *Surveying crime in the 21st century* (pp. 33–53). Monsey, NY: Criminal Justice Press.

Forrester, D., Chatterton, M., & Pease, K. (1988a). *The Kirkholt Burglary Prevention Project, Rochdale* (Home Office Crime Prevention Unit Paper 13). London: Home Office.

Forrester, D., Chatterton, M., & Pease, K. (1988b, November). Why it's best to lock the door after the horse has bolted. *Police Review, 4,* 2288–2289.

Forrester, D., Frenz, S., O'Connell, M., & Pease, K. (1990). *The Kirkholt Burglary Prevention Project, phase II* (Home Office Crime Prevention Unit Paper 23). London: Home Office.

Foster, J., & Hope, T. (1993). *Housing, community and crime: The impact of the Priority Estates Project* (Home Office Research Study 131). London: HMSO.

Hedström, P. (2005). *Dissecting the social: On the principles of analytical sociology.* Cambridge: Cambridge University Press.

Hope, T. (2007a, 28 February). *Differential immunity: A general theory of crime victimization.* Seminar to the Centre for Criminological Research, University of Sheffield.

Hope, T. (2007b). The distribution of household property crime victimization: Insights from the British Crime Survey. In M. Hough & M. Maxfield (Eds.), *Surveying crime in the 21st century* (pp. 99–124). Monsey, NY: Criminal Justice Press.

Hope, T. (2007c). Theory and method: The social epidemiology of crime victims. In S. Walklate (Ed.), *Handbook of victims and victimology* (pp. 62–90). Cullompton: Willan.

Hope, T., Bryan, J., Trickett, A., & Osborn, D. R. (2001). The phenomena of multiple victimization. *British Journal of Criminology, 41,* 595–617.

Hope, T., & Trickett, A. (2004). La distribution de la victimation dans la population. *Déviance et Société, 28,* 385–404.

Hughes, G. (1998). *Understanding crime prevention: Social control, risk and late modernity.* Buckingham: Open University Press.

Kleemans, E. R. (2001). Repeat burglary victimization: Results of empirical research in The Netherlands. In G. Farrell & K. Pease (Eds.), *Repeat victimization* (pp. 53–68). Monsey, NY: Criminal Justice Press.

Kronman, A. T. (1983). *Max Weber.* London: Edward Arnold.

Kuhn, T. S. (1996). *The structure of scientific revolutions* (3rd ed.). Chicago: University of Chicago Press.

Lauritsen, J. L., & Davis-Quinet, K. F. (1995). Repeat victimization among adolescents and young adults. *Journal of Quantitative Criminology, 11,* 143–166.

Lauritsen, J. L., & Laub, J. H. (2007). Understanding the link between victimization and offending: New reflections on an old idea. In M. Hough & M. Maxfield (Eds.), *Surveying crime in the 21st century* (pp. 55–75). Monsey, NY: Criminal Justice Press.

Laycock, G. (2001). Hypothesis-based research: The repeat victimization story. *Criminal Justice, 1,* 59–82.

Maguire, M. (2007). Crime data and statistics. In M. Maguire, R. Morgan, & R. Reiner (Eds.), *The Oxford handbook of criminology* (4th ed., pp. 241–301). Oxford: Oxford University Press.

Mawby, R. I. (1979). *Policing the city.* Farnborough: Saxon House.

Mayhew, P., Maung, N. A., & Mirrlees-Black, C. (1993). *The 1992 British Crime Survey* (Home Office Research Study 132). London: HMSO.

Morgan, F. (2001). Repeat burglary in a Perth suburb: Indicator of short-term or long-term risk? In G. Farrell & K. Pease (Eds.), *Repeat victimization* (pp. 83–118). Monsey, NY: Criminal Justice Press.

Nelson, J. F. (1980). Multiple victimization in American cities: A statistical analysis of rare events. *American Journal of Sociology, 85,* 870–891.

Osborn, D., Ellingworth, D., Hope, T., & Trickett, A. (1996). Are repeatedly victimized households different? *Journal of Quantitative Criminology, 12,* 223–245.

Osborn, D., & Tseloni, A. (1998). The distribution of household property crimes. *Journal of Quantitative Criminology, 14,* 307–330.

Pease, K. (1998). *Repeat victimisation: Taking stock* (Crime Detection and Prevention Series Paper 90). London: Home Office Police Research Group.

Pease, K. (2008). Victims and victimization. In S. G. Shoham, O. Beck, & M. Kett (Eds.), *International handbook of penology and criminal justice* (pp. 587–611). Boca Raton, FL: CRC Press.

Planty, M., & Strom, K. (2007). Understanding the role of repeat victims in the production of annual US victimization rates. *Journal of Quantitative Criminology, 23,* 179–200.

Polvi, N., Looman, T., Humphries, C., & Pease, K. (1990). Repeat break-and-enter victimization: Time course and crime prevention opportunity. *Journal of Police Science and Administration, 17,* 8–11.

Polvi, N., Looman, T., Humphries, C., & Pease, K. (1991). The time course of repeat burglary victimization. *British Journal of Criminology, 31,* 411–414.

Sparks, R. F. (1981). Multiple victimization: Evidence, theory and future research. *Journal of Criminal Law and Criminology, 72,* 762–788.

Sparks, R. F., Genn, H., & Dodd, D. (1977). *Surveying victims.* Wiley: London.

Spelman, W. (1995). Once bitten, then what? Cross-sectional and time-course explanations of repeat victimization. *British Journal of Criminology, 35,* 366–383.

Trickett, A., Osborn, D. K., Seymour, J., & Pease, K. (1992). What is different about high crime areas? *British Journal of Criminology, 32,* 81–90.

Tseloni, A., & Pease, K. (2003). Repeat personal victimization: "boosts" or "flags"? *British Journal of Criminology, 43,* 196–212.

Wiles, P., & Costello, A. N. (2000). *The "road to nowhere": The evidence for travelling criminals* (Home Office Research Study 207). London: Home Office.

Wittebrood, K., & Nieuwbeerta, P. (2000). Criminal victimization during one's life course: The effects of previous victimization and patterns of routine activities. *Journal of Research in Crime and Delinquency, 37,* 91–122.

In the Frame: 20th-Century Discourses about Representations of Crime in Fictional Media

3

CHAS CRITCHER

Contents

Introduction

The debate about whether the mass media cause crime or other deviant behavior is alive and well. American academics, especially psychologists, often consider it to have been resolved. Here is a recent example. "Basically, the scientific debate over *whether* media violence has an effect is over and should have been over by 1975" (Anderson, 2004, original emphasis). The same article undertakes a "scientific meta-analytical review" of studies of violent video game playing. Its conclusions, once again, are unequivocal: "exposure to violent video games is significantly linked to increases in aggressive behaviour, aggressive cognition, aggressive affect, and cardiovascular arousal and to decreases in helping behaviour" (Anderson, 2004). Such a linkage is claimed to be causal and "linked to serious, real-world types of aggression" (Anderson, 2004). To confuse matters, reviews by other psychologists come to precisely the opposite conclusion (Bensley & van Eenwyk 2001): "current research is not supportive of major concern that video games lead to real life violence."

This accusation against a media form, that it induces violent, aggressive, or even criminal behavior among the otherwise law-abiding, is nothing new. British historical studies, such as those by Pearson (1983) and Springhall (1998), have concurred. "The monologue of fears about the moral downfall of the common people as the result of debased amusements, stretching back across more than two centuries, must be counted as one of the determining traditions within the unfolding preoccupation with the decline and fall of the 'British way of life'" (Pearson, 1983). At the heart of such debates has been the question about the effects of the new medium, whatever it is, on violent, deviant, or criminal conduct among the young. In the 20th century, the debate sharpened, but it had been evident well before in reactions to earlier forms of mass culture.

Popular amusements attracted criticism in mid-19th-century Britain. Young people congregated at nightly penny gaffs, especially in London. These provided a mixture of song, comedy, magic, and dance. Middle-class observers were alarmed. There was opportunity for lewd intercourse between the sexes. The dramatization of the exploits of highwaymen and other notorious criminals encouraged criminal thoughts and deeds among the audience (Springhall, 1998). In America, in the 1870s, there was a crusade against cheap dime novels (Starker, 1989). These mainly cowboy and detective stories were alleged to affect their readers by arousing their sexual desires, inciting them to commit criminal acts and diverting their minds from hard work and thrift. The 20th century would bring new types of electronic media, able to transmit graphic images instantaneously to mass audiences. Crime, an established theme of popular culture, inevitably appeared on page and screen.

Dire consequences were anticipated if any of the audience sought to imitate the fictional images to which they were exposed.

This chapter analyzes three significant episodes in the history of the mass media in the United Kingdom: films before and after the First World War, comics in the 1950s, and so-called video nasties in the early 1980s and again in the early 1990s. For each episode, we will review the emergence of the new technology or genre and the immediate reaction to it, the remedial measures adopted, and the characteristics of the campaigners. Lastly, we will apply the framework of moral panic, as originally outlined by Cohen.

> Societies appear to be subject, every now and then, to periods of moral panic. A condition, episode, person or group of persons emerges to become defined as a threat to societal values and interests; its nature is presented in a stylized and stereotypical fashion by the mass media; the moral barricades are manned by editors, bishops, politicians and other right-thinking people; socially accredited experts pronounce their diagnoses and solutions; ways of coping are evolved or (more often) resorted to; the condition then disappears, submerges or deteriorates and becomes more visible. Sometimes the object of the panic is quite novel and at other times it is something which has been in existence long enough, but suddenly appears in the limelight. Sometimes the panic passes over and is forgotten, except in folk-lore and collective memory; at other times it has more serious and long-lasting repercussions and might produce such changes as those in legal and social policy or even in the way the society conceives itself (1973, p. 9).

The conclusion will identify some empirical generalizations and their theoretical implications.

Film: Reel Life Fantasies

Emergence and Reaction

Cinematograph shows first appeared in the United States and the United Kingdom during 1896, showing mostly in variety theaters. Specialist film theaters were built from 1909 onward. Thus, produced was "a mass audience for what became known as the cinema which far outstripped any previous form of commercial entertainment in its appeal to the young" (Springhall, 1988). Immediate reaction to this unprecedented form of mass entertainment was often fearful.

> In 1910, people not only marvelled at the technical virtuosity of the screen, they also feared its effects. First there were its physical dangers: that darkened and ill-ventilated cinemas could damage the eyesight and encourage the spread of infection: that children who went regularly to the cinema would forfeit the

exercise necessary to healthy development; that the realistic terrors and excitement viewed would over stimulate young minds, making them subject to night terrors; that late nights and lack of sleep would impair concentration on school work. But the moral dangers were even more to be feared. Attempts were made to screen films in lighted cinemas, for there was a risk that young couples would take advantage of the darkness for immoral activities, or perverts would molest young people sitting next to them. Perhaps children would be encouraged to steal or beg to get the price of admission to their favourite entertainment, or people would imitate the behaviour seen on the screen, and so a rise in crime and immorality would result. Most serious of all, perhaps the subtle influence of the cinema would give young people false values, encouraging them to reject chastity and virtue, to despise marriage, home, and family, and to decide that the only drawback to crime was getting caught (Bertrand, 1978, pp. 15–16).

The composition of the audience was especially problematic because, as one Australian police inspector put it in 1918, cinema was unlike the "adult" audience for theater since, "here the audiences are comprised largely of women, young children and boys" (Bertrand, 1978). Boys would be incited to commit crimes, girls to indulge in illicit romances. The movies appeared to portray real events with direct emotional appeal. A professor of philosophy complained that the movies "represent real flesh and blood characters and import moral lessons directly through the senses." For boys in the audience, the film "forces upon his view things that are new, they give firsthand experience" (Black, 1994).

Remedy

Though some critics of film argued that more suggestive adults, notably women, might have their heads turned by films, most arguments centered on the vulnerability of children. In their name censorship was inaugurated in all nations where the cinema became a mass pastime. In the United States the Catholic Legion of Decency campaigned for films to adhere to Christian morality. Using propaganda effectively and threatening to organize boycotts of immoral films, they were instrumental in forcing the industry to undertake self-regulation, in the form of the Hays Code. For public showing, all films had to comply with this set of strict moral prohibitions that governed the content of American films from the late 1920s to the mid 1960s (Black, 1994, 1997). In Britain, the first form of censorship appeared in the guise of concern over health and safety. After a series of fires in ramshackle venues, the Cinematograph Act of 1909 aimed to improve safety standards by requiring licensing of premises showing films. Some local authorities exploited the act to try to censor what was shown.

Eventually the British Board of Film Censorship (BBFC) was founded by the industry amid mounting pressure for a government censorship body.

It began work in 1913 "with only two rules – no nudity and no personification of Christ" (Smith, 2005). Films would be given two types of certificate, U for Universal and A for Public. Both were regarded as suitable for children but the former would be especially recommended for matinees. Local authorities were initially suspicious of the film industry's own body and continued to censor films themselves but the BBFC established its preeminence, especially after issuing stricter censorship guidelines in 1917. Despite the new rules, the association of film with crime continued to be troublesome, as noted in the BBFC annual report for 1919.

> One of the most difficult subjects with which the Board has had to deal is the question of crime…Stories of crime make a strong appeal to the imagination of the public, especially to the less educated sections. When a story of crime is accompanied with the further elements of daring adventure, or romance, and of mystery, there are the elements of a popular success. It is also true that to young people, especially boys, with their ingrained instinct for adventure, uncorrected by experience of life, such 'crime' films make a special appeal, and it may be added, a dangerous appeal. (Smith, 2005, p. 30)

The BBFC code, revised in 1925, explicitly referred to a need to censor "dangerous mischief easily imitated by children" (Smith, 2005).

A specific challenge for the censors was the Hollywood gangster movie. Seventy-eight were made between 1930 and 1933 before the Hays code began to bite in 1934. In the US films had endings altered, moralizing prologues or epilogues added, and crucial speeches rewritten. By the time they reached the United Kingdom there was no need for any censorship nor much apparent inclination for it. The prevailing view that American crime fiction bore no relationship to British realities was comforting. More disconcerting were horror movies, notably *Dracula* and *Frankenstein* in 1931. Though films of horror classics had been made in silent versions, the addition of sound added a new and disturbing dimension. The prospect of children being exposed to such films provoked religious organizations, already disturbed by the genre's play with Christian symbolism, and the child saving lobby.

In the early 1930s the Home Office and local authorities debated the status of the A certificate. Councils wanted it to become exclusively for adults; the BBFC demurred. The Home Office compromise was that children should only be admitted accompanied by a responsible adult. In 1933 the same Home Office circular which resolved the A certificate dispute, also advocated adding the label H for horror films. This was still only advisory, that such films were unsuitable for children, but in 1937 it became a stand-alone category to which children would be refused admission. The new certificate represented the first formal exclusion of children from film-going. This had resulted from shifts in perceptions of the ill effects of cinema. Less emphasis was now placed on what behavior the cinema might provoke and more on the ways in which it might upset children's emotional balance. Smith (2005) cited one statement that 'the interest has altogether changed. We are concerned not with the morals of the children but with their fear, of wolves foaming at the mouth and that sort of thing.' This source was a former member of the London County Council education committee, a fairly typical monitor of the new medium.

Activist Critics

Who objected most to the cinema and on what grounds? Richards (1984) identified three groups as very active in responding negatively to the cinema in the United Kingdom: teachers, the clergy, and "the moralists." But "one group almost always in favour of the cinema was the police" on the grounds that it kept young people out of the pub or off the street. Clues about cinema's critics, their arguments and motives can be found in various semi-official inquiries conducted into the matter. In 1917 the Cinema Trade Council asked the National Council of Public Morals to undertake "an independent enquiry into the physical, social, moral, and educational influence of the cinema, with special reference to young people" (Smith 2005). It took evidence over six months from major institutions, eventually producing a 400-page report that was largely positive. It specifically tackled the alleged connection between the cinema and crime. Juvenile crime, it argued was too complex to be attributed to a single cause, especially a marginal one: "While a connection between the cinema and crime has to a limited extent in special cases been shown, yet it certainly has not been proved that the increase in juvenile crime generally has been consequent upon the cinema, or has been independent of other factors more conducive to wrongdoing" (Smith 2005).

Nevertheless, the advent of talkies provoked another flurry of inquiries, four between 1930 and 1933. The Birmingham National Council of Women asked for stricter censorship and set up its own inquiry when rebuffed by Home Office. It was clearly biased against film from the outset. A Birkenhead enquiry followed the Birmingham model and reflected the same prejudices. London County Council instigated an inquiry when frustrated by its inability to prevent children seeing some films. It involved over 20,000 children. An inquiry in Edinburgh conducted by the city's "Juvenile Organisations Committee" based its evidence on a survey of schoolchildren. The latter two found little cause for concern, suggesting that "within key institutions, including the church, education and the media, there was a large range of opinion and a significant amount of qualified support for children's cinema-going" (Smith 2005). Smith makes two main observations about those involved in these inquiries. First, particular kinds of organizations were prominent: "their members were nearly all from religious, educational, youth and women's organisations" (2005). Second, women were very prominent, comprising for example 62 per cent of the Edinburgh inquiry membership. Married women especially made great play of their concerns as mothers.

Critics rather resented the intrusion of cinema into the socialization process normally dominated by family, school, and church. Loss of control over the socialization process could at different times produce concerns with imitations of criminal behavior or with emotional disturbance among children. Regulation would realign the messages from films with those from other governing agents.

Moral Panic and Regulation

Before the First World War the government, like local authorities, believed that film provoked crime. Meeting their representatives in 1916, Home Secretary Herbert Samuel said: "I have lately obtained the opinion of a number of Chief Constables, who declare with almost complete unanimity that the recent increase in juvenile delinquency is, to a considerable extent, due to demoralising cinematograph films" (Smith, 2005). Appearing yet again as Home Secretary in 1932 in a Commons debate on juvenile crime, Samuel expressed precisely the opposite view: "my very expert and experienced advisors at the Home Office are of the opinion that on the whole the cinema conduces more to the prevention of crime than to its commission...In general, the Home Office's opinion is that if the cinema had never existed there would probably be more crime than there is rather than less" (Springhall, 1988).

Nevertheless, the censorship system was tightened throughout the 1930s, with the A certificate theoretically requiring an adult to accompany a child, and the H certificate excluding children altogether. Children tried to circumvent the rules. They would ask an adult to pretend they were with them to gain entry to an A certificate – though this could not be done with the new H certificate. A regulatory system was in place that successfully prescribed who could watch which films in the cinema. The question is whether this was the outcome – Cohen's "measures resorted to" – of a moral panic. Smith argues it was not, for four reasons. First, it was not a sudden reaction. The debate lasted from before the war into the late 1930s. Second, the reaction was not "hostile, groundless or irrational" (2005). Cinema did have effects, there was a genuine debate about what they were, and attempts were made to establish "the facts." Third, there was no discernible folk devil since the objection was to a form of entertainment. Finally, the campaign against the cinema was fragmented into local pockets of concern and lacked a national spearhead. Overall the reaction to cinema was "too gradual, complex and varied to be described as a classic moral panic" (2005). This position seems well justified but may not extend to our next case study of comics.

Comics: Lines of Conflict

Emergence and Reaction

A wholly new style of comic, which "came from a tradition of publishing very different from that previously known in Britain," because "aimed at adults" (Barker, 1984c), was launched in 1934. Their growth was phenomenal. By 1941, thirty publishers were producing 150 titles and selling 15 million to 18 million copies each month to about 60 million readers. By 1943, because widely read by the armed forces, monthly sales had increased to 26 million (Springhall, 1998). Ten years later in 1953-4 sales had tripled to 75 million a month.

These comics, including cowboy, crime, horror and war genres, soon attracted criticism. Especially influential was a book *Seduction of the Innocent* by American psychiatrist Fredric Wertham, published in 1954. Wertham accused the comics of espousing abhorrent moral views, including racism and sexism. More damningly, he argued that they caused criminal behavior among boys. Wertham's book influenced campaigns everywhere. Its key assumptions were that comics invited readers to identify with perpetrators of violence, that children would automatically do so, and that this would have a negative effect on their moral development. Alleged effects were deduced from the texts so that "claims about effects are logically tied up with claims about what the comics are like" (Barker, 1984c).

Several of the states in America attempted to ban comics but the legislation was ruled unconstitutional. In response—and following the lead of the film industry 20 years earlier—the industry formulated a Comic Books Code in 1954. This effectively put an end to horror comics, though crime comics were able to continue. Overall, the U.S. comic book industry lost its mass market until Superman and other comic heroes came along in the 1960s. In Britain, campaigners founded the Comics Campaign Council in 1953. Its objectives were to:

1. make known as widely as possible the variety and dangers of the more vicious types of comics;
2. discourage the production, sale and distribution of these publications;
3. encourage the production of more attractive and desirable literature for children, both in strip form and other styles. (Barker, 1984c, pp. 12–13)

Influential members of the CCC included a teacher, a psychologist, a youth leader, and a teacher turned full-time mother. Nearly all were members of the British Communist Party. Such activists could not succeed alone. They needed support from a larger and more respectable organization. Crucial for this was the intervention of the National Union of Teachers (NUT). They had been discussing the issue from 1952 but only decided to act in 1954, following a letter to the *Times Education Supplement* by campaigner George Pumphrey drawing attention to a specific comic, *The Haunt of Fear,* which the national press picked up. The issue dovetailed with the NUT's efforts to establish the teaching profession as a moral touchstone. They decided to hold an exhibition of comics in 1955. It had immediate impact: "MPs, and many powerful people attended it, and left duly shocked. The BBC filmed it for the TV news, and most newspapers covered it. Several MPs were to express their gratitude for exposing the matter" (Barker, 1984c). In the British tradition, a new law was proposed.

Remedy

The Children and Young Persons (Harmful Publications) Act was passed in 1955 and renewed in 1965. The opening paragraph clarified its scope:

> This act applies to any book, magazine or other like work which consists wholly or mainly of stories told in pictures (with or without the addition of written matter), being stories portraying–
>
> 1. the commission of crimes; or
> 2. acts of violence or cruelty; or
> 3. incidents of a repulsive or horrible nature;
> 4. in such a way that the work as a whole would tend to corrupt a child or young person into whose hands it might fall (whether by inciting or encouraging him to commit crimes or acts of violence or cruelty or in any other way whatsoever) (Barker, 1984c, p. 17)

Penalties consisted of "four months imprisonment or a £100 fine, or both, for the printing, publishing or selling such material."

The United Kingdom was not alone in passing such a law. Canada (1949) and New Zealand (1954) had been the first (Watson & Shuker, 1998). Equivalent measures were adopted in many parts of the world, across Europe and into Asia (Lent, 1999).

Activist Critics

Barker found astonishing "just how much the campaign had depended on the organised intervention of the British Communist Party" (1984c), especially in its early stages. One motive for their involvement was to attack American culture. With very little coverage or build-up in national newspapers before the 1955 Act, the media were not significant players in the campaign, serving mainly to report on its progress. When the press did take an interest, the discourse was a familiar one of (British) civilization under threat, as in this *Times* editorial on November 11, 1954:

> The problem which now faces society in the trade that has sprung up of presenting sadism, crime, lust, physical monstrosity, and horror to the young is an urgent and grave one. There has been no more encouraging sign of the moral health of the nation than the way in which public opinion has been roused in condemnation of the evil of "horror comics" and the determination to combat them (Springhall, 1998, p. 142).

Criticism of the comics often depended on the belief that comics invoked the worst kind of emotional reaction, as in this extract from a CCC pamphlet: "Comics fascinate children because most people, and probably all children, react first with their feelings rather than their minds, and the more primitive the emotions stimulated, the stronger the reaction. Comics appeal to the primitive feelings, and these drown out other and higher emotions" (Barker 1984c).

The early emphasis on comics as directly causing criminal behavior was gradually displaced by a moral objection to the inherent depravity of the comics involving "the idea of 'horror' as the focus of the disturbance of children's minds" (Barker, 1984c). Crime comics were actually ideologically conventional. Those becoming criminals typically lost all decency and sense of proportion, so behaving in ways that guarantee their capture and punishment. "Here is a threshold between society and a kind of nether world of crime. In that nether world, all the laws of connectedness of events change. And once you are in it, you are on a slippery slope, to worse and worse crimes and thus to self-destruction" (Barker, 1984c).

By contrast, horror comics were much more complex. The genre depends on "shock-logic" where apparently normal interactions are suddenly undermined by the manifestation of an alternative, horrific logic of action. Barker gives his own interpretation of the complexity of a notorious strip *Lucy's Tale*, in which a young girl frames her parents for the murder of her mother's lover, so she can start a new life without them. Springhall's (1998) review of typical plots comes to a similar conclusion that they "offer a domesticated version of horror centred on the modern American family, invariably involving mutual antipathy, hidden secrets, divorce, adultery and violent impulses." Appreciation of the genre depends on understanding its conventions and its capacity for self-parody. This deliberate distancing cannot justify assumptions about the reader's "identification" with the perpetrator of the horrific acts. Crucial to the whole argument was "the inability of politicians to read comic books in a figurative or satirical sense" (Springhall, 1998).

Moral Panic and Regulation

The problem identified by campaigners was the adaptation of the comic format for a teenage or young adult male audience. Their stories about war, crime, and horror seemed devoid of moral content and concentrated on action of a violent and sometimes horrific kind. The self-evident danger was that less mature readers would emulate the actions drawn on the page. Springhall (1998) identifies campaigners' more hidden motives including intellectual disdain for the latest manifestation of mass culture, the need to explain rising juvenile crime, and anti-American sentiments. Barker sees the campaign as a defense of an increasingly fragile sense of Britishness against the corrupting forces of Americanism. It depended crucially on intuition/commonsense for understanding of both the comics and their effects. As would be the case with video nasties later, it was only necessary to put the offending material on display for all decent people to appreciate how dangerous it was. The campaign was an unqualified success. The comics were effectively banned from Britain and largely ceased publication. For Barker, "the lack of opposition is amazing" (1984c).

Springhall specifies why the comics campaign met the requirements of a moral panic:

> All the symptoms of a classic "moral panic" had been made manifest in the British "horror comic" scare; the media definition of a "threat"; the stereotyping of comic books as "horror comics"; a spiralling escalation of the perceived "threat" through the media and censorship lobbying: and, finally, the emergence of a parliamentary "solution" in terms of tough legislation, moral isolation and symbolic court action. British reaction to the Americanised threat was more than slightly hysterical, temporarily effective, and then completely forgotten (Springhall, 1998, p. 146).

The comics campaign seems to be an almost perfect moral panic. Barker is not so sure—critical of the tendency of moral panic theorists to overemphasize the role of the media and downplaying the importance of understanding the (genuine) motives and tactics of campaigners. Differences between media are also likely to be elided. Yet, overall, the model apparently holds for this example in ways it did not for film.

Video Nasties: Cutting Up Rough

Our third case study, of video nasties, produced in the United Kingdom two separate episodes in 1982–1984 and 1992–1994, almost exactly 10 years apart—a "double" panic. The narrative—the emergence/reaction and remedy phases—will be presented separately for each episode first. Then, the activists and the process of moral regulation will be considered across both episodes.

Emergence and Reaction: 1

The first episode followed the rapid take-up of the videocassette recorder (VCR) in the early 1980s. By 1982, a third of households owned or rented one. Six thousand tapes could be rented from 20,000 locally owned video shops. Coincidentally, Hollywood produced a crop of gruesome horror films. Their irresponsible marketing—on covers, posters, and magazines—prompted complaints that the Advertising Standards Authority largely upheld in 1981 (Petley, 1984). Video magazine editors agreed new standards for adverts. The press was alerted. Articles in the *Daily Mail* and *Sunday Times* in late May stressed the extreme violence of such films, including sadism, mutilation, and cannibalism. The precise origins of the term *video nasty* are unclear, but it was diffused by the *Sunday Times*. The British Board of Film Classification (BBFC) set up a joint working party with the British Videogram Association (representing distributors) to devise a mandatory classification scheme. The National Viewers and Listeners Association (NVLA), formed in the 1960s to campaign against sex and violence on television, was advocating stricter controls than for cinema. Throughout 1982, the government favored a voluntary code.

Over the summer the distributors of five videos (*Death Trap, Cannibal Holocaust, SS Experiment Camp, I Spit on Your Grave,* and *Driller Killer*) were successfully charged under the Obscene Publications Act and forfeited all copies. By August 1982, "the video nasty moral panic was well established" (Petley, 1984). The industry now reluctantly recognized the need to clarify the law. Few voices were raised in protest.

In December 1982, Labour MP Gareth Wardell proposed a law to prohibit renting of 18 certificated films to children. The motion was passed, but the government declined to back it. The opponents of video nasties were not to be fobbed off. In February 1983, the *Daily Mail* launched a "Ban the Sadist Videos" campaign. In a letter to NVLA leader Mary Whitehouse, Prime Minister Margaret Thatcher indicated her concern. Whitehouse then "came up with her master stroke" (Petley, 1984) in the planning of a screening for MPs of selected extracts from the nastiest videos. In April 1983, the government called a general election. The Conservative Party's election manifesto promised measures to deal with "the spread of dangerous and obscene video cassettes" (Barker, 1984b). Throughout June and July, the press discovered court cases where violent offenders blamed videos for their behavior. Films on general release were often implicated. "By this time the term 'video nasty' had unmistakably become synonymous simply with 'horror film'" (Petley, 1984). Legislation soon followed.

Remedy: 1

After its June election victory, the government supported a Private Member's Bill. It sought to outlaw the sale or hire of any video without a certificate from an authority and the sale or hire of adult-certificated videos to children, with maximum penalties of a £1000 fine and 2 years in prison. The bill passed its first reading in September 1983 and its second reading in November. In between, the NVLA held its screening for MPs. The amended bill required the BBFC to be "aided" by guidelines from the Director of Public Prosecutions and to pay "due regard" to the fact that videos were likely to be seen in the home. The maximum fine was increased to £20,000. The Bill became law as the Video Recordings Act 1984.

Emergence and Reaction: 2

On February 12, 1993, 2-year-old James Bulger was abducted from the Strand shopping center in Bootle, taken to a nearby canal and then two and a half miles to a railway track, where he was brutally beaten to death, his body left on the rails to be cut in half by a passing train. Shock at this horrific murder was compounded when two boys, aged 9 and 10, were charged with the crime. The boys, Jon Venables and Robert Thompson, were tried for 70 days in November 1993, found guilty of murder, and sentenced to be "detained at Her Majesty's pleasure." The trial judge, on this rare occasion, made a statement in open court after the boys had been taken away. He observed that "it is not for me to pass judgement on their upbringing but I suspect violent video films may in part be an explanation." He singled out *Child's Play 3*, which "had some striking similarities to the manner of the attack on James Bulger." The police officer in charge of the case told *The Guardian*, "he had no evidence to suggest that the boys had access to any videos worse than might be found in many households."

After the verdict, press opinion blamed moral decline on liberal permissiveness, the collapse of family life, and the failings of schools. However, the real culprit was obvious: "the Bulger case came to be dominated by arguments about the effects of the media" (Buckingham, 1996). Broadsheet papers debated the issue, but popular papers eschewed logic. The front page of *The Sun* the day after the trial simply declaimed "for the sake of our kids BURN YOUR VIDEO NASTY."

Remedy: 2

Much of the campaign was orchestrated by a fundamentalist religious organization, the Movement for Christian Democracy (MCD). In January 1994, they drafted an amendment to the Criminal Justice Bill about to go through parliament, calling for the banning on video of all films "likely to cause psychological harm to children." David Alton, a Catholic and Liberal MP who spearheaded the campaign, claimed the support of more than 200 MPs from all parties. Nevertheless, Home Secretary Michael Howard rejected the amendment as unworkable, effectively banning from video many films already granted a cinema certificate. He instead offered a tighter guidance to the BBFC. However, it became clear that Howard would lose the vote. In eleventh-hour negotiations with Alton and Labour leader Tony Blair, Howard agreed to change the legislation. Penalties for supplying unlicensed videos or adult videos to children would be increased and the BBFC would have to pay regard to videos that "present an inappropriate model for children or are likely to cause psychological harm to a child." The *Daily Mail*'s leader (April 13, 1994) was ecstatic about a measure that signaled "nothing less than a return to responsible censorship by popular demand." This remains the current law of the land on video certification.

Activist Critics

Barker identifies "an hysterical press campaign (which) got going through 1982 and climaxed in 1983" (Barker, 1984a). The key newspaper was the *Daily Mail*, with the *Sunday Times* a close second. The mid- and down-market press relished the prospect of a moralistic campaign. A *Daily Mail* editorial on June 30, 1983, was typical: "The failure of our politicians to turn back this tide of degenerate filth and to prevent it fouling the minds of children and adolescents is nothing short of a national scandal" (Barker, 1984a). Ten years later, an editorial in the *Express* (November 26, 1993) declared: "More and more children are growing up in a moral vacuum, which for so many is being filled with fetid junk from the lower depths of our popular culture—video nasties, crude comics and violent television." Analyzing press coverage of the Bulger verdict, Franklin and Petley argue that "the 'normal' requirements of reporting were abandoned in favour of undiluted, vitriolic editorialising" (1996).

Outside the press, the chief actors in the double moral panic were fundamentalist religious groups, the NVLA led by Mary Whitehouse in the first episode and the MCD led by David Alton in the second. The NVLA's tactics proved successful. "The NVLA's lobbying on the issue of video nasties is an object lesson in How To Do It" (Petley, 1984). They had found an issue that was novel, newsworthy, and brooked no opposition. Some insight into the views of such campaigners came from a book published subsequently. Hill (1985) makes four specific objections to video nasties: they are viewed unregulated in the home; offer realistic and sadistic portrayals of violence; are devoid of moral messages; and invite emotional identification with the perpetrator. The evil is popular culture, undermining public (and implicitly Christian) morality. Adopting similar views, the MCD was crucial in 1993–1994. Its newsletter revealed that £13,000 had been raised to support the campaign, a parliamentary draftsman employed to draft the amendment, and a petition circulated with 100,000 signatories (Petley, 1994). Even the upmarket press made no sustained attempt to reveal the religious agendas of the NVLA or the MCD.

Newspapers and Christian lobbyists combined to put pressure on the government, largely through backbench MPs. Although it is unclear how far concern about video nasties in 1983–1984 spread beyond the elites of church, parliament, and press, opposition to "the media hysteria and the ill-conceived legislation" remained "almost non-existent" (Petley, 1984).

Moral Panic and Regulation

In the case of video nasties, the object of regulation was the viewing of graphic horror movies on videotape in the home. No attempt was made to regulate the production or importation of horror videos. Regulation was directed first at distributors and second at retailers. Unlike film or comics, this campaign did not start in the United States where the issue never arose in that form. The first reaction occurred in Sweden. New Zealand and Australia followed the United Kingdom, but elsewhere, response was muted (Critcher, 2003).

In the first episode, the identified problem was that the VCR-enabled films that either could not be seen in the cinemas or only under age restrictions to be watched at home. Its lack of regulation was compounded by the coincidental rash of "slasher" films. Such films did exist, could be obtained, and just possibly might be seen, by children. In the second episode, the focus was on horror films that already had certificates and were, like *Child's Play 3*, even being shown on satellite television. Uncertificated films were no longer the problem. Rather, it was the viewing of films by those supposed to be excluded by the certification category. There is no reliable evidence that significant numbers of children ever saw the 30 or so films originally defined as "video nasties." By the later episode, the video industry had expanded massively. Horror films only constituted 3% of the overall market, but some children did have the opportunity to see on video films they could not see in the cinema. Exposure does not, however, guarantee effect. *Child's Play 3* as a test case does not provide a model for violent imitation. It had been given a "15" certificate in cinema and an "18" on video. Whatever its quality, the film is clearly an ironic fantasy in which the villain, Chucky, is defeated.

Neither act had much long-term impact. The 1984 Act outlawed uncertificated videos, but these were already being prosecuted under the Obscene Publications Act. The 1994 amendment introduced a different system of classification for videos from cinema that delayed some releases, but many so-called video nasties were eventually certificated, albeit some years later. The measures were more symbolic than repressive.

Academic commentators suggest that the first episode was a "moral panic…whipped up by the National Viewers and Listeners' Association, the tabloid press, teachers, churchmen and others" (Petley, 1984). Buckingham (2000) accepts that the second episode was one of "a series of interdependent moral panics about children" in the last two decades of the 20th century, although wary of dismissing the often genuine concerns of campaigners and the public. The campaigns over video nasties were indeed almost perfect examples of moral panics, meeting virtually all of Cohen's requirements. Yet this generic model cannot quite specify how this issue came to be dominated by organized religious fundamentalism, "how, in many apparently secular societies, forms of evangelical Christianity have been so successful in defining the terms of the public debate" (Buckingham, 2000).

Conclusion: Regulation Rules

The influence of those accusing the media of prompting deviant behavior might appear to have waned. They may have won the occasional battle, but they have lost the war. It has not proved viable to demonstrate "that media violence makes people more aggressive *than they would otherwise have been*, or that it causes them to commit violent acts *they would not otherwise have committed*" (Buckingham, 2000, original emphases). If this is true for the United Kingdom, it is patently not so for the United States. There can be found a much wider acceptance for the idea "that violence, as it is dramatized on-screen in all its forms, affects our children and conditions them to be more violent than they would naturally become without being exposed to it" (Grossman & Degaetano, 1999).

American media policy has followed this new orthodoxy. The preamble to the 1996 Communications Decency Act stated unequivocally that the representation of sex and violence on television directly affects audience behavior. The outcome was the V-chip amendment requiring all new standard television sets to be fitted with a filtering device that could be activated to block identified programs. Broadcasters would rate each program so that parents could prevent unsuitable programs appearing on their TV screens. This technology is disputed by some broadcasters and apparently ignored by parents (Price, 1998). This contemporary effort to regulate television programming is unusual by international standards, yet in keeping with the history of efforts to regulate media representations of crime, sex, and other forms of deviance. Closer consideration of our case studies yields some empirical generalizations that have theoretical implications.

Empirical Observations

Three common threads emerge from our three case studies: the problematic status of the horror genre, the assumed susceptibility of working-class boys to imitate deviant behavior, and the objections to media images on moral grounds, as distinct from claims about effects. We started this discussion with the expectation that selected examples from the history of debates about mass media fictions would center on crime. We expected to find that fictional representations of criminal activity would be criticized for encouraging audiences to accept or indulge in criminal behavior. Censorship proposals or policies would be based on the fear that real crimes would occur as a result of fictional ones.

Such expectations have only been partly met. Some of the anticipated arguments were found in discussions of gangster movies in the 1930s, comics in the 1950s, and video nasties in the 1980s and 1990s. Acts of criminal violence were singled out for disapproval, yet each case study suggests that as a genre, crime proved less problematic than horror. Crime narratives could be, and were, altered in various ways to ensure the correct message: crime does not pay. In the United Kingdom, American gangster movies could be regarded as wholly unrealistic because nothing like that ever happened here. Horror, however, was another matter altogether. Its very essence was to disturb and shock. Such experiences were regarded as intrinsically unacceptable for the very young, less because they would imitate what they saw but more because it would disturb them emotionally. In the British system of film censorship, the first classification to exclude children totally was the H certificate. Legislation about comics effectively prohibited the horror comic because unlike its crime counterpart, it could not be infused with a moral message. Finally, video nasties were not crime films but the slasher variation of horror movies.

Critics refused to acknowledge the importance of genre. Films, comics, and video nasties were all interpreted literally by critics as intending to advocate whatever human behavior they showed. As Shubart (1995) notes, "hallmarks of the horror genre" are "the violent breaking of social and sexual taboos," "images of death," and "extreme sensations of shock and excitement." Kermode (1997) agrees, "Essentially a surrealist genre, contemporary horror demands to be read metaphorically rather than literally." How the meaning of any deviant act is embedded in the genre and thus interpreted by audiences is largely ignored. The culture's moral guardians understand little about the artifacts it produces.

They are, however, quite clear about the second recurrent theme— which parts of the audience are most at risk. It was in all cases taken for granted that boys, especially working-class boys, were especially at risk from media fictions about either crime or horror. (No campaign has ever been mounted against a media form or genre on the grounds that it would trigger widespread deviance among middle-class girls.) Debates about media violence have always been shot through with assumptions about sex and class. The socialization process for working-class boys is always regarded as tenuous. Anything that threatens to undermine it, even slightly, is regarded as jeopardizing the basis of civilization by releasing the barbarian within. Class bias is evident from those who led the attack on each occasion: local councilors and educationalists on film, members of the Communist Party and the NUT on comics, and religious fundamentalists in alliance with popular newspapers on video nasties. The middle class felt compelled to intervene to head off the threat from working-class boys exposed to dangerous influences. Class distaste and vitriol was especially apparent in media discussion of life on council estates in the aftermath of the Bulger trial. Here is columnist Lynda Lee Potter in the *Daily Mail* (April 13, 1994): "There are thousands of children in this country with fathers they never see and mothers who are lazy sluts. They are allowed to do what they want, when they want. They sniff glue on building sites, scavenge for food and, until now, they were free to watch increasingly horrific videos. By 16, they are disturbed and dangerous."

The third recurrent theme is the strain of moral repugnance among critics of the media. Direct effects were claimed to be the real danger, but equally, the objectors opposed the (lack of) moral code in media fictions. For example, some of Wertham's criticisms of comics have a distinctly modern ring. He claimed that they overtly condoned racism and sexism. It may be debatable whether this characterization is accurate, yet its viability does not depend on any claims about effects. Wertham was objecting in principle to the tacit approval of such attitudes in a medium of popular culture. We do not have to agree with his other views about comics, or his claim that they caused criminal behavior, to concede that this moral argument has some force. Rather too many video nasties involved violence against women, albeit highly stylized, for them to be absolved from moral critique.

Theoretical Implications

There is a pattern common to our three case studies about the emergence of a medium or technology, who reacts to it and how, and the remedies prescribed. Such regularities have been observed for a wide range of media innovations on both sides of the Atlantic (Springhall, 1998; Starker, 1989). The pattern approximates to that Cohen described for a moral panic. An *innovation* is defined as a threat, its nature is stylized and stereotyped by the media, moral entrepreneurs denounce it, experts confirm its heinousness, a legal solution is found, and the concern then dissipates. However, in important ways, panics about media deviate from the general model. For example, there are no human folk devils because the objection is to a cultural form or technology. The alleged threat, that audiences might imitate deviant behavior, is quite specific and narrow.

Drotner (1999) has consequently offered "media panic" as a subspecies of moral panic. Its specific characteristics are that new media are debated by old media, that opinions are polarized, and that the debate is about children but conducted by adults, with professional interests in the area. Often precipitated by a single case, the debate peaks quickly and then fades away as some kind of resolution is found. Following this suggestion, we can specify even more closely what is involved in a "media panic."

1. It is an immediate reaction to a new medium or genre.
2. It takes the new technology or form of it to be more graphic than anything before and thus more likely to persuade the audience of its realism.
3. The fictional representation of deviant behavior of some kind is problematic because of the dangers of imitation.
4. The meaning of the narrative is derived from a literal interpretation of its alleged content with little or no acknowledgment of the characteristics of the medium or genre.
5. Regulatory polices are predicated on the need to prevent such fictions being exposed to very young children and especially working-class boys.

These characteristics are shared by the three cases reviewed here, those preceding them such as dime novels, and those that have followed, notably computer games. However, this pattern is not automatically reproduced for every media innovation. Neither radio nor television was seriously alleged to threaten the moral order (Critcher, 2008). Why some innovations provoke panic while others do not is a question for future research.

It remains insufficient simply to establish whether or not a media/moral panic has occurred. Barker (1984c) finds moral panic an inadequate account of the British comics campaign because it assumes that the media are the key actors when his own study suggests the importance of organized pressure groups and their deeper motives. Springhall (1998) argues that the concept of moral panic stresses continuities in social reaction but actually disguises significant shifts and nuances. Smith (2005) adds the objection that the model imputes irrationality to campaigners, denying their claim to logical argument. Buckingham (1996) suggests moral panic analysis cannot itself reveal important underlying themes such as the contemporary resonance of apparent threats to and from children.

Overall, whether in its conventional form, or revised to apply specifically to the media, moral panic analysis only takes us so far. What may be required is to see moral panics as extreme instances of a wider process of moral regulation defined as "practices whereby some social agents problematise some aspect of the conduct, values or culture of others on moral grounds and seek to impose regulation upon them" (Hunt, 1999). All instances of moral regulation involve a specified target, moralizing agents, a range of tactics to be used, a set of persuasive discourses, and a process of political contestation. While moral panics are discrete episodes, moral regulation is a continuous process. The moral nature of the issue is not given; middle-class reformist organizations have to establish it. The scope of moral regulation is much wider than that of moral panics. Current debates about healthy living, for example, would not qualify as moral panics but can be seen as forms of moral regulation. Moral panics are much more about deviants and deviance. Media panics are about the alleged capacity of media technologies or forms to promote imitatory behavior among impressionable audience members.

We have identified some specific characteristics of reactions to fictional representations of crime in new media technologies or forms, which transpired to match those of moral panics. Their specific characteristics appear to justify a subspecies of media panic. The theoretical deficiencies of both kinds of panic analysis may be remedied by using the framework of moral regulation. Such conceptual advances may enable more sophisticated analysis of the next panic about media representations of crime, wherever and whenever it appears.

References

Anderson, C. (2004). An update on the effects of playing violent video games. *Journal of Adolescence, 27*, 113–122.

Barker, M. (1984a). Introduction. In M. Barker (Ed.), *The video nasties* (pp. 1–6). London: Pluto Press.

Barker, M. (1984b). Nasty politics or video nasties? In M. Barker (Ed.), *The video nasties* (pp. 7–38). London: Pluto Press.

Barker, M. (1984c). *A haunt of fears: The Strange story of the British horror comic campaign*. London: Pluto Press.

Bensley, L., & van Eenwyk, J. (2001). Video games and real-life aggression: Review of the literature. *Journal of Adolescent Health, 29*, 244–257.

Bertrand, I. (1978). *Film censorship in Australia*. St. Lucia: University of Queensland Press.

Black, G. (1994). *Hollywood censored: Morality codes, Catholics and the movies*. Cambridge: Cambridge University Press.

Black, G. (1997). *The Catholic crusade against the movies 1940–1975*. Cambridge: Cambridge University Press.

Buckingham, D. (1996). *Moving images: Understanding children's emotional responses to television*. Manchester: Manchester University Press.

Buckingham, D. (2000). *After the death of childhood*. Cambridge: Polity Press.

Cohen, S. (1973). Folk devils and moral panics. St. Albans: Paladin.

Critcher, C. (2003). *Moral panics and the media*. Milton Keynes: Open University Press.

Critcher, C. (2008). Making waves: Historical aspects of public debates about children and mass media. In S. Livingstone & K. Drotner (Eds.), *International handbook of children, media and culture* (pp. 90–104). London: Sage.

Drotner, K. (1999). Dangerous media? Panic discourses and dilemma of modernity. *Paedogogica Historica, 35*, 593–619.

Franklin, B., & Petley, J. (1996). Killing the age of innocence: Newspaper reporting of the death of James Bulger. In S. Wagg & J. Pilcher (Eds.), *Thatcher's children: Childhood, politics and society in the 1990s* (pp. 134–154). London: Falmer Press.

Grossman, D. G., & Degaetano, G. (1999). *Stop teaching our kids to kill.* New York: Crown.

Hill, C. (1985). Conclusion. In G. Barlow & A. Hill (Eds.), *Video violence and children* (pp. 160–170). Sevenoaks: Hodder and Stoughton.

Hunt, A. (1999). *Governing morals: A social history of moral regulation.* Cambridge: Cambridge University Press.

Kermode, M. (1997). I was a teenage horror fan, or, "How I learned to stop worrying and love Linda Blair." In M. Barker & J. Petley (Eds.), *Ill effects: The media/violence debate* (pp. 57–66). London: Routledge.

Lent, J. (Ed.). (1999). *Pulp demons: International dimensions of the postwar anti-comics campaign.* Madison, NJ: Fairleigh Dickinson University Press.

Pearson, G. (1983). *Hooligan: A history of respectable fears.* Basingstoke: Macmillan.

Petley, J. (1984). A nasty story. *Screen, 25*, 68–74.

Petley, J. (1994). In defence of video nasties. *British Journalism Review, 5*, 52–57.

Price, M. (Ed.). (1998). *The V-chip debate: Content filtering from television to the internet.* Hillsdale, NJ: Erlbaum.

Richards, J. (1984). *The age of the dream palace: Cinema and society in Britain 1930–1939.* London: Routledge.

Shubart, R. (1995). From desire to deconstruction: Horror films and audience reactions. In D. Kidd-Hewitt & R. Osborne (Eds.), *Crime and the media: The post-modern spectacle* (pp. 219–242). London: Pluto Press.

Smith, S. J. (2005). *Children, cinema and censorship.* London: I. B. Taurus.

Springhall, J. (1998). *Youth, popular culture and moral panics.* Basingstoke: Macmillan.

Starker, S. (1989). *Evil influences: Crusades against the mass media.* New Brunswick, NJ: Transaction.

Watson, C., & Shuker, R. (1998). *In the public good? Censorship in New Zealand.* Palmerston North, NZ: Dunmore Press.

Wertham, F. (1955). *Seduction of the innocent.* New York: Museum Press.

Fingerprint and Photograph: Surveillance Technologies in the Manufacture of Suspect Social Identities

4

PAUL KNEPPER
CLIVE NORRIS

Contents

Introduction

In 2001, the Home Office announced its "modernizing" criminal justice agenda with an emphasis on expanding the scientific and technological tools associated with the policing function. The Home Office has sought to upgrade electronic registries and databases available to police and capabilities for cataloguing fingerprints, vehicles, DNA, and other criminal identification information. This is consistent with the rationale that tackling the problem of the "persistent offender" would bring about a significant reduction in national crime statistics (Norris, 2006).

The idea that surveillance technology can be used to isolate "professional criminals" is by no means new. The technical apparatus has advanced, but the rationale is as old as the Victorian era. In this chapter, we focus on the period between 1881 and 1914 that saw the establishment in England of the "modern information state" (Higgs, 2001; Porter, 1987; Torpey, 2000). Our discussion combines perspectives of social critique and historical criminology. Norris has written extensively about the sociology of surveillance (Norris, 2003; Norris & Armstrong, 1999; Norris & McCahill, 2006), and Knepper has contributed to a historical criminology focusing on the late Victorian and Edwardian eras (Knepper, 2007a, 2007b, in press). Our purpose is not to offer a systematic account of the origins of state surveillance; rather, we are interested in the relationship between individual suspects and suspect populations.

In the last decades of the 19th century and first decades of the 20th, the authorities looked to photographic and fingerprint technologies as a means of isolating various suspects. Looking back, it becomes clear that the technical aspect of surveillance was never enough. The authorities celebrated each advance in technological apparatus, but the advances failed to achieve stated ambitions. As we will show, there was a social aspect to the technology in the sense that the technical aspects of identifying, classifying, and monitoring require an understanding of the population to be monitored and the rationale for monitoring them. Although the authorities looked to scientific language as a means of locating individuals within populations, the definition of the populations of interest relied on larger prejudices expressed in social and political language.

Our discussion draws on the views of three early directors of criminal investigation at the Metropolitan Police: Edward Henry, Robert Anderson, and Howard Vincent. We use a variety of sources, including their own writings, parliamentary reports, and newspaper accounts. In the first section, we point to "colonial criminality" and the role of criminal identification technologies in the context of the British Empire, specifically, India and Malta. In the next section, we discuss the use of these technologies in Britain and the concern about "professional criminality." In the third and fourth sections, we discuss the interest in fingerprints and photographs in relation to "anarchist criminality" and "alien criminality"; concern with alien criminality led to passage of the Aliens Act in 1905. Although the threat posed by individual suspects changed, the source of the threat always found its way back to the usual suspects: foreigners, immigrants, and ethnic minorities.

Colonial Criminality

During the first decade of the 20th century, Scotland Yard established fingerprint analysis as the preferred method of criminal identification. The fingerprint bureau opened in 1901, and within a few years, fingerprint bureaus had been established in cities across the United States, Holland, Belgium, Austria-Hungary, and Germany. Yet contrary to the image of Scotland Yard triumphing over London's criminal underworld, fingerprints did not emerge in England but in India. Fingerprint identification was born in British India where, as Sengoopta (2003) concludes, "the curious combination of despotic rule and intense insecurity" led colonial administrators to devise a means of identification for wide-scale surveillance.

British rule over the Indian subcontinent presented a staggering prospect. The scale of the land, diversity of languages, and inscrutability (from the British point of view) of cultures overwhelmed colonial administrators. The Sepoy Mutiny of 1857 confirmed how little they knew and engendered a lingering uneasiness about their mismanagement precipitating another revolt. For the knowledge to govern India, British colonial authorities turned to science, and classification became the centerpiece of this approach. Colonial ethnologists inventoried "criminal tribes" in the belief that these groups originated in ancient times and were compelled by hereditary to crime as a vocation. This sort of research led to the "discovery" that criminality was pervasive in Indian society (Brown, 2001). Frederic Mouat, Inspector-General of Gaols in India, referenced this outlook when he commented in 1891 on the importance of devising an unerring test of identity for habitual criminals. "Organised bodies of criminals, some hereditary, and all more or less dangerous, required special agencies for their detection and repression" he said, and added that identification would render it more "difficult and dangerous to live by criminality as a profession, than any of the sentences passed" (Mouat, 1891).

When in 1891 Edward Henry became Inspector-General of Police in Bengal, Bertillon's anthropometric system represented the state of the art in establishing personal identity. In the 1880s, Alphonse Bertillon organized an identification bureau within the Paris police, and his system became the basis for similar bureaus throughout Europe. Bertillon assigned personal identity from a series of body measurements; the measurements focused on the head, arms and hands, and other unchangeable aspects of the adult skeletal structure. Bertillon's bureau also included a photographic studio. Although French authorities had been making photographs of prisoners for several years, he standardized the procedures to produce consistent images: one full face, one profile (Rhodes, 1956). Bertillon's chief accomplishment, however, was a card file catalog of criminal records or "search cabinet." Trying to find a match for an individual's description, even with a photograph, took weeks. Bertillon solved this problem by translating the body measurements into a number for cataloguing. Five body measurements, subdivided into three categories, corresponded with particulars drawers in the cabinet; and the combination yielded a practical search-and-retrieval system (Sekula, 1986).

Henry implemented Bertillon's system, but its major limitation became apparent: the results depended on consistency of measurement. The Paris police achieved good results with the system because the measurements taken by Bertillon himself, or under his supervision, were made in the same way.

When responsibility for the system relied on police with varying levels of training, using instruments of uneven calibration, the results varied. Henry tried to improve the system, by reducing the number of measurements to be taken and by introducing finger impressions (Fosdick, 1915).

Henry learned of fingerprint analysis by way of the Victorian polymath Sir Francis Galton. During the 1880s, Galton opened his anthropometric laboratory at the International Health Exhibition in London to collect statistics needed for his research into heredity. His decision to add fingerprints to his inventory of body measurements proved of little value in revealing the production of genius but suggested the police might have a new method for recognizing repeat criminal offenders (Brookes, 2004). In a series of articles in the 1880s and 1890s, Galton explained the use of fingerprints as a means of personal identification. He worked out the mathematics to confirm uniqueness, demonstrated the permanence of patterns throughout the life course, and described a classification system (using the language of arches, loops, and whorls). He also described methods of photographic enlargement to facilitate the process of matching prints (Galton, 1888a, 1888b, 1891a, 1891b). Galton's book, *Finger Prints*, was published in 1892. The year before, he said that he looked forward to the day when prison photographers had the added duty of fingerprinting convicts and establishing a central register (Galton, 1891b). Following correspondence with Galton, as well as a visit to Galton's laboratory in 1894, Henry agreed to collect all 10 fingerprints in addition to the measurements on Bertillon's card.

In conjunction with two Indian subinspectors, Azizul Haque and Hem Chandra Bose, Henry devised the classification system that would make him famous. The "Henry system" assigned letters of the alphabet to the five basic fingerprint patterns, linked these patterns to further divisions of subpatterns, and incorporated this into the anthropometric card catalog system. Henry substituted the alphabetic fingerprint code for Bertillon's number and, in this way, created a practical and efficient search-and-retrieval system for use with fingerprints. In 1897, the governor-general directed police throughout India to cease collection of anthropometric information altogether and declared Henry's fingerprint system to be the basis for criminal identification. A year later, police authorities opened the fingerprint bureau at Calcutta, the paradigm for criminal identification in Great Britain and Europe (Sodhi & Kaur, 2005).

The Colonial Office recognized criminal identification as an essential tool of colonial policing. The authorities urged use of fingerprint classification not only for large and complex colonial populations, as in India, but even in much smaller and less complex populations, such as Malta. In 1814, Britain annexed the island of Malta to establish a naval base in the Mediterranean. Compared with the Indian subcontinent, Malta presented a manageable geographic space, an understandable European culture, and an agreeable population that seldom made trouble. British observers in the 19th century commented, in fact, on the lack of crime. "In the criminal court," R. Montgomery Martin exclaimed, "it does not appear that there is much business of a serious nature. The common offence is stealing and pilfering; but there is a remarkable absence of all crimes of a very aggravated nature" (Martin 1837). During the first decade of the 20th century, the most serious "crime" problem concerned boys begging or hawking in Valletta. Tancred Curmi, the superintendent of police in 1903, complained in his annual report to the British government about young beggars who "uncared for by their parents, infest the streets, causing trouble to police, and nuisance to the public" (Malta Police, 1905).

Nevertheless, British authorities felt the need for a comprehensive system of monitoring the inhabitants. Their anxieties extended from a specific concern about foreigners in Malta and a general suspicion of "otherness" that coincided with colonial rule elsewhere. In 1899, the British government in Valletta promulgated the Aliens Law to clarify procedures for reception of foreigners. The law required masters of ships to present a list of passengers (names, professions, place of embarkation) to the collector of customs. Police had the authority to require foreigners to present a passport at the collector of customs or superintendent of police and make declarations, including name and surname; rank, profession, or trade; and national origin. Those seeking to establish residence in Malta were entered into the "Register of Resident Aliens" kept by the police. The law provided that foreign residents could be deported for conviction of crime or "leading an idle and vagrant life" (*Malta Government Gazette,* 1899).*

In response to concern about foreigners, and particularly foreign criminality, the Malta Police created the Aliens Branch and Criminal Record Office. Many foreigners came to Malta during the "boom years" of 1903–1906, attracted by employment on civil engineering projects. Construction of the breakwater in the Grand Harbour by the Admiralty and the barracks by the War Office led to a doubling of wages, and contractors imported laborers from Italy and Spain to supplement the Maltese workforce. Curmi, the superintendent of police, reported "much difficulty" in enforcing the aliens law: "undesirable aliens continue to give trouble, and their misdeeds are only kept in check with difficulty" (Malta Police, 1908). In 1909, the secretary of state for the colonies sent Edward B. McInnis to review police organization, and he

---

* Foreign residents also had to provide, within 2 days of arrival, surety against becoming a burden to the government. During the first 5 years, hundreds of prosecutions were carried out each year, mostly for failing to provide surety. Few foreigners were prosecuted for crimes—approximately 23 between 1899 and 1904 (Malta Police, 1905).

offered a series of recommendations for defense against foreign criminality. He suggested creation of a detective force and the establishment within the detective office of a registry of "known thieves and offenders." It was "most essential" that the detectives be trained in "the taking and classification of 'finger prints' as this method of identification is absolutely infallible." He further recommended the aliens branch be amalgamated into this new detective branch and a new aliens law passed along the lines of the legislation in force in England (McInnis, 1910). McInnis was the first of several British police sent by the Colonial Office to urge the Malta Police to establish a fingerprint bureau.

Photography was not an invention of colonial administration in the same sense as fingerprint classification, although it proved useful in the context of empire. Governors of British goals had made portraits of prisoners as early as 1847, but "criminal photography" did not become common practice until the 1870s. In 1871, Parliament passed the Prevention of Crime Act that required all prisons to adopt photography and set up a central registry at Scotland Yard. By 1886, this registry contained some 60,000 photographs (Popple, 2005). Police officials did, however, see in photography an important means of thwarting colonial criminality. In *The Police Code and General Manual of the Criminal Law for the British Empire* (1895), Sir Howard Vincent put it simply: "The utility of photography in the pursuit of criminals cannot be overestimated." In Great Britain, he explained, prison warders made portraits of all persons sentenced to penal servitude before release and entered their names in registry at the convict supervision office within the Home Office. A copy of the photograph was also sent from the prison to the police of the district in which the convict was to be released. Vincent went on to explain that owing to the similarity between portraits of different people, Bertillon's body measurement system should be used to establish identity (Vincent, 1895).

Photographs became a tool in the search for international fugitives. During the first decade of the 20th century, the Malta Police received notice of persons wanted by police forces in Europe and North America. In 1907, for example, police in the districts were asked to look for J. Edward Boeck, wanted by the New York City Police on a charge of grand larceny. The circular contains a verbal description of age, height, hair color, and so on (Malta Police, 1907a). A number of these announcements indicated that a photograph of the suspect could be viewed. The description of Ross W. Douglass, a clerk with the U.S. Signal Corps in the Philippine Islands, was distributed in 1908. The announcement also includes information that "A photograph of Douglass with a more detailed description of him and a photograph and description of the woman with whom he practised are with the Inspector On Duty, Main Station, Valletta" (Malta Police, 1907b).

Professional Criminality

Although British authorities were willing to put the new science of identity to work in the colonies, the introduction of fingerprint classification at home was another matter. Until well into the 20th century, British policing avoided the use of scientific methods. There were no forensic laboratories, research staff, or criminal museums of the sort associated with policing on the continent. The police declined to introduce scientific methods believed to jeopardize the good will and cooperation of the public, methods the ordinary person would have considered "unfair" (Craven, 1933). To convince a skeptical public about the value of fingerprints and photographs in establishing personal identity, police officials emphasized the problem of "professional criminality."

During the final decades of the 19th century, Parliament became increasingly interested in habitual criminals. In 1869, Parliament passed the Habitual Criminals Act providing longer sentences for "old offenders." The act gave judges the authority to detain arrested persons (while the police searched for evidence of previous criminality) and to lengthen sentences for those determined to be hardened criminals. The Prevention of Crimes Act (1871) provided for establishment of a register of "habitual criminals," identified as those convicted of a crime with a previous conviction on record. From this register, the Home Office prepared the annual Habitual Criminals Register and the Register of Distinctive Marks for circulation to all police forces in Great Britain. In addition, the Metropolitan Police maintained its own archives of the names and distinctive marks of convicted criminals, supplemented by albums of photographs, beginning in 1887, of habitual criminals (Spearman, 1894).

Robert Anderson led the campaign against professional criminality. He became director of the Criminal Investigation Division (CID) at the Metropolitan Police in 1888 and served in this capacity until 1901. During the first decade of the 20th century, he published a series of articles advancing his belief in the need to tackle "professional criminals." The end of the gallows and transportation to the colonies had ended the system of dealing with professional criminals, Anderson maintained, and reconviction statistics showed "the professional criminal is developing and becoming a serious public danger" (Anderson, 1901). The Home Office was particularly interested in criminal identification in the 1890s given the widespread conclusion that the nation's prison policy had been a failure. The Gladstone Committee Report on Prisons in 1895 confirmed what many had been thinking for some time: short prison stays failed to redirect lawbreakers. One of the primary lines of criticism had to do with increasing rates of reconviction, indicating the growth and persistence of a distinct population who had decided to make a vocation of crime (Harding, 1988).

Consistent with logic advanced in the Gladstone Committee Report, Anderson argued that misadministration of the prison system was to blame. A high-class detective force was in place to identify habitual criminals, but only to see that these criminals were "duly photographed and measured," before they would be "promptly released." Releasing habitual criminals after a short prison stay was an "absurd" and "stupid" response Anderson claimed. The "systematic, organised crime against property is entirely the creature of our present penal system," and specifically, the system of professional theft was an artifact of short sentences (Anderson, 1901). He argued that a single prison could be built to hold all of the nation's professional criminals and thereby reduce the amount of crime in the nation to a remarkable degree. "Professional criminals never change…" Anderson wrote, "if and when they are convicted of crime, they receive a sentence of a few years' duration, and are then let loose again upon society. How long will the public tolerate this scandalous and stupid system?" (Anderson, 1910a).

The promise of criminal identification enabled professional criminality to become a major crime-reduction strategy; photographs held out the possibility of verifying the personal identity for each of the 35,000 persons convicted each year.

However, as a practical method of recognizing professional criminals, the registers, even with the addition of photographs, proved unreliable. Persons arrested could defeat attempts to identify them by using aliases. As late as the 1890s, some other method was required to safeguard against incorrect identification of habitual offenders. One of the primary means of identifying the habitual criminal was face-to-face knowledge of a local constable. Three times a week, remanded prisoners from across London were brought to Holloway, to be inspected by some 30 detectives and police officers to see if any could be recognized as old offenders (Spearman, 1894). The registers also proved unmanageable. By 1886, the registry at Scotland Yard held the images of nearly 60,000 criminals (and Paris police had some 100,000 photographs). Various police forces had instituted additional registries of their own, which before the end of the century, amounted to an avalanche of some 10,000 photographs (Garson, 1900). It was impractical, if not impossible, to search the photographs looking for a particular face.

Anderson argued that given the technology was in place to identify hardened criminals, the authorities should use it to forestall crime. However, he was also arguing the technology was superfluous in the sense that he already knew how to forestall crime; the population of professional criminals over-lapped, he alleged, with foreign criminals. Anderson cited a question in Parliament of November that year, alleging that some 4,943 persons charged in the previous 12 months at the Metropolitan Police Court were of "foreign nationality." Although small in number, this foreign criminal population was significant; according to the adage, it was a matter of quality rather than quality. Anderson pointed to forgery prosecutions as evidence that the foreign aliens represented the "most skilful and dangerous" of the professionals. "It is plain," Anderson (1903) declared, "that our criminal population would be appreciably reduced if the criminal aliens were expelled from our shores." Essentially, Anderson contended that the British character was essentially honest and peaceful, and if it were not for the "alien leaven in our midst, the volume of crime would be marvellously small" (Anderson, 1910b).*

In 1893, the Secretary of State for the Home Department, Herbert Asquith, appointed a committee to inquire into the Bertillon system as used in France (and much of the continent) and the new fingerprint system championed by Galton. Named after its chair (Charles Troup), the Troup Committee recommended the implementation of a fingerprint system for criminal identification. By 1914, even the Francophone nations of Europe conceded the passing of the Bertillon system. At the International Police Congress held in Monaco, conferees predicted it would only be a few years before all police records in Europe would be on based on fingerprints (Fosdick, 1915). Looking back, it is easy to see how, when combined with Henry's classification system, fingerprint technology emerged as the superior system for accuracy and simplicity. What is less well understood is that the advocates of both systems believed them to have the power to characterize groups as well as individualize suspects.

John Garson, the scientific advisor to Scotland Yard on criminal investigation, also served as vice president of the Anthropological Institute of Great Britain. He pointed to anthropometry as a means of characterizing individuals and also claimed, in a text on anthropology, that the same procedure was used to investigate differences between races. At a lecture to the Anthropological Institute in 1900, a member of the audience questioned the overlap of the two

---

* Montague Crackanthorpe did not support Anderson's conception of professional crimi-nality, but his response references wider ideology of a criminal class. Crackanthorpe, a barrister and social critic, disagreed on legal grounds. He felt that juries would be reluc-tant to pronounce a person as being a "professional criminal" because such a verdict was tantamount to outlawry; a legal determination of professional criminality would brand a lawbreaker a social outcast and end the possibility of making an honest livelihood. He expressed his belief, however, in the general proposition of "distinguishing one class of criminal from another." Lombroso was right to claim, Crackanthorpe concluded, in the existence of occasional, habitual, and professional criminals (1902).

purposes: "The measurements referred to must either show racial characteristics and be of use to the ethnologist, or they must show individual peculiarities and therefore be of value to the prison expert. They certainly cannot do both at once" (Garson, 1900). In his reply, Garson claimed that body measurements were important for both criminal identification and race science. The measurements of the convicted in Britain reflected the balance of various races, Garson (1900) explained, as well as elements of "degeneracy," particularly in towns (Garson, 1900).*

Garson was not alone in his views. In *Finger Prints* (1892), Galton insisted that fingerprint technology had the power to confer a unique identity on every individual and establish that identity beyond doubt. Yet he also believed the same fingerprints revealed the characteristics of a race. Although he confessed to finding no systematic differences in ridge patterns across races, he continued to suppose that fingertips encoded racial identity. "The impressions from Negroes betray the general clumsiness of their fingers, but their patterns are not, so far as I can find, different from those of others" (Galton, 1892). Despite the lack of data, he concluded the fingertips of Africans revealed a "greater simplicity," the cause of which did not lend itself to measurement. Henry Faulds, a Scottish doctor who pursued fingerprint science while working in Japan, also thought he could see racial differences in fingerprint patterns. He commented on the considerable difference between ridge patterns on hands of the Japanese and the English (Faulds, 1880).

Similarly, photographs did not merely record the identity of an individual suspect, they revealed a criminal type, a category of human being with a penchant for criminal behavior. In 1879, Galton reported to the Anthropological Institute the results of his experiments with composite photography. His instruments for superimposition of portraits allowed for production of "the portrait of a type and not of an individual" (Galton, 1879). Galton conceived of the possibility of using photographic technology to reveal "the principal criminal types" after viewing a large collection of photographs of criminals maintained by Sir Edmund Du Cane, the Director-General of Prisons. Galton commissioned a set of "composites" in which he superimposed portraits of

---

* In referencing the degeneracy theme, Garson linked the criminal identification project with criminality presumed to be heritable. Nordau, who authored the widely read *Degeneration* (1892), insisted that degeneracy was passed on to children by parents' intoxication, cocaine use, overwork, and lunacy. Nordau suggested that crime had increased and that some portion of this increase should be attributed to degeneracy. He did allow that some criminals could not be classified as degenerates but were "normal human beings" who had become members of the criminal class due to defective child-rearing, education, and a depraved environment. The "great majority of professional criminals," Nordau concluded, engaged in crime owing to their "inability to check their impulses, bluntness of conscience, lack of judgment, etc." (1912).

criminals convicted of a murder, manslaughter, and violent robbery. These revealed, he suggested, "not the criminal, but the man who is liable to fall into crime" (Galton, 1879). Composite photography, he concluded, would prove useful for establishing "typical pictures of different races of men" (Galton, 1879).

Anarchist Criminality

While Anderson continued to argue the merits of attacking professional criminality, a new threat emerged requiring extension and advancement of surveillance technology: anarchism. Beginning with the assassination of Tsar Alexander II in 1881, British newspapers carried stories of assassinations and explosions on the continent and in America. In Paris, bombs were thrown into magistrates' houses, police stations, and boulevard cafés. In Barcelona, explosions occurred at a theater and a religious procession. Anarchists stabbed president Carnot of France, shot the Spanish prime minister Canovas del Castillo, and shot King Hubert of Italy.

To counter the anarchist threat, Scotland Yard applied methods they had developed over the years to detect and arrest criminals, which generally meant physical surveillance and use of informants.* Specifically, Scotland Yard extended structures put in place to counter the "dynamitards." In 1881, an explosion occurred at Salford military barracks, killing a 7-year-old boy and injuring three other people. In 1887, a series of attacks occurred in London, Liverpool, and Glasgow. The bombings were the work of the Fenians, an Irish nationalist organization operating in Ireland and America. The bombers hoped to force Westminster to withdraw from Ireland and allow for development of a free and independent Irish state. Scotland Yard formed an Irish Bureau within the CID, and it was out of this group that the anti-anarchist surveillance network was organized (Short, 1979). Inspector Patrick Macintyre, a founding member of the Irish Bureau, was among those assigned to watch the anarchists. He and William Melville became so well-known at anarchist gatherings that they only bothered to disguise their appearance for Sunday evening lectures (Latouche, 1908).

However, unlike the violence linked to Irish nationalists, the anarchist threat was more ambiguous. Who the anarchists were, and what they hoped to achieve, was never clear. One individual who was prepared to supply the

---

* Covert and overt intelligence gathering became systematized, and cooperation with police forces in other countries became routine. Forensic science and photography were applied to the task. The traditional detective philosophy, of dealing with threats on a case-by-case basis, gave way to a more generalized approach of gathering, recording, and retrieving evidence (Clutterbuck, 2006).

"who" and "why" of anarchism was Howard Vincent, the first person to direct the CID. He had convinced himself that the anarchist threat coincided with the alien threat and sought to enlist immigration policy in the fight for Britain's security. During his years as an MP, he pushed for legislation to restrict immigration. While at Scotland Yard, his biographer explained, Vincent had been occupied with watching the arrival and observation of anarchists and political conspirators. Despite the English tradition of offering political asylum, the government should not expose itself to "harbouring the authors of murder plots." The preventive work of the Metropolitan Police would be easier if the Home Secretary had the authority to turn away persons "reasonably suspected of criminal purposes" (Jeyes & How, 1912).

London was never the address of an anarchist movement but a roundabout of individuals and groups with sundry motivations and ideologies. Café intellectuals, trade unionists, political organizers, and self-proclaimed bohemians gave lectures, distributed leaflets, and peddled newspapers. There were English anarchists, but they failed to attract concern. The English anarchists convened at the Autonomie Club in Tottenham Court Road, a "dingy, badly furnished, ramshackle place," and several smaller neighborhood clubs (Latouche, 1908). "There are very few English anarchists and they are of little account" said *The Times* (1911). However, there were also the "foreign anarchists," particularly Jews from Russia and Poland, and they represented a different kind of threat. The Jewish anarchists convened at Berner Street, a club established by Morris Winchevsky to "spread true socialism among Jewish workers." The International Workers' Educational Club housed the Society of Jewish Socialists and the *Arbeter Fraint*, "Worker's Friend," newspaper. Berner Street staged Yiddish theatricals and Russian dramas; communists and socialists sought converts there and trade unionists lectured to cabinet makers. The club was also a venue for cosmopolitan intellectuals such as William Morris and Prince Kropotkin (Fishman, 1975).*

Suspicion focused on Jews after a bomb blast at Greenwich Park in 1894, the first anarchist bombing to occur on British soil. Like anarchism itself, exactly what was intended and who may have been behind it remains

---

* Suspicion focused on Jewish anarchists in 1888 when one of "the ripper's" victims was found outside the club. The body had been discovered in a yard, adjacent to the International Workingmen's Club, by Louis Diemschütz, the club's steward. Anderson was among those who suggested that the crimes attributed to Jack the Ripper must have been done by a Jew as no Englishman could have committed such atrocities. The murders had occurred in Whitechapel leading to rumors about a Jewish murderer, a kosher butcher. Anderson made public his suspicion that the perpetrator and "his people" were "low-class Jews." He decided that the murderer lived in the immediate area and was known to other people, people that would not surrender him to the authorities. The unwillingness of the police to find the murderer was explained by the "fact that people of that class in East End will not give up one of their number to Gentile justice" (1910c).

a mystery. In February of that year, *The Times* carried the story of an explosion at Greenwich Park and an injured man found at the site (*The Times*, 1894a). The man, who died in hospital, was identified as Martial Bourdin, a "foreigner" who had killed himself while attempting to attack the Royal Observatory. Bourdin had ties with the Autonomie Club in Tottenham Court, the site of anarchist meetings, and knew the French anarchist, Emile Henry, who had, 3 days earlier, tossed a bomb into a café killing one person and injuring 20 others. As revealed at the inquest, Scotland Yard had been shadowing Bourdin, but when informed that he had left the Autonomie with dynamite, lost track of him (*The Times*, 1894b).

Vincent saw in the Greenwich blast a moment to advance the cause of immigration restriction. On February 19, 1894, he put a question to the Secretary of State for the Home Department about whether the secretary was aware that "considerable numbers of dangerous characters" had been sent to England from France and elsewhere. Considering the "circumstances of the day," Vincent asked, would the government propose placing any limit on foreign immigration, to avoid entry of "the refuse population of Europe?" The secretary, Herbert Asquith, answered that although "dangerous and objectionable characters" did find their way to England, the government was inclined to pursue cooperation with other countries in information sharing rather than in making a change in the law (Hansard, 1894). Vincent maintained a long-term preoccupation with Jews. As far as he was concerned, Jews had foisted the "sweating system" on British labor, created a housing shortage from London to Leeds, and introduced an influenza epidemic (in Sheffield) in 1891 (Jeyes & How, 1912).

Vincent was one of three representatives sent by the British government to Rome for the International Conference for Defence Against Anarchism. The conference began in November 1898, about 3 months after the murder (in Geneva) of Empress Elisabeth of Austria. The event caused an immediate clamor across Europe for international police countermeasures, and 22 states sent delegates. The conference had three goals: to define anarchism so as to make professing anarchist doctrines a criminal offense across Europe, to produce an international agreement regarding the response to anarchists, and to devise a system of sharing information about known anarchists among the participating states. Of the three goals, only the third was successful. Sir Philippe Currie, another of Britain's representatives, defended British liberalism. He declared that anyone who committed murder, or conspired to commit murder, would receive severe punishment afforded by British law. He also stated that "we do not in England place under police surveillance individuals against whom no charge of plotting a crime or inciting to a crime can be levied" (Liang, 1992).

At least not "officially." Vincent participated in a series of closed-door meetings of police officials at the Rome conference, and the group reached an understanding concerning surveillance of anarchist suspects. Each police force agreed to establish a central office for surveillance of anarchists and to communicate to the other offices information concerning those individuals under their watch. All foreign anarchists were to be deported to their home states for legal action. Several European police forces agreed to forward on a monthly basis the names and descriptions of persons expelled. Robert Anderson had pressed Vincent with the need for taking "exceptional measures" to keep the threat of anarchists in check. Britain should not adopt a tolerant attitude toward anarchists; it was unfair to provide a comfortable home to those avoiding capture by other governments for terrorist activities (Anderson, 1911).

One outcome of the antianarchist conference concerned the *portrait parlé*; the states agreed to adopt it as the method of criminal identification. The *portrait parlé* had been devised by Bertillon to assist detectives in locating suspects at large by providing a clear, intelligible description of the person wanted. The name refers to a written description, adhering to a specific protocol, of the particulars from the profile photograph and record of body measurements. The nose, ears, and forehead were divided into three categories (large, medium, small), the outline of the nose divided into three classes (concave, rectilinear, convex), and so on. Edmund R. Spearman, one of Bertillon's English advocates, had proposed this very system several years earlier. To catch international culprits, the means of personal identification shared by various police forces had to be the same: "If the system were the same in every country, the interchange of information would be easy and rapid" (Spearman, 1894). The *portrait parlé* was particularly useful for surveillance. Not only could the description be squeezed onto a folded card carried in a pocket, it could be transmitted across international borders by telegraph (Jensen, 1981).*

By 1908, police in several nations had achieved a measure of organization with respect to sharing information about suspicious persons, specifically photographs. The Paris police were said to have a gallery of 4,000 known anarchists, each with photograph, and resume, and duplicated this material for English and American authorities (Latouche, 1908). The usefulness

---

* During the 1890s, the CID saw the telegraph primarily as a means of communication and may have been more consistent in this than other police organizations in the country. Such was the state of communications technology in 1894 that Scotland Yard failed to investigate Bourdin's contacts in the immediate aftermath of the Greenwich explosion. Searches of the Autonomie Club and other places frequented by Bourdin and his associates were not carried out until the following day, apparently because the Greenwich constable notified Scotland Yard of the explosion by letter rather than telegram (Oliver, 1983).

of these photographs, however, remained questionable. Robert Anderson recalled how a detective from the Police of Paris came to London with the photograph of a fugitive thought to have taken up residence: "'You want me, then, to find this man among the 7,000,000 of people in London,' I said with a laugh, 'nothing could be easier—I'll go and get him for you!'" (1910b).

Alien Criminality

Doubts about the usefulness of photographs and fingerprints coincided with an increasing reliance on public policy. Although the means of classification improved, certainly with respect to fingerprints, the authorities increasingly realized such technologies could resolve neither the problem of persistent criminality nor that of anarchist violence. Rather than attempting to iden- tify and monitor particular individuals, increasing attention was placed on policies for excluding categories of alleged troublemakers. Immigration restriction became a primary means, and in the discussion surrounding pro- visions of such legislation, notions of professional criminality and anarchist subversion often fused into a notion of "alien criminality."

In 1901, a group of MPs led by Howard Vincent succeeded in their call for appointment of a Royal Commission on Immigration. The commission sat for 13 months at Caxton Hall, Westminster, and heard from some 175 "experts" and "qualified persons." Although the commission ostensibly con- cerned itself with the "alien question," most witnesses testified about problems of Jewish immigrants in London's East End. The activities and problems of immigrant Jews were characterized with the good and familiar behaviors of the English working class (Steyn, 1999). One of the themes to emerge was the overlap of foreign criminality and professional criminality. Richard Hyder, a subdivisional inspector, testified that foreign criminals who did not speak English had an advantage over the police. Yiddish-speaking individuals could more easily conceal their crimes (Royal Commission, 1903). The chair of the County of London Sessions, W. R. McConnell, testified that immigrants, but principally the "German and Yiddish-speaking nationalists" were responsible for an increase in a particularly worrisome category of burglary: a "scientific" form of house-breaking, enabled by specialized tools and specific knowledge (Royal Commission, 1903).

When Vincent testified before the Royal Commission, he cited Anderson's argument about the need for immigration restriction. Anderson's statement about the "criminal alien invasion" was, Vincent said, "in no way exagger- ated." Vincent not only linked aliens with professional criminality, but sought to make them suspect in other ways as well. He urged the government to protect "its own people" from the "unfair competition" of foreigners and from contamination by "loathsome diseases" from which many of the aliens were afflicted (Jeyes & How, 1912). In Leeds, Vincent believed he had seen the sweating system at work and believed it could be curbed by "cutting off the supply of Russian, Polish and Hungarian Jews" (Jeyes & How, 1912). He marveled at the lack of support for alien exclusion among working classes; he attributed this lack of support to a "sentimental regard" for political refugees. There were also "false ideas" in the air about the intent of the legislation constituting an attack on the poor by the rich. Vincent attributed these false ideas as an attack on the Unionist party (Jeyes & How, 1912).

Edward Henry, the chief commissioner of the Metropolitan Police (1903–1918), agreed with Vincent about the importance of excluding persons from entry who had been *convicted* of crimes in their country of origin, but he did not believe in turning away individuals for *suspicion* of political or other crimes. Primarily, his reluctance had to do with the difficulty of establishing identity. In the case of convicted criminals, identity could be established by means of fingerprints. The French had recently introduced the practice of fingerprinting prisoners (consistent with the British convention); and Henry surmised that in the future, such classification would enable identification of former prisoners "at once" (Royal Commission, 1903). However, in the case of suspects, identity would be problematic because such means of identification were unavailable. Kenelm Digby, a member of the Royal Commission, pressed Henry on the matter. Supposing you had a description from foreign police that a suspect was due to arrive in a particular port at the certain time, Digby asked. Henry replied that just that sort of case had happened just the other day: "We had a wireless message giving very specific details and description of a person, and of his luggage, and saying that his luggage would contain very valuable bonds that he had carried away. We searched this luggage and he proved to be an official of very high rank, and I had to go and make the most abject apology to him" (Royal Commission, 1903).

Henry did not want the police to be manipulated by political forces. The system of acting on "private information" from foreign political sources was easily abused. It would be "impractical" for the police to act on information about suspects given the difficulty of establishing identity. The French police maintained a substantial collection of photographs of people without something specific against them but who were regarded as troublesome. Henry emphasized the deficiency of photography for surveillance: "I could produce photographs before this Commission of three or four different men, and you would be prepared almost to swear they were photographs of the same person" (Royal Commission, 1903). Photographs could be used to identify foreign suspects at the ports of entry only when a foreign police officer arrived in person along with the photograph and declared that he was prepared to recognize the person. This required a great deal of time and energy for one suspect (Royal Commission, 1903).

Some British Jews agreed with the need for immigration restriction. N. S. Joseph, secretary of the Russo-Jewish Committee that had been set up in 1882 for relief of Jews facing persecution in Russia, advocated an alien expulsion act. Under Joseph's proposal, the Home Secretary would have the authority to expel several categories of aliens, beginning with "aliens who are notorious anarchists" (Royal Commission, 1903). Colonel Albert Goldsmid, founder of the Jewish Lads Brigade (modeled after the Church Lads Brigade), said that after reading a "powerful pamphlet" by Vincent, "no unprejudiced Jew" could deny the arguments for immigration restriction (*Jewish Chronicle*, 1901a). Such statements were co-opted by antialien MPs in the parliamentary debate leading to passage of the Aliens Act. Harold Lawson, MP, declared that the great number of those appearing in criminal courts belonged to the Jewish community. Britain was receiving the "black sheep of their own community and of which they themselves are rightly ashamed." He also pointed to denunciations of Jews in the radical and socialist press. Another member claimed that Jews already settled in the East End welcomed the measure for alien restriction because they wished to protect the good living they enjoyed (Hansard, 1905).

Other leaders of London's Jewish community recognized the uses to which statements such as Colonel Goldsmid's would be put, particularly his endorsement of Vincent's arguments. Charles Emanuel, solicitor to the Jewish Board of Guardians, wondered whether Goldsmid had bothered to investigate the matter of Jewish immigration before suggesting that Jews clasp hands with Vincent, "the leader of the anti-alien agitators." Emanuel explained that he had on more than one occasion needed to correct inaccurate figures Vincent had supplied to Parliament (*Jewish Chronicle*, 1901b). The Aliens Act was passed in 1905, making Britain the first state to establish a modern structure for immigrant restriction. The act designated "immigration ports" at which immigration officers had the power to reject "undesirables," including those unable to support themselves, lunatics, idiots, and those sentenced for a crime in a foreign country. The act also gave the secretary of state authority to deport certain convicted alien criminals (Pellew, 1989). Vincent and Anderson viewed the act as too little, too late. During the sitting of the Royal Commission in fact, Vincent introduced an unsuccessful criminal aliens bill. In the years after the passage of the act, radical secretaries of the Home Office, they suggested, interpreted provisions to make its exclusion aspect ineffective (Jeyes & How, 1912).

Anderson made use of the Houndsditch murders in 1910 to complain about the ineffectiveness of immigration restriction. The police surprised the perpetrators during the robbery of a jeweler's shop on Houndsditch in the East End, and the robbers killed three of the police. After a shoot-out involving an automatic pistol and army detachments, several suspects were brought to trial. These were mostly Russian and Lithuanian immigrants. For Anderson, these events confirmed the "peril" at hand. The murders proved that the Home Office had failed to administer the act in the way it had been intended. He argued that by ridding the country of Houndsditch-type criminals, the nation would be protected from "alien criminals of the ordinary type" as well (1911).

Anderson went on to argue that surveillance technology allowed for interception of foreign anarchists, if only the British government would awake to the necessity of it: "They [foreign anarchists] are well known to the police in their own country and foreign police would supply us with their *dossiers* and in many cases with photographs and fingerprints." It would be desirable to "make all foreign visitors liable to the kind of supervision to which English people are subjected in Continental countries" (1911). Major William-Evans Gordon, an MP and founder of the British Brothers (the first quasifascist organization in Britain), agreed with Anderson. The exclusion of criminal aliens should take place at ports, but this would not in itself detect professional criminals, "expert burglars and other skilled criminals." Professional criminals could only be dealt with by a system of registration. Scotland Yard should establish and maintain a detailed scheme for registration of aliens as had been implemented in Germany (Gordon, 1911).*

The *Jewish Chronicle* argued against the effort to prevent crime by foreigners through more restrictive provisions to the Aliens Act. Amending the Aliens Act in the direction of restricting immigrants would not prevent a "foreign anarchist" from arriving in England. The editors hinted at a class bias in the practice of searches at port, leading to greater restriction of Jewish immigrants. The legislation did not provide for searching first-class passengers, and Russian or other anarchists could easily disguise themselves as first class when they were only third class (*Jewish Chronicle*, 1910). Existing provisions may not be adequate, but there was "no ring which the law could place around the United Kingdom through which a Russian anarchist could not find a loophole in admission" (*Jewish Chronicle*, 1911). The *Jewish Chronicle*

---

* By 1915, the identifying information once collected for prisoners became required of everyone. The National Registration Act (1915) obliged all UK citizens to carry identity cards. That same year, the government introduced a new passport design incorporating a photograph. The passport, consisting of a single sheet of folded paper, was protected by board covers wrapped in blue cloth bearing a gold crest (Lloyd, 2003). Lloyd observes that by the end of the war, the movement to abolish passports was defeated by governments who had discovered just how closely a population could be monitored and how easy it was to justify this monitoring. The International Conference on Passports, Customs Formalities and Through Tickets in 1921 fixed the content and dimensions of modern passports.

endorsed surveillance of individual suspects as an alternative to restrictive immigration policy, and specifically, Edward Henry's recommendation that police monitor suspicious individuals within the population rather than attempt wholesale screening at the point of entry (*Jewish Chronicle,* 1910).

Conclusions

Technologies for personal identification represented aspects of the surveillance state that emerged during the last decades of the 19th century and first decades of the 20th century. Fingerprint and photographic techniques enabled authorities to respond to threats of criminality and violence, or so they believed. Photography became an important supplement to anthropometric measurement, and by the end of the period, fingerprint classification had established itself as superior to them both. However, even the science of fingerprint identification proved unreliable as a means of isolating dangerous individuals. Despite the promise of such technological advances, identifying the source of threats fell back to familiar fears and anxieties. Conceptions of individual suspects, constructed in scientific language, relied on ideas about suspect populations, understood in political and cultural terms.

The modern practice of criminal identification began as a colonial science of fingerprint classification. The practical use of fingerprints by police to assign personal identity originated in India. British rulers sought a means of monitoring a diverse population and responding to (what they believed to be) the serious problem of hereditary criminality. The Colonial Office extended this technology to other colonies, including one of the smallest. In Malta, colonial administrators encountered a European population and a negligible crime problem. However, they still urged to use of fingerprints, particularly to deal with crimes committed by foreign residents. Foreigners had come to Malta to work on British civil engineering projects and authorities worried about the amount of crime they introduced into Maltese society.

Fingerprint science became the premiere means of establishing personal identity in Britain, but the British population could not be monitored in the same way as colonial populations. Police officials endorsed fingerprints as a means of tackling the problem of professional criminality, of growing concern in the wake of a widespread perception in the 1890s that the nation's prisons had failed. The Home Office, the Metropolitan Police, as well as local prisons and police forces, photographed offenders and created voluminous registries of images in an effort to identify professional criminals. The avalanche of information made it difficult, even impossible, to find specific individuals, but this did not weaken support for criminal identification technologies. To compensate for the lack of precision in identifying specific criminal threats, the commissioner of the Metropolitan Police described the threat from the populations in which these individuals could be found: foreigners. In addition, the founders of the new technologies described the science of identity as a "dual science," capable of revealing individual and racial characteristics.

The link between criminal suspects and the usual suspects—foreigners, immigrants, and ethnic minorities—became stronger with the rise of anarchist violence. Ambiguity surrounding the "who" and "why" of the anarchist danger gave way to the belief that the foreign element was responsible, particularly, Jewish immigrants. Jewish anarchists were said to have been behind the explosion at Greenwich Park, the first anarchist outrage on British soil. In response to the anarchist threat, Britain participated in the first international conference concerning anarchism and agreed to share information on those suspected of holding anarchist views with police forces on the continent. The "speaking portrait" was adopted for physical surveillance in Britain and for sharing intelligence with other police.

By 1905, the concerns about professional, foreign, and anarchist criminality culminated in the Aliens Act, the first modern legislation to restrict immigration. The police advocates of criminal identification urged Parliament to adopt measures for registration and monitoring of immigrants. Although the technology of identity should have made this unnecessary—the whole point was to identify and isolate dangerous individuals—police authorities conceded the limitations of stopping criminals at entry. Photographs and fingerprints of individual foreign suspects did not offer much in the way of identifying dangerous individuals at ports nor in tracking or monitoring such individuals once they had gained entry. Instead, the authorities emphasized measures aimed at the population of suspects, defined in social and political terms, and talked of blanket registration and wide-scale monitoring.

References

Anarchists in London. (1911, 4 January). *The Times*, p. 8.
Anderson, R. (1901). Our absurd system of punishing crime. *The Nineteenth Century and After, 49*, 268–284.
Anderson, R. (1903). The crusade against professional criminals. *The Nineteenth Century and After, 53*, 496–508.
Anderson, R. (1910a). Some Scotland Yard experiences and incidents. *Blackwood's Magazine, 187*, 508–519.
Anderson, R. (1910b). Sharps and flats. *Blackwood's Magazine, 187*, 678–690.
Anderson, R. (1910c). At Scotland Yard. *Blackwood's Magazine, 187*, 357–358.
Anderson, R. (1911). The problem of the criminal alien. *The Nineteenth Century and After, 69*, 217–224.
Brookes, M. (2004). *Extreme measures: The dark visions and bright ideas of Francis Galton*. London: Bloomsbury.
Brown, M. (2001). Race, science and the construction of native criminality in colonial India. *Theoretical Criminology, 5*, 345–368.

Clutterbuck, L. (2006). Countering Irish Republican terrorism in Britain: Its origin as a police function. *Terrorism and Political Violence, 18,* 95–118.

Crackanthorpe, M. (1902). The criminal sentences commission up to date. *The Nineteenth Century, 52,* 847–863.

Craven, C. (1933). The progress of English criminology. *Journal of Criminal Law and Criminology, 24,* 230–247.

Criminal aliens. (1911, 6 January). *Jewish Chronicle,* pp. 5–6.

Evans-Gordon, W. (1911). The stranger within our gates. *The Nineteenth Century and After, 69,* 210–216.

Explosion in Greenwich Park. (1894a, 16 February). *The Times,* p. 5.

Faulds, H. (1880, 28 October). On the skin-furrows of the hand. *Nature, 22,* 605.

Fishman, W. (1975). *East End Jewish radicals 1875–1914.* London: Duckworth.

Fosdick, R. (1915). The passing of Bertillon system of identification. *Journal of American Institute of Criminal Law and Criminology, 6,* 363–369.

Galton, F. (1879). Composite portraits. *Journal of the Anthropological Institute of Great Britain and Ireland, 8,* 132–144.

Galton, F. (1888, 21 June). Personal identification and description. *Nature, 38,* 173–177.

Galton, F. (1888, 28 June). Personal identification and description. *Nature, 38,* 201–202.

Galton, F. (1891a). Method of indexing finger marks. *Nature, 44,* 141.

Galton, F. (1891b). Identification by finger-tips. *The Nineteenth Century, 30,* 303–312.

Galton, F. (1892). *Finger prints.* London: Macmillan.

Galton, F. (1900). Identification offices in India and Egypt. *The Nineteenth Century, 48,* 118–126.

Garson, J. G. (1900). The metric system of identification of criminals as used in Great Britain and Ireland. *Journal of the Anthropological Institute of Great Britain and Ireland, 30,* 161–198.

Hansard. (1905). *House of Commons parliamentary debates, 13 April to 10 May* (Vol. 145). London: Author.

Harding, C. (1988). The inevitable end of a discredited system? The origins of the Gladstone Committee report on prisons. *The Historical Journal, 31,* 591–608.

Higgs, E. (2001). The rise of the information state: The development of central state surveillance of the citizen in England, 1500–2000. *Journal of Historical Sociology, 14,* 175–197.

Jensen, R. (1981). The International Anti-Anarchist Conference of 1898 and the origins of Interpol. *Journal of Contemporary History, 16,* 323–347.

Jeyes, S. H., & How, F. D. (1912). *The life of Sir Howard Vincent.* London: George Allen.

Knepper, P. (2007a). "Jewish trafficking" and London Jews in the age of migration. *Journal of Modern Jewish Studies, 6,* 239–256.

Knepper, P. (2007b). British Jews and the racialisation of crime in the age of empire. *British Journal of Criminology, 47,* 61–79.

Knepper, P. (2008). The other invisible hand: Jews and anarchists in London before the First World War. *Jewish History, 22,* 295–315.

Lambourne, G. (1984). *The fingerprint story.* London: Harp.

Latouche, P. (1908). *Anarchy: Its methods and exponents.* London: Everett and Co.

Liang, H.-H. (1992). *The rise of the modern police and the European state system from Metternich to the Second World War.* Cambridge: Cambridge University Press.

Lloyd, M. (2003). The passport: The history of man's most travelled documents. Stroud, U.K.: Sutton Publishing.

Malta Police. (1905). Annual Report for 1903-4. National Archives of Malta (GMR 523).

Malta Police. (1907a). Circular of 20 July. National Archives of Malta (POL 10/1).

Malta Police. (1907b). Circular of 11 July. National Archives of Malta (POL 10/1).

Malta Police. (1909). Annual Report for 1907-8. National Archives of Malta (GMR 412).

Martin, R. M. (1837). History of the British possessions in the Mediterranean. London: Wittaker.

McInnis, E. (1910). Report on the re-organisation of the Malta Police Force. Malta: Government Printing Office, National Library of Malta.

Mouat, F. J. (1891). Notes on M. Bertillon's discourse on the anthropometric measurement of criminals. Journal of the Anthropological Institute of Great Britain and Ireland, 20, 182-198.

Nordau, M. (1912). The degeneration of classes and peoples. Hibbert Journal, 10, 745-765.

Norris, C. (2003). From personal to digital: CCTV, the panopticon, and the technological mediation of suspicion and social control. In D. Lyon (Ed.), Surveillance as social sorting: Privacy, risk and digital discrimination (pp. 249-281). New York: Routledge.

Norris, C. (2006). The intensification and bifurcation of surveillance in British criminal justice policy. European Journal on Criminal Policy and Research, 13, 139-158.

Norris, C., & Armstrong, G. (1999). The maximum surveillance society: The rise of closed circuit television. Oxford: Berg.

Norris, C., & McCahill, M. (2006). CCTV: Beyond penal modernism? British Journal of Criminology, 46, 87-118.

Oliver, H. (1983). The international anarchist movement in Late Victorian London. London: Croom Helm.

Ordinance No. 1: The Aliens Act, No. 4093. (18999 February). Malta Government Gazette.

Pellew, J. (1989). The Home Office and the Aliens Act, 1905. The Historical Journal, 32, 369-385.

Popple, S. (2005). Photography, crime and social control. Early Popular Visual Culture, 3, 95-106.

Porter, B. (1987). The origins of the vigilant state. London: Weidenfeld and Nicolson.

Rhodes, H. (1956). Alphonse Bertillon: Father of scientific detection. London: George Harrap.

Royal Commission. (1903). Report of the Royal Commission on Alien Immigration with minutes of evidence and appendix, Vol. 2. Minutes of evidence. London: HMSO.

Sekula, A. (1986). The body and the archive. October, 39, 3-64.

Sengoopta, C. (2003). Imprint of the Raj: How fingerprinting was born in colonial India. London: Pan Books.

Short, K. R. M. (1979). The dynamite war. Dublin: Gill and Macmillan.

Sodhi, G. S., & Kaur, J. (2005). The forgotten pioneers of fingerprint science. Current Science, 88, 185-191.

Spearman, E. (1894, September). Known to the police. The Nineteenth Century, 36, 356-370.

Steyn, J. (1999). The Jew: Assumptions of identity. London: Cassell.

The Aliens Act. (1910, 30 December). *Jewish Chronicle*, pp. 7–8.

The Jewish Lads Brigade. (1901a, 9 August). *Jewish Chronicle*, p. 18.

The Jewish Lads Brigade and the alien immigration question. (1901b, 30 August). *Jewish Chronicle*, p. 6.

The explosion in Greenwich Park. (1894b, 17 February). *The Times*, p. 5.

Torpey, J. (2000). *The invention of the passport: Surveillance, citizenship and the state.* New York: Cambridge University Press.

Vincent, H. (1895). *The police code and general manual of the criminal law for the British Empire.* 9d. London: Francis Edwards.

Electronically Monitoring Offenders and Penal Innovation in a Telematic Society

5

MIKE NELLIS

Contents

Introduction

This chapter will consider the emergence of the electronic monitoring (EM) of offenders as an instance of penal innovation—a relatively new way of controlling (and punishing) offenders in the community—that has been taken up in some degree (either as localized experiments or fully national schemes) in approximately 25 countries over the last 25 years. The United States, British Columbia, Australia, and Singapore were the early adopters. England and Wales briefly experimented with it in 1989/1990, but Sweden was the first European county to develop a national scheme in 1996. Most European countries now make use of it (Mayer, Haverkamp, & Levy, 2000). Poland is committed to it; Russia (at least Moscow) is establishing it. Mexico, Argentina, and Hong Kong have schemes; and at least one African country is showing interest. Although there is (as yet?) no country in which EM constitutes the dominant approach to community supervision, considered globally it is not an insignificant development. Indeed, the political and commercial momentum behind it shows no sign of waning. This chapter seeks to explain—a little schematically, paying only limited attention to the nuanced circumstances of its adoption in different countries—how and why this innovation has come about and to suggest how it may evolve in the future. It will be a little speculative—and more focused on Europe than the United States—although it is grounded in things that are already happening but that are still improperly understood.

"Electronic monitoring" is no longer a single technology. In its original (and still predominant) form, it enabled the use of curfews and home detention as forms of community supervision. The offender has a tag attached to his ankle and is told to stay within close proximity to a transceiver installed in his home, which transmits radio frequency signals from the tag to a computer in a distant control center, via either the landline telephone system or the cellular radio system. By this means, the offender's presence or absence from his home can be verified and recorded. This system is widely used in England and Wales for both young and adult offenders sentenced by the court, bail defendants, released prisoners, and, in a very small number of cases, terrorist suspects (Nellis, 1991, 2004, 2007). In Scotland, the same technology is also used to enforce exclusion zones—the transceiver is placed at a victim's home or at the entrance to a public space (shopping mall or harborsides)—which the offender has been forbidden to visit. In the United States, and in some mainland European countries, curfew monitoring can be augmented by remote alcohol monitoring—in effect linking a breathalyser to the monitoring equipment. Early versions of this device used photographic or voice verification technology to confirm the identity of the person using the mouthpiece; the newest version uses automated biometric facial recognition technology.

After its widespread introduction in the United States, particularly in Florida, various European countries (England and Wales, the Netherlands, Sweden, and France) have experimented with tracking technology, using America's GPS satellites. Different companies market equipment with slightly different capabilities, but offenders are still tagged at the ankle and, in addition, carry a transceiver that picks up signals from the satellites, enabling their whereabouts outdoors to be pinpointed with considerable accuracy (although tall buildings, subways, and atmospheric conditions can affect signal quality) (Monmonier, 2002; Shute, 2007). To enable pinpointing indoors as well, the GPS technology can be combined with cellular radio (mobile phone) systems. Some transceivers store data and require it to be downloaded to the control center each night, via a monitoring (and battery recharging) unit in the offender's home, creating a record of movement that is only available to supervisors some hours afterward; others (more expensively) emit a constant signal, enabling the monitoring of movement in real time. Some equipment enables direct communication with the offender, by voice or text. In different jurisdictions, tracking is used in different ways: mapping an offender's routes on a day-to-day basis and maybe matching them automatically with maps of known crime incidents; more usually, monitoring the perimeter of specified exclusion zones. The same technology can be used to create small inclusion zones, thereby making curfews and home detention possible. Various technology companies currently are competing with each other to develop a "one-piece" tracking unit, making the transceiver small enough to fit into an ankle tag.

It is important that the EM of offenders is understood not simply as a technology but as an "automated sociotechnical system" (Lianos & Douglas, 2000), a partly autonomous technology serviced and sustained by a range of human operatives. There are several groups of such operatives. First, the equipment manufacturers provide support teams for customers whose systems malfunction. Second, trained people are required to fit tags and install transceivers in offenders' homes, and to staff control centers on a 24/7 basis, liaising with criminal justice agencies, and dealing with any problems that come up for the offenders and their families. Third, some countries embed EM in rehabilitative and reintegrative programs and provide social work support to all who undertake them; although to a greater or lesser degree, there are tensions between EM and the probation services on whose traditional supervisory territory it has impinged. In addition, legal and administrative regulations relating to EM's use, devised by politicians, lawyers, and civil servants, vary between countries and can alter its intensity, impact, and meaning, both to offenders and to the surrounding system of supervision. The United States tends to use EM more punitively, readily accepts that ankle tags might well be stigmatizing, and permits longer periods on monitoring than European countries: several states have legislated to use it for life on released sex offenders.

Explaining the Emergence of Electronic Monitoring

To explain these developments requires, depending on one's standpoint, either going "beyond criminology" on the one hand or stretching the boundaries and enlarging the focus of the field on the other. The core of the explanation is the claim that EM is a somewhat belated application, in the sphere of criminal justice, of technologies and practices associated with the wider telecommunications revolution; from that insight, something about the future trajectory of EM might be inferred. EM cannot properly be understood purely as a self-contained penal initiative, conceived and operated by penal administrators alone in response to a perceived "control deficit" in the preexisting repertoire of community penalties. It did not even originate in established penal policy networks. Something approximating to EM had indeed been imagined and desired by electronic engineers, behavioral psychologists, and science fiction writers from the mid-20th century onward (and imagined and feared by liberal intellectuals who took their cues from George Orwell), but it could never have been actualized and mainstreamed without the prior availability of miniature electronic components and a cable and wireless communication infrastructure that had been developed for purposes quite independent of crime control (Castells, 2000). Urban theorist Stephen Graham succinctly describes the complex material reality of this new near-global infrastructure:

> New telecommunication networks tend to be largely *invisible* or *silent* or, at most relatively hard to discern, weaving through or under the fabric of cities, using very little space. Urban telecommunications networks consist of underground networks of ducts and cables and aerial lattices of wires over which speed-of-light flows of electrons or photons carry information. Radio and satellite-based telecommunications networks rely on the truly invisible flows of electromagnetic radiation across space between antennae, transmitters and aerials (1997, p. 33).

Commentators on the growth of digital technology have devised various shorthand characterizations of the society that it is in the process of transforming—the network society, the digital society, the wired society, and the telematic society among them. I opt here for William Bogard's (1996) term *telematic* because it denotes societies "that aim to solve the problem of perceptual control at a distance through technologies for cutting the time of transmission of information to zero." Significantly, this definition captures important aspects of EM itself. Bogard is primarily concerned with the *imaginary* of telematic society—an extrapolation of what it could become in the future, the projected end point toward which it leads—the very attraction of which allegedly lures (some of) us forward toward its realization. I am more concerned with specific here-and-now empirical realities than Bogard, but I am convinced that EM's political and commercial champions are indeed guided by an imaginary that seemingly promises vastly greater levels of control over offenders than any previous form of community supervision, notably those associated with probation. Bogard himself fears where the imaginary is luring us; the champions of EM, needless to say, welcome the prospect. Indeed, the rhetoric used by politicians (in Britain) to promote EM as a form of "punishment in the community" has sometimes come close to claiming that it actually achieves the kind of "hypercontrol" over people which Bogard believes certain applications of digital technology makes possible, taking "the disciplinary functions of surveillance to their imaginary limit" (idem). In practice, the reality of EM in its present technological forms has fallen well short of hypercontrol. Although it has indeed introduced an entirely new mechanism for gaining compliance in community supervision—remote surveillance—it is not incapacitative in the manner of a ball-and-chain or a prison cell. Even in the rare instances where EM house arrest lasts a full 24 hours, over several days and weeks, the offender can always make the choice to disregard the constraint: EM prohibits, but it cannot (yet) inhibit. It is not especially "disciplinary" in the Foucauldian sense, although an element of internalization of externally imposed regulation pertains. EM is not as comprehensively educative as the attitude-changing and character-building programs associated with probation. Precisely because it is not inherently incapacitative, EM has come to seem, from the standpoint of "populist punitivism," as a lenient and ineffective penalty; and there have been a handful of well-publicized occasions, in England and Scotland, where tagged offenders have committed serious crimes, including murder. This does pose a challenge for the future of EM—or at least the future forms of EM—and it is in part by understanding "the telematic imaginary" that one can gauge what these might (and might not) be.

Conceptualizing Telematic/E-Topian Society

The expansion of global capitalism—the compression of time and distance by digital technologies that facilitate vast flows of data, primarily to increase capital accumulation, extend and consolidate political, economic and social networks, and to enhance consumption—is invariably seen as the driver of telematic society (with the American military having pioneered specific inventions—communication satellites, the Internet) (Agger, 2004). In contrast to Bogard, William J. Mitchell (1999), dean of Architecture and Planning at MIT, optimistically believes that the increases in "connectivity" that this new, real-time, communication technology will bring about—the augmenting of face-to-face encounters (between employers and workers, politicians and citizens, entrepreneurs and consumers, or just between friends)—will foster mutual understanding among diverse peoples and thereby increase conviviality and social integration. He dubs this brave new world "e-topia" a substantively similar concept to "the telematic imaginary" but without the sense of threat with which Bogard deliberately freights the latter. Mitchell is equivocal about the extent to which new forms of connectivity might supplant rather than augment older forms but insists that the old ways will not—cannot—survive unaltered; an electronic communication grid has now been "superimposed on the residues and remnants of the past," and entirely new options for making, maintaining, and recording contact with people, for whatever reason, have now been created (1999).

Mitchell says nothing about the technology's potential for surveillance, policing, and punishment (possibly to avoid tainting it with "negative" connotations), but there is no reason to suppose that the emergence of "electronic networks within which *new forms of human interaction, control and organisation* [italics added] can actually be constructed in real (or near-real) time" (Graham, 1998) will not also affect penal innovation and the practice of community supervision. Just as commercial organizations can now gauge when face-to-face encounters are essential to business and when communication can be "virtual," so cost-conscious crime controllers can now consider, when deciding how offenders should be supervised, "the different grades of presence that are now available...and weigh these against the costs" (Mitchell, 1999). This "economy of presence" (idem) has been a significant factor in the way that EM has become a rival to probation (and prison). Where community supervision is deemed to require the making of a personal relationship with an offender (in order to bring about change), sustained face-to-face encounters between offender and social worker may be deemed vital. Where supervision is deemed to require nothing more than an impersonal transaction—the delivery (or exchange) of information, a gesture of acquiescence, proof of compliance with a particular rule—not only are social workers unnecessary, but telepresence, even automated telepresence, may be deemed sufficient. EM enables the balance between the relational and the transactional in community supervision to be struck differently than hitherto.

EM is consistent with—and expressive of—telematic society in other ways too. Late modern life is permeated with location monitoring technologies, a multiplicity of embedded tags and sensors that can rapidly identify what things are, where they are, and (in very varying degrees) regulate their movement. Some systems are optical (barcodes and readers), some biometric (fingerprint, iris and facial and voice recognition systems), some acoustic (using ultrasonic emissions), and some electromagnetic (ATM cards, RFID chips). In cities, "grids of terrestrial transceivers can keep track of vehicles and cell phones" (Mitchell, 1999). America's GPS satellites can accurately pinpoint any object or person fitted with a transceiver to within a few meters. Within buildings, various motion-sensitive, electromagnetic, optical, and acoustic sensors can follow the movements of people and artefacts. "Remote summoning capabilities"—smoke detectors that summon fire services, burglar alarms that summon police, stress detectors in bridges, and dams that signal impending malfunctions to maintenance agencies—are already commonplace. "In a ubiquitously networked world this idea will increasingly be extended," not least to old and ill people, via telecare and telemedicine (the remote monitoring of health signs) by "unobtrusive wearable devices" that relay information to medical centers (idem)—as well as to offenders. As equipment and information transmission costs come steadily down, so remote sensing systems will multiply: "video cameras, for example," notes Mitchell (1999) "are evolving into single chip devices costing only a few dollars; they can become cheap "eyes" for almost anything."

Shifts in the locus and trajectories of once readily identifiable penal innovation processes (Ryan, Savage, & Wall, 2001; see also Franko Aas, 2004, Haggerty, 2004) have become harder to pinpoint and map in telematic societies. Old routes of influence (via the established penal reform network) close down, or become narrower and intermittent, while new ones, emanating from new sources (in the commercial sector), open up. These shifts occur when the "affordances" in respect of surveillance and crime control offered by the preexisting telecommunications infrastructure become apparent to key state actors—a process stimulated by a political desire for "modernization" but shaped in practice by a welter of contingencies. Once the affordances are recognized, new ways of doing things present themselves—as, significantly, does its corollary—the prospect of dispensing with old ways (it is partly in such terms that the slow demise of the Probation Service in England and Wales can be understood). When the new champions of ostentatious crime control, committed to protecting the public in the here-and-now—not at some point in the future, when an offender's rehabilitation may or may not have occurred—scan the horizons of possibility, it is not to advances in social welfare or improvements in social justice that they look but to managerial and telematic technologies that seemingly offer the prospect of policing social spaces and processing transgressions with a degree of near ubiquity and instantaneity that has never before been possible. As Bogard (1996) notes, the allure of meticulous regulation (rapid, decisive, and sometimes preemptive responses to all foreseeable contingencies) is "an imaginary that runs deep in telematic societies," which has at least as much of an appeal to crime controllers as it does to the corporate entrepreneurs and financial traders whose global ambitions generated the telecommunications infrastructure in the first place. To understand how processes of penal innovation are changing, we must first examine the emergence of "the managerial state."

The Managerial State and Penal Innovation

Clarke and Newman (1997) define the managerial state as "a cultural formation and distinctive set of ideologies and practices which form one of the underpinnings of an emergent political settlement," in which traditional relationships between state and citizen, public and private agencies, providers and receivers of social care, and management and politics itself are all altered. Computer technology was so central to the operation of "the managerial state" that its strategies could quite aptly be called "technomanagerialism." These were infused into existing public sector bureaucracies, with destabilizing effects. Although it was understood from the outset that the core ingredients of the "new public management"—economy, efficiency, effectiveness—would affect traditional approaches to the community supervision of offenders, the precise consequences of this (in England) were less easily discerned. From a managerial standpoint, the work of the humanistically oriented probation service in effecting change in offenders' behavior seemed unpalatably slow, distant (any effects of rehabilitative initiatives were not immediate), and imprecise, leading first to attempts to redesign "effective practice" within the service, and later to the reconfiguring of the service itself. Its humanistic sentiments came to seem obsolete in a managerialist age, while EM, on the other hand, seemed to have an "elective affinity" with managerialist prescriptions and was more self-evidently modern (Mainprize, 1996; Scheerer, 2000). This affinity is mediated both by the potential of information technology and by the interpellated image of offenders (like managerialist subjects generally) as shallow, rational and malleable actors, easily rendered compliant, and has three distinct dimensions, namely, time, contractual governance, and (less strongly) contracting out.

First, computer-augmented managerialism attempts to accelerate administrative processes, to reduce the time lapse between action and reaction, instruction and compliance, authorization, and feedback (via speedier information flows). In criminal justice generally this has heightened concerns about delays in court, speeding up police decision making (by getting computerized information to them faster), and in some instances enabling them to administer "on the spot" penalties. In the context of community supervision, managerialism has created expectations that the schedules of offenders will be more tightly regulated, that the monitoring of compliance will be intensified, and that reoffending will be reduced more quickly than in the past. The ideal—the imaginary—of continuous, real-time monitoring is latent within contemporary managerial approaches to offenders. This cannot readily be achieved by human staff without undue intrusiveness and high financial cost, but it can be achieved by remote monitoring technology. For the duration of their curfew period, the whereabouts of compliant tagged offenders are known in real time and are capable of verification to within a matter of seconds, as well as being retrievable, if necessary (for use as evidence in court). Satellite tracking technologies are marketed as offering control "24/7/365," extending the spatial arena in which offenders' movements are knowable, and vastly improving (from the vendor's viewpoint) on the temporal regimes imposable by standard probation interventions (Nellis, 2008).

Second, at a micro level, managerialism drives the growing adoption of "contractual governance"—or "regulated self-regulation" (Crawford, 2003)—of individuals, in which transgressors or potential transgressors sign a contract with an institutional authority agreeing to abide by certain conditions regarding their present and future conduct, on pain of specified sanctions for noncompliance. Many community sentences (not only the civil measures on which Crawford dwells) nowadays possess this contractual element—it is a means of enlisting the offender's active cooperation to ease the practical administration of the sentence, even where formal consent is not required by law. EM adds a remote surveillant element to the repertoire of compliance strategies available to supervisors—giving incentives, showing trust, and implying threats—but this in no way makes EM incapacitative. The wearing of a tag, its presence on their body, potentially "responsibilitizes" offenders in a direct and immediate way; it structures their choices, reminding them to regulate themselves, to calculate their chances, and to abide (or not) by the rules laid down in their "contract."

Third, at a macro level, managerialism can lead to the outsourcing/ contracting-out of various state functions to private and voluntary organizations, on the understanding that this will make service delivery cheaper, more efficient, and (sometimes) more innovative. Such "governing-at-a-distance" requires the establishment of an audit and inspection regime to ensure accountability, and demands new flows of information, which computerization facilitates. Group4Securicor (G4S) and Serco (and previously Reliance Monitoring Services), the companies that deliver EM in England, Wales, and Scotland, are contracted in this way. To a degree they have become emblematic of New Labour's belief that the private sector is much more adept at delivering technological innovation than the public sector (Nellis, 2006). Something akin to Mitchell's conception of "e-topia" inflects New Labour's managerial vision (McLaughlin, Muncie, & Hughes, 2001): such is the dynamism that it calls forth that it might as aptly be called "technomanagerialism." This was a significant element in New Labour's Strategic Plan for Criminal Justice 2004–2008 (Home Office, 2004) and was latent in the Carter Report (2004), which, among other things, promoted contestability (greater use of the private sector) and announced the establishment of satellite tracking pilots.

Two further points need to be made about the managerial state. As noted earlier, EM was initially imagined (by both its champions and its detractors) as more controlling than it turned out to be, and perhaps its merits as a penal innovation had to be discursively exaggerated in order for it to gain space in debates on the future of community supervision. William Mitchell's (1999) analysis, however, enables us to see this exaggeration in a somewhat broader perspective. The 1990s were the period in which e-topian (or techno-managerialist) possibilities first seriously began to destabilize a whole range of public and private institutions: "familiar regimes were being swept away by simultaneously unfolding, causally intertwined processes of technological innovation, capital mobilisation, social reorganisation and cultural transformation." Many first-generation digital innovations were overhyped in this period, both by those who welcomed and those who feared their likely impact: Mitchell's pithy observation that many were promoted as "Viagra versions of older, tireder predecessors that cannot do the job anymore" (idem) captures exactly how EM was portrayed by the Home Office—as a smarter, superior, and more robust form of community supervision than that provided by the seemingly anachronistic probation service.

The managerial state consciously empowered the private sector, as a penal innovator, in a way that previous state formations had not done. As states began to show interest in EM, they signaled to commercial organizations—particularly security companies and technology manufacturers, many with a global reach—that a new crime control market was opening up (exactly as some entrepreneurs had already anticipated). Although states retained tight contractual control over the organizations that sold equipment and/or delivered monitoring services, the subsequent global evolution of the market itself, the range of products available, and the discourse about their utility and significance became impossible to regulate in the same way. A self-described "electronic monitoring industry" came into being, initially to service the United States, then to service Europe, whose internal dynamics (takeovers, buyouts, patent wars) and external relations (with state and supra-state agencies) then began to shape the market, to generate its own telematic vision of what was possible and desirable in crime control and its own cross-national information flows about options and opportunities.

Penal Innovation on the State–Commercial Interface

There are three types of commercial organizations in the EM field—technology-producing companies, operational service-providing companies, and combined technology and service-providing companies. The development of commercial organizations in this field has mirrored the development of commercial organizations in digital telecommunications more generally, which developed "incrementally and messily through a complex ongoing process of technological innovation, new infrastructure construction, adaptive reuse of existing infrastructure, alliances and mergers among telecommunications providers and reformulation of regulatory regimes" (Mitchell, 1999). Since the advent of EM in the United States in the early 1980s, technological innovation has been constant, legal battles have been fought over patents, smaller companies have been progressively bought up by larger ones, and various forms of service delivery structure have emerged in different countries (EM is embedded in Probation in Sweden and the Prison Service in Belgium, contracted out to private organizations in England, Wales, and Scotland). Some of the companies involved—those involved in running private prisons or selling commercial services to state-based prison systems (Securicor, Serco, Wackenhut)—were already constituent parts of "the commercial correctional complex" (Lilly, 1992; Lilly & Deflem, 1996; Lilly & Knepper, 1993); others, such as Elmotech and On Guard Plus, were newcomers. Before the emergence of EM, the commercial corrections complex had shown little interest in the supervision of offenders outside prison and had largely aligned itself, ideologically, with the perceived need to expand imprisonment (Christie, 2001). EM opened up another potentially lucrative market. The state's role in regulating commercial enterprise should not be underestimated, but it is nonetheless on the interfaces between statutory criminal justice bodies and commercial organizations that processes of penal innovation in the 21st century are being dramatically reconfigured. In the course of modernizing the infrastructure of criminal justice, the old circuits of penal reform are being circumvented— IT companies such as Fujitsu, British Telecom, and Siemens are becoming as, and maybe more, important to the Home Office than Nacro, the Prison Reform Trust, and the Howard League in exploring what it is possible and desirable to do. The mentality—the imaginary project—might aptly be called "e-topian correctionalism." New options for creating and maintaining order are being hatched on these interfaces, which at best are transforming existing criminal justice agencies (the police; Chan, 2001) and at worst rendering them obsolete (probation; Nellis, 2006). On the interface between state and commercial organizations, in the EM world, there are three broad processes that are shaping penal possibilities: the state stimulation of innovation, transnational showcasing, and customizing new developments in telecommunication technology for the corrections market. I will comment on each in turn.

The State Stimulation of Innovation

This occurs in three ways. First, at a political level, senior ministers construct the modernizing discourses against which existing forms of community supervision are made to look inadequate, creating the problem to which EM can then be presented as the solution. Ministers also champion EM in the media and among the public as a vital tool in the fight against crime, creating expectations, promising results, and simultaneously signaling to the companies that a market is emerging. Second, at an operational level, the task of procuring and implementing EM has largely been given (across Europe) to young and ambitious civil servants who are staking their careers on making it a success—rising stars who are neither too embedded in existing policy networks nor loyal to traditional approaches to practice. Third, such people tend to be technologically savvy and are able to specify and commission continual upgrades in equipment quality from the EM suppliers. This then gives the EM companies an incentive to engage in research and development and to scan the market for ways of improving current technology. In a section of contract with an EM supplier-headed "continuous development and innovation," the Scottish Executive (2002) specified that "the contractor will be expected to demonstrate flexibility in bringing into use improved equipment should this become available." In addition, contractors must commit to providing EM to support not only the applications at present in use or planned but also any ad hoc arrangements that may need to be made during the lifetime of the contract. Contractors must also undertake to provide EM to support new applications the Scottish Executive wishes to introduce, whether or not these schemes are statutory. Payment for additional services will be determined by agreement. Contractors must ensure the software capacity of any monitoring unit includes additional platforms to accommodate additional uses (idem).

Perhaps the most striking instance of the state stimulating technological development is arguably the Home Office legislating for satellite tracking in 2000, without specific plans (at that time) to implement a program but in anticipation of suitable technology becoming available. Although satellite tracking technology was already in use in the United States, the Home Office wanted equipment that was more reliable. Elmotech, which had not initially expected there to be a European market for satellite tracking, came up with the STaR system partly to meet the Home Office's tight specifications.

Transnational Showcasing

Private companies showcase their successes in one country in the hope of stimulating interest in other countries. This is most easily accomplished by visits from one country to another but also by the biannual workshops of the kind organized since 2001 by the Conference Permanente Europeene de la Probation (CEP). These have been funded by the commercial organizations that are either doing business or hoping to do business in Europe and bring vendors together with policy-makers, practitioners, and, to a lesser extent, researchers. In October 2004, Elmotech organized a conference in Italy to celebrate 10 years of doing business in Europe and to cultivate more.

Conferences and exhibitions give the companies not only a chance to pitch their wares to the market but also an opportunity to learn what state agencies are looking for. Most companies are aware that European governments are modernizing their probation services and seeking, largely for cost reasons, to reduce their prison populations. Most are aware that their "product" creates some unease in probation services and, in Europe at least, have sought to avoid being perceived as threatening. Nonetheless, the companies have always emphasized the control EM exerts at night, implying that in the modernizing world, an offender management service restricted to the daytime is inadequate and anachronistic: the night remains emblematic of lawlessness (Melbin, 1987). More recently, and particularly since the advent of GPS tracking, they have emphasized their capacity to devise strategies of incessant oversight: "Securicor," for example, "currently monitors over 2200 offenders [on EM] at any one time, providing a comprehensive 24/7 installation, monitoring and follow-up service," while Reliance Monitoring Services works "silently and unobtrusively 24 hours per day, 365 days per year to ensure the protection of the community."

Most companies are well aware that governments can and do claim more control for EM technology than it can in fact deliver, and are wary of being set up to fail, jeopardizing profit in the long run. Some have realized the danger of allowing EM to be associated with "populist punitivism" and have made a point of emphasizing how their technology could support and augment probation rather than displace it. This was particularly true of Reliance Monitoring Services in Scotland, where a strong social work culture still prevailed and where social work staff was recruited to manage Reliance precisely because they understood how to pitch it (Johnson, 2002). However, even some of the purely technology-manufacturing companies have adopted this strategy and advertise their wares in a probation and youth justice-friendly language:

> Advances in technology have significantly increased the sentencing and supervision options available to courts, prison authorities, police and probation services throughout the world for the monitoring and surveillance of offenders. Research shows that reduced custodial terms or, alternatively, non-custodial sentencing can improve family relationships and help offenders to resist the pressure to re-offend. [They offer] the flexibility to allow offenders to continue with or find paid work and to participate in structured education, training and reparation programmes designed to tackle offending behaviour. [They] also help ease prison overcrowding while at the same time saving authorities and taxpayers considerable costs (On Guard Plus, publicity brochure, 2004).

To acquire the capacity to speak in this way, most of the companies have acquired probation expertise, either in the form of consultants or employees. In England, former chief probation officer Dick Whitfield played an important part in persuading the service to be less hostile to EM and has subsequently acted as a consultant for Securicor and as an adviser to the Scottish Executive. Some probation staff transfers directly to the private sector. This is perhaps more apparent in the United States, where Richard Nimer, a former deputy director of Florida Department of Corrections, joined Pro Tech, but it happens elsewhere too: in England and Wales and Scotland Securicor recruited a senior manager from the probation service; Reliance recruited probation officers in England and criminal justice social workers in Scotland to head up its EM operation, partly on the understanding that such people would have credibility as salespeople with the probation and social work services, respectively.

Customizing New Developments in Telecommunications Technology for the Corrections Market

Even without state stimulation, the EM companies, specifically those involved with technology manufacture, constantly become aware of possibilities for upgrading—improved equipment and/or cost-savings—as new developments occur in the wider field of telecommunications which can be adapted to corrections. The promise of upgrades becomes part of what the company offers its customers. Pro Tech, which sells itself in terms of having been the first provider of GPS offender tracking technology in the United States, makes this clear: "As GPS technology continues to evolve, you can be sure Pro Tech Monitoring will be in step, providing you with systems that utilise the latest technology." A similar message is apparent from G4S: "By *continually innovating* [italics added] and providing excellent service, EM will possibly contribute to a safer society both now and in the future." On Guard Plus defined itself as "the only organisation in its sector able to offer a true perspective on the relative merits of existing equipment types *and/or emerging technology* [italics added]."

It is because the private organizations are best positioned to anticipate, understand, and customize new developments in information technology that they have become major contributors to penal innovation. State governments may have opened up the possibility for them, and indeed licensed them to innovate; but once the innovation process has begun, it is not easy to constrain the process. There is no necessary intention on the part of states to fully supplant existing community supervision agencies like probation but the longer term consequences of the advent of EM are hard to predict. As Mulgan (1991) states, "information technologies continue to be most revolutionary not in creating the new out of nothing but rather in restructuring the way old things are done" (Graham, 1997); but one might still wonder how far "restructuring" might go—does it simply mean modernizing probation, or dispensing with probation altogether? Can anything constrain the momentum of telematic technology in penal policy-making?

Telematics, Managerialism, and Populist Punitivism

It is not difficult to show that EM is one particular expression of "the telematic imaginary," but whatever the future of telematics more generally, the future of EM in its present forms is not guaranteed. Contemporary crime control structures are shaped and constituted by the interplay of three conceptually (if not always empirically) distinct discourses—one (to put it rather simplistically) emphasizing punishment and repression; the second rehabilitation, help, and social justice; and the third (in which "the telematic imaginary" is grounded) managerialism and control. The humanistic ethos of the rehabilitative discourse is in serious decline (more so in some jurisdictions than others); and although decline may have been slowed by the advent of restorative justice and the articulation of a human rights perspective, it has not been arrested or reversed. The respective fortunes of managerialism and "populist punitivism," and the ways and contexts in which they might clash or converge, are less clear. Fionda (2000) affirms the long-term ascendancy of managerialism. Crawford (2003) sees elements of reciprocity between the two discourses, punitive means being held in reserve to sanction noncompliance with predominantly managerial interventions. Bottoms (1995) suggests that populist punitivism remains powerful enough to constrain and impede the pure logic of managerialism: if true, this does have implications for EM (Nellis, 2003a).

The reality of contemporary EM certainly falls short of the "hypercontrol" envisaged by Bogard. EM systems do in part illustrate "the conversion of persons and social relations into the universal ether of information" (Bogard, 1996), but the acquisition of onscreen information at unprecedented speed does not necessarily translate into—or equate with—automatic compliance on the part of the tagged offender. Current forms of EM approximate to, but do not in any final sense constitute, the "transfiguration of discipline…[the] higher, more devious order of discipline" (idem) that Bogard (and Baudrillard) believes telematics entails. Compliance rates for EM, even in Britain, are indeed reasonably high; and that is largely because they have been applied to low- and medium-risk offenders who have weighed up the risks of noncompliance, feared worse punishments, and accepted the rules imposed on them. There have, however, been sufficient high-profile instances of noncompliance—offenders choosing to disregard the constraints of the tag and committing further crime—to mock any talk of "hypercontrol" in this context. The conservative parties in both England and Wales and Scotland, who are mostly oriented toward punishment, have become deeply skeptical of EM for all but the lowest risk offenders, precisely because its putative constraints seem so easy to evade. Victim advocate organizations and relatives of murder victims—increasingly powerful voices (when amplified by the media) in the politics of late modern crime control—have prominently questioned the value of tagging as a means of protecting victims (Bra, 2007).

Populist punitivism does constitute a check on the expansion of EM but has by no means sapped long-term political commitment it. This perhaps is the surprising thing; EM survives despite serious criticism of it. Neither governments nor commercial vendors seem unduly anxious about the future of EM. "In the UK we've had a bit of negative publicity about electronic monitoring," Paul Moonan (2005), EM director for G4S, admitted ruefully, adding "most of it based on half-truths." Criminology in fact understands that a fair amount of failure in community supervision has always been tolerated (Cohen, 1985); the failure is simply managed by the state to spur the development of new and better versions, often more of the same, but tougher. In respect of EM, the pattern was noted early in the United States: a pioneering EM scheme, embedded in social work and administered by a not-for-profit organization in Palm Beach Florida, was discontinued because it was not considered intrusive enough by its state funders—"there is no place left for caring for people," its director complained, "all the state wants is to have offenders watched" (Lilly, 1992). Some commentators at this point believed that EM would be a passing fad; however, precisely because it was embedded in the commercial correctional nexus, Lilly doubted this, concluding correctly that EM "is likely to return in a stronger form" (in Florida's case, satellite tracking). What Lilly foresaw in microcosm in Florida held true on a grander scale throughout EM's history.

Nonetheless, at any given moment in time, a combination of technical limitations and populist punitive sentiments may impede particular initiatives. The satellite tracking pilots in England and Wales proved the viability of the technology in many respects but left doubts among practitioners about its capacity (contrary to the political hype that attended their launch) to control high-risk sex offenders who were tempted to cross the perimeter of an exclusion zone (Nellis, 2005; Shute, 2007). The police response time to such an event might never be sufficiently rapid to prevent harm being done. Some of the satellite tracking technologies used had the capacity to communicate (by text or cell phone) with the offender; but this may not only fail to guarantee compliance, it may also increase agency liability for the offender's behavior. The future of satellite tracking in England and Wales has finally become uncertain because, once the government was forced by rising prisoner numbers to begin building more prisons, money for rolling out satellite tracking beyond the pilots ceased to be available. It is still used on a small scale in the Netherlands and France, but compared with its rapid expansion in the United States, the market for satellite tracking in Europe is not seen to have "taken off" in the way that the commercial organizations anticipated and hoped (Mark Griffiths, G4S, personal communication, September 2006). This may change when Galileo, Europe's own network of geolocation satellites, established to rival the United States's GPS satellites, becomes operational after 2012; as digital infrastructure, it will certainly create new possibilities and may stimulate new thinking in a range of agencies.

Managerialism survives in part because it can absorb and transform some elements of populist punitiveness. So, if stand-alone EM curfews come to be perceived as an "inadequate" form of offender control, there are a number of ways in which they might be modified to compete better against more viscerally punitive measures or simply to increase compliance rates. EM can be embedded in a social work support program, as in the Belgian and Swedish models, rather than used as a stand-alone measure. More likely, some kind of compromise with punitiveness itself would need to be effected, such as Julian Roberts' (2004) idea of "community custody," a package of intensive support and surveillance strategies including curfews/house arrest (modeled on some Canadian initiatives).

Compliance with stand-alone versions of EM may be increased by the threat of a massive custodial penalty in the event of breach (common in the United States). Such ingredients have been present in the EM-monitored control orders used on unconvicted terrorist suspects in England since 2005, but even this has not prevented some absconding (Nellis, 2007). At the extreme, the prospect of remote pain infliction via EM has existed in science fiction writing since the 1970s and indeed figured in the Spiderman story that helped trigger the first official uses of EM (Nellis, 2003). Only recently, in 2007, has it become technically possible to inflict a remote, temporarily immobilizing electric shock on a tracked offender heading into an exclusion zone; but whether it will ever be marketed or used is a moot point.

The respective fortunes of managerialist and punitive approaches in the future will depend in large part on the intensity and rigidity of social divisions between the affluent and the poor, and on the perceived violence of any impending threats to social order. Existing—arguably liberal—uses of EM will not survive a sense of severe threat. Architect Lieven de Cauter (2002) has already recognized that "the technological devices, with their soft, almost invisible thresholds, do not suffice" to create control under conditions of extreme disorder. Under such conditions, public and politicians alike will be inclined to adopt tried and tested forms of urban crime control and crime prevention—"the fence, the wall, the gate, the stonghold" (idem)—as well as the prison. The affluent and comfortable will lock, light, and zone themselves out of harm's way, segregating themselves from the perceived "dangerous classes" (Bauman, 2007; Caldeira, 2000; Davis, 2006). Under such circumstances, "the telematic imaginary" does not wither away, but it lures us less toward the personalized surveillance packages for offenders exemplified by contemporary forms of EM and more toward means of regulating whole classes of marginalized people, monitoring mobility (a proxy for regulating behavior) within and between class-differentiated zones using biometric access controls at borders and checkpoints (Jones, 2006) and an array of visual surveillance technologies—CCTV, satellite cameras, helicopters, and unmanned spy planes.

Even if (as seems likely) imprisonment continues to expand and flourish, the private security companies still have a product to sell. EM need no longer be associated, as it has been, with community supervision and alternatives to prison: ElmoTech's TRaCE technology permits "inmate tracking and area-monitoring capabilities inside correction facilities and around them" (company brochure, 2006). Its "wireless area monitoring system" can produce "real-time headcounts" and check continuously whether inmates are in the right place (zone-based monitoring) at the right time (schedule-based monitoring). It can also indicate where within a penal institution an officer's wrist alarm goes off, identify the officer concerned, and list which inmates are present. This technology was first applied in a federal penitentiary in the United States but has also been taken up in three prisons in the Netherlands and in one open prison in Sweden (with plans to extend to three more). The aim in all three cases was the reduction of staff costs—making adjustments to the "economy of presence"—and the improvement of security within the institution.

It is perhaps not too difficult—if one factors in smart building technology and telerobotics (the remote manipulation of intelligent machines)—to extrapolate from this development to the concept of the fully automated prison, controlled by a handful of personnel many miles from the institution itself. Although he does not specifically mention prisons, William Mitchell (1999) envisages telerobotics being particularly useful "where services must be delivered to dangerous locations." Alongside the comprehensive visual and location monitoring of inmates, telerobots of the near future could undertake all the routine menial processes of physical confinement—opening and closing cell doors, sealing and unsealing corridors, giving instructions, turning lights on and off, serving food, laundering clothes, activating preprogrammed e-learning machines at set times, arranging video links to relatives and lawyers. Guarding prisoners in many U.S. jails is already itself a menial task, requiring no significant educational qualifications or complex interactional skills; and with dangerous prisoners in supermax regimes, inmate–guard contact is already minimized. The emerging sense that prison guarding is essentially "dirty work"—too distasteful and too stressful to be undertaken by ordinary people (like the equivalent burgeoning sense that modern warfare is too dangerous for ordinary soldiers)—stimulates in the international research and development community a desire to design machines that could and should be capable of impersonally executing such tasks.

Conclusions

I have sought in this chapter to show that the existing forms of EM are expressions of what, following William Bogard, might be called "the telematic imaginary" or, adapting William Mitchell's "e-topian correctionalism," a mentality that optimistically envisages an expanding role for electronic/digital technology in offender management. "E-topian correctionalism" is a new, and still evolving, factor in penal innovation. The various forms of EM that have developed since the early 1980s are its first concrete instances—the ones that first signaled that the process of penal innovation was changing—but they are unlikely to be the last. The mentality is most evident on the interface between state and commercial organizations involved in the EM field, in which each one stimulates the other to imagine and realize new ways of regulating offender's behavior. It is grounded, at root, in managerialism. Although "e-topian correctionalism" bears little resemblance to the humanistic philosophy that dominated mid-20th century attempts to control offenders in the community, it is similarly vulnerable to the populist punitive criticism that it is in fact insufficiently controlling and exists in constant tension with demands for more overtly painful responses to criminal behavior. It is, nonetheless, arguably too deeply embedded in contemporary sociotechnical developments ever to be eradicated now, although the forms it takes—and the forms in which it is imagined—will adapt to suit the perceived realities of crime and disorder, and the perceived levels of desirable security.

"E-topian correctionalism" both contributes to and is legitimated by wider surveillance practices. "Surveillance societies" were emerging in Europe anyway as a consequence of the telecommunications revolution. Official concern about organized crime and migration pointed up a need for more registration and monitoring of citizens. Mathiesen (2000) noted that "the likely development toward a more or less integrated, totalised registration and surveillance system in Europe implies a development toward a vast 'panoptical machine' which may be used for registration and surveillance of individuals as well as whole categories of people, and which may well become one of the most repressive political instruments of modernity." The post 9/11 "war on terror" intensified these trends, and security needs—above and beyond commercial needs—became stronger drivers of innovation in surveillance. The emergence of a wider surveillance culture has a paradoxical effect on EM. On the one hand, it legitimates it and stimulates its expansion. On the other, the very normalization and routinization of a range of surveillance practices in the everyday lives of all citizens make it difficult to effectively project an image of geolocating offenders as something distinctively and decisively punitive—geolocation (via mobile phones) is something we all experience to a greater or lesser degree and perhaps appreciate as a convenience. This in turn creates a space in which the voices of populist punitiveness can still impinge on penal policy-making.

The more standardized and commodified community supervision processes become—the more like a transaction than a relationship—the more easily they are automated. With the past decade's worth of automation in banking and financial services in mind, Mitchell (1999) observes that "the service agent on the end of the line can often become an unsleeping piece of software rather than a human operator." Some aspects of EM presage this; whatever future forms it takes, automation will be one of its legacies. Even in respect of its current forms many elements of the monitoring process are automated—recording compliance patterns, issuing alerts, verifying identity, passing information between agencies, even some verbal/telephone communication with offenders themselves. The current presence of human operatives in EM control centers reflects both the limitations of the technologies-in-use and the continuing belief that human/personal contact with offenders still contributes both to the legitimacy and effectiveness of the monitoring process. If, for whatever reason, human contact was deemed optional or expendable, such that monitoring became merely transactional, rather than relational, all communication processes with offenders under electronic supervision in the community could be further automated. The "image of man" and "the image of justice" that is interpolated within policy on, and work with, offenders is thus of vital moral importance in critiquing these developments and setting limits on technologically based initiatives in crime control. The subtle objectification of offenders by managerial, actuarial, and risk-oriented approaches, combined with their demonization by tabloid media, serves over time to foster a sense of them as so loathsome, so incorrigible, so fundamentally "other," that they may be thought less deserving of human company or contact and fit only to be managed by machines. Such sentiments are arguably latent within "the telematic imaginary," and Bogard is right to fear the future toward which, in extremis, it lures us—less the convivial "e-topia" as envisaged by Mitchell, more "the inhuman" as envisaged by Lyotard (1991).

References

Agger, B. (2004). *Speeding up fast capitalism*. London: Paradigm.

Bauman, Z. (2007). *Liquid times: Living in an age of uncertainty*. Cambridge: Polity.

Bogard, W. (1996). *The simulation of surveillance: Hypercontrol in telematic societies*. Cambridge: Cambridge University Press.

Bottoms, A. E. (1995). The politics and philosophy and sentencing. In C. Clarkson & R. Morgan (Eds.), *The politics of sentencing reform*. Oxford: Clarendon Press, 17–49.

Bra (2007). *Extended use of electronic tagging in Sweden: The offenders' and victims' views* (Report 2007:3). Stockholm: Swedish National Council for Crime Prevention.

Carter, P. (2004). *Managing offenders, reducing crime—A new approach*. London: Home Office Strategy Unit.

Caldeira, T. P. R. (2000). *City of walls: Crime, segregation and citizenship in Sao Paulo*. Berkeley: University of California Press.

Castells, M. (2000). *The rise of the network society*. Oxford: Blackwell.

Chan, J. B. L. (2001). The technological game: How information technology is transforming police practice. *Criminal Justice, 1*, 139–159.

Clarke, J., & Newman, J. (1997). *The managerial state: Power, politics and ideology in the remaking of social welfare*. London: Sage.

Christie, N. (2000). *Crime control as industry*. London: Routledge.

Cohen, S. (1985). *Visions of social control*. Cambridge: Polity Press.

Crawford, A. (2003). Contractual governance of deviant behaviour. *Journal of Law and Society, 30*, 479–505.

Davis, M. (2006). *Planet of slums*. London: Verso.

de Cauter, L. (2002). The capsular city. In N. Leach (Ed.), *The hieroglyphics of space: Reading and experiencing the modern metropolis*. London: Routledge.

Fionda, J. (2000). New managerialism, credibility and the sanitisation of criminal justice. In P. Green & A. Rutherford (Eds.), *Criminal policy in transition*. Oxford: Hart, 109–130.

Franko Aas, K. (2004). From narrative to database: Technological change and penal culture. *Punishment and Society, 6,* 379–393.

Graham, S. (1997). Imagining the real-time city: Telecommunications, urban paradigms and the future of cities. In S. Westwood & J. Williams (Eds.), *Imagining cities: Scripts, signs, memory*. London: Routledge, 31–49.

Haggerty, K. (2004). Displaced expertise: Three constraints on the policy relevance of criminological thought. *Theoretical Criminology, 8,* 211–231.

Home Office. (2004). *Confident communities in a secure Britain: The Home Office strategic plan 2004–2008*. London: Home Office.

Johnson, I. (2002, May). Electronic monitoring—maintaining the balance. *Criminal Justice Management, 5,* 14–15.

Jones, R. (2000). Digital rule: Punishment, control and technology. *Punishment and Society, 2,* 5–22.

Lianos, M., & Douglas, M. (2000). Dangerisation and the end of deviance: The institutional environment. In D. Garland & R. Sparks (Eds.), *Criminology and social theory*. Oxford: Clarendon Press.

Lilly, J. R. (1992). Selling justice: Electronic monitoring and the security industry, *Justice Quarterly, 9,* 493–503.

Lilly, J. R., & Deflem, M. (1996). Profit and penalty: An analysis of the corrections–commercial complex. *Crime and Delinquency, 42,* 3–20.

Lilly, J. R., & Knepper, P. (1993). An international perspective on the privatisation of corrections. *Howard Journal, 31,* 174–191.

Lyotard, J.-F. (1991). *The inhuman: Reflections on time*. Oxford: Blackwell.

Mainprize, S. (1996). Elective affinities in the engineering of social control: The evolution of electronic monitoring. *Electronic Journal of Sociology.*

Mathiesen, T. (2000). On the globalisation of control: Towards an integrated surveillance system in Europe. In P. Green & A. Rutherford (Eds.), *Criminal Policy in Transition*. Oxford: Hart, 162–192.

Mayer, M., Haverkamp, R., & Levy, R. (Eds.). (2003). *Will electronic monitoring have a future in Europe?* Freiburg: Max Planck Institute.

McLaughlin, E., Muncie, J., & Hughes, G. (2001). The permanent revolution: New labour, new public management and the modernisation of criminal justice, *Criminal Justice, 1,* 301–318.

Melbin, M. (1987). *Night as frontier: Colonizing the world after dark*. New York: Free Press.

Mitchell, W. (1999). *E-topia: Urban life, Jim, but not as we know it*. Cambridge: MIT Press.

Monmonier, M. (2004). *Spying with maps: Surveillance technologies and the future of privacy*. Chicago: Chicago University Press.

Mulgan, G. (1991). *Communication and control: Networks and the new economies' of communication*. Cambridge: Polity Press.

Nellis, M. (1991). The electronic monitoring of offenders in England and Wales: Recent developments and future prospects. *British Journal of Criminology, 31,* 162–185.

Nellis, M. (2003a). Electronic monitoring and the future of the probation service. In W. H. Chui & M. Nellis (Eds.), *Moving probation forward; evidence, arguments and practice*. Harlow: Longmans, 244–260.

Nellis, M. (2003b). News media and popular cultural representations of electronic monitoring in England and Wales. *Howard Journal, 42,* 1–31.

Nellis, M. (2004). "I know where you live": Electronic monitoring and penal policy in England and Wales 1999–2004. *British Journal of Community Justice, 2,* 33–59.

Nellis, M. (2005). "Out of this world": The advent of the satellite tracking of offenders in England and Wales. *Howard Journal, 44,* 125–150.

Nellis, M. (2006a). NOMS, contestability and the process of technocorrectional innovation. In M. Hough, R. Allen, & U. Padel (Eds.), *Reshaping probation and prisons: The new offender management framework.* Bristol: Policy Press, 49–68.

Nellis, M. (2006b). Electronic monitoring, satellite tracking and the new punitiveness in England and Wales. In J. Pratt, D. Brown, M. Brown, S. Hallsworth & W. Morrison (Eds.), *The new punitiveness: Trends, theories and perspectives.* Cullompton: Willan, 167–188.

Nellis, M. (2007). Electronic monitoring and control orders for terrorist suspects in England and Wales. In T. Abbas (Ed.), *Islamic political radicalism.* Edinburgh: Edinburgh University Press, 263–276.

Nellis, M. (2008). 24/7/365. Mobility, locatability and the satellite tracking of offenders. In K. Franco Aas, H. O. Gundhus, & H. M. Lomell (Eds.), *Technologies of Insecurity: The surveillance of everyday life.* London: Routledge, 105–124.

Roberts, J. V. (2004). *The virtual prison.* Cambridge: Cambridge University Press.

Ryan, M., Savage, S., & Wall, D. (Eds.). (2002). *Policy networks in criminal justice.* London: Palgrave.

Scheerer, S. (2000). Three trends into the new millennium: The managerial, the populist and the road towards global justice. In P. Green & A. Rutherford (Eds.), *Criminal policy in transition.* Oxford: Hart.

Scottish Executive. (2002). *Contract between the Scottish Executive and Reliance Monitoring Services Ltd for the provision of electronic monitoring.* Retrieved from www.scotland.gov.uk/publications (Accessed 16 August 2007).

Shute, S. (2007). *Satellite tracking of offenders: A study of the pilots in England and Wales. Research Summary 4.* London: Ministry of Justice.

Key Elements of Restorative Justice Alongside Adult Criminal Justice

6

JOANNA SHAPLAND*

Contents

Introduction

In this chapter we will be focusing on some of the key aspects of restorative justice as it may be used in cases involving adult offenders. Using restorative justice with adult offenders has tended to be a rarer occurrence than its now mainstream use with young offenders in various countries. Statutory provisions for conferencing or direct mediation for young offenders are now in force in New Zealand, Northern Ireland, Poland, and parts of Australia (Campbell

* The research reported on in this chapter was undertaken with Anne Atkinson, Helen Atkinson, James Dignan, Lucy Edwards, Marie Howes, Jennifer Johnstone, Gwen Robinson, and Angela Sorsby. James Dignan is now at the University of Leeds, UK. Jennifer Johnstone is now at the University of Newcastle, UK.

et al., 2006; Daly, 2001, 2004; Morris & Maxwell, 2001; Wozniakowska, 2005), with the discretionary use of restorative justice and restorative practices being widespread in England and Wales, Canada, and the United States. The scarcity of schemes and evaluations of restorative justice for cases involving adult offenders can be seen from the fact that the recent review of effectiveness by Sherman and Strang (2007) considered 9 schemes for violent crime and 11 schemes for property crime involving young offenders or young adult offenders (from Australia, Canada, the United States, and the United Kingdom) but only one scheme for violent crime (from the United States) and one scheme for property crime (from Canada) involving adult offenders.

Yet restorative justice initiatives are one of the main new policy initiatives for dealing with offending in many Western countries (Council of Europe, 1999; van Ness, 2003). The European Union's (2001) decision states that "Each Member State shall seek to promote mediation in criminal cases for offences which it considers appropriate for this sort of measure" (Article 10). In England and Wales, the Home Office (2003) has encouraged a wide range of measures for both young and adult offenders, which span conferencing, direct and indirect mediation, and restorative practice. Let us differentiate what may be important in different circumstances and in relation to different disputes.

Restorative justice with adult offenders and their victims poses some additional challenges and raises questions only rarely considered in relation to younger offenders. These include the stronger tradition of prosecution and traditional criminal justice sentencing (as opposed to diversion) with adult offenders; a greater emphasis on punishment and deterrence, as opposed to education and rehabilitation, particularly in a culture of punitive populism (Garland, 2001); the rather more routine processing of adult cases, at least in the lower courts (Carlen, 1976; Sudnow, 1965); and the traditionally more open and less private context of adult criminal courts, at least in common law countries. Restorative justice, with its emphasis on communication, problem solving, change for offenders, and a participative role for victims, seems less immediately applicable to our stereotype of the adult criminal case, whether that be of the very serious case of violence, tried and sentenced through the majesty of the law in the higher courts, or the long list of cases of more or less persistent minor offenses in the lower courts. It is probably this misfit in stereotypes that has led to restorative justice being used so far predominantly with younger offenders.

Our own research, however, has been primarily in relation to cases involving adult offenders and often serious offenses, which received both restorative justice and the traditional criminal justice processes in England and Wales. Restorative justice and criminal justice were run in parallel—with victims and offenders receiving both. This allows us to consider the extent to which restorative justice was found by victims and offenders to be applicable to their cases—and the key aspects that seemed to be important in these adult cases. In this chapter we will concentrate on three such key aspects:

- participation, communication, and safeguards to ensure procedural justice;
- apologies and symbolic reparation;
- restorative justice and security.

First, however, it is important to describe the schemes, their evaluation, and the model of restorative justice they were using.

The Restorative Justice Schemes

The three schemes we have evaluated were funded by the Home Office (now the Ministry of Justice) in England and Wales, as part of their Crime Reduction Programme. The evaluated work of the schemes started in 2001, with cases being actively taken until 2003/2004 (Shapland et al., 2004, 2006a). The schemes ran in five different areas of England and Wales and dealt only with offenses involving individual personal victims, not organizational victims (businesses, community facilities) or offenses without obvious victims (public order offenses, drugs offenses, etc.).

Restorative justice is a very broad term, which includes conferencing, direct and indirect mediation, circle sentencing, and peace-making and dispute resolution processes, which have ranged in scale from work in divided countries (e.g., the South African Peace and Reconciliation Commission) to disputes between landlords and tenants, within schools, and in companies. The three schemes we have evaluated all took the definition of restorative justice set out by Marshall (1999): "Restorative justice is a process whereby parties with a stake in a specific offense collectively resolve how to deal with the aftermath of the offense and its implications for the future." This means that, to count as a case in which restorative justice had occurred, there had at least to be some collective resolution by victim and offender, using a neutral facilitator or mediator. A case in which there was only a flow of information in one direction (e.g., the offender answering the victim's questions as to how the offense came about, but the victim then not expressing anything to the offender) could not count as such collective resolution—and so, although it might involve restorative practices, it could not fall within our definition of restorative justice (Shapland et al., 2004). The minimum number of participants included a victim, offender, and facilitator/mediator, although many restorative justice events included far more (offender and victim supporters, relevant professionals invited by the offender or victim). The cases all involved direct victims who were individuals. No victim was an organization unless there were participating individuals who themselves were direct victims (e.g., in a robbery of a shop or post office where the shop assistant, manager, or cashier was threatened).

It is important to recognize that restorative justice in these schemes involved only cases where the offender had either pleaded guilty or admitted responsibility for the offense. The restorative justice hence did not influence the trial of the offender, in which guilt or innocence was established, but was, in criminal justice terms, relevant to sentencing or parts of the penal process postsentence/disposal. Both victim and offender had to agree to take part in the restorative justice: This was a voluntary element. If either did not agree, then the criminal justice process would continue in the normal way. Where the restorative justice took place just before decision-making stages in criminal justice (sentence, release from a custodial sentence, during a community-based sentence), a report was made by the scheme to relevant professionals in the criminal justice system (judge, probation officers, corrections authorities).

Nonetheless, the three schemes, between them, involved different restorative justice processes (conferencing, direct mediation, indirect mediation) and took place at many different stages of the criminal justice process. Details of the processes involved in setting up the schemes, their experiences with criminal justice, the numbers of cases, and attrition rates are given by Shapland et al. (2004, 2006a).

Justice Research Consortium

Justice Research Consortium (JRC) was the largest scheme, and it is directed by Larry Sherman and Heather Strang. It offered only conferencing, in which both offenders and victims were invited by professional facilitators to attend a conference with supporters. The model of conferencing used was very similar to that run by them in Canberra, Australia, in the RISE scheme (Sherman et al., 1997). The scheme was run at three sites in England, with random controlled trials being run at each. Cases were randomized to experimental and control groups after the process of preparation for restorative justice and after both offender and victim consent to take part had been obtained. After that point, the experimental groups experienced the conference, but the control groups returned to the criminal justice process without the conference taking place. No case involved violence between partners (domestic violence) or sexual assaults.

The random controlled trials involved:

- restorative justice presentence (between conviction and sentence) for cases at all the London Crown Court centers for adult offenders and offenses of burglary of a dwelling, robbery, and other forms of street crime involving a direct victim (e.g., theft from the person);

- presentence restorative justice for both property crimes and violent crimes at magistrates' courts (lower criminal courts) in Northumbria;
- diversionary restorative justice for youth cases given final warnings and some adult cases involving formal cautions in Northumbria (in these cases, the formal criminal justice process had finished before the restorative justice, but these cases will not be considered further in this chapter);
- conferences run before release from prison or during community-based sentences for offenses of violence for adult offenders in the Thames Valley area of England (involving several prisons and probation areas).

Because of the stage of criminal justice and the nature of the offenses, many conferences took place in prison. They were facilitated by police officers, assigned to a special restorative justice unit (in London and Northumbria) or by probation officers, prison officers, or community mediators (in Thames Valley).

The conference itself started with the facilitator introducing everyone present, who were sitting in a circle. The offender would then be asked to say how the offense came about. After this, the victim would be asked to describe the effects of the offense on them and ask anything they would like to say, after which both victim and offender supporters would comment on the effects on them. After this, all would turn to think about what might happen in the future. Suggestions were incorporated into an outcome agreement, which all present agreed and signed and which was subsequently sent to criminal justice authorities. When the formal part of the conference finished, refreshments were served and participants could continue to chat informally.

REMEDI

REMEDI has been delivering mediation in South Yorkshire for many years. The Home Office's money enabled it to expand its operation over the South Yorkshire area. It offered victim–offender mediation, both direct mediation (meeting between victim and offender, with a mediator) and indirect mediation (sometimes called shuttle mediation, involving an exchange of information between the victim and offender, carried by the mediator). It worked with adult offenders undertaking community sentences or about to be released from prison and with young offenders who had been diverted to final warnings or were appearing before a referral panel.

Both direct and indirect mediation were driven by the victim and offender, who tended to concentrate on how the offense occurred and the effects of the offense. There was less emphasis on any future-oriented problem solving, and outcome agreements were rare. Two mediators were used on each case, with some mediators being employed by REMEDI and some being volunteers.

Where cases were referred from the probation service (for adults) or the Youth Offending Team, a report was made back to the referring body.

CONNECT

CONNECT worked primarily within the areas covered by two magistrates' courts in London, taking referrals from the court during conviction and sentence. A wide range of offenses was covered, for adult offenders only, including both property and violent offenses but not those including domestic violence or sexual assaults. A few cases came from much later in the criminal justice process and were victim-initiated, where victims who were in touch with the probation service in relation to very serious offenses of violence said that they would like to meet the offender. CONNECT offered participants direct and indirect mediation as well as conferencing, but most cases were indirect mediations. CONNECT workers wrote a report to the court or the relevant referring authority after the end of the mediation.

The Evaluation

The evaluation involved being in touch with the schemes over their whole period of operation, analyzing their databases, interviewing staff members and relevant agency personnel, interviewing victims and offenders after the completion of restorative justice, and observing all conferences and direct mediations it was feasible to attend. Detailed results can be found in Shapland et al. (2004, 2006a, 2007). The evaluation is continuing to look at reoffending rates and the cost of the schemes, but these data are not included in this chapter.

Unlike many schemes in other countries, these schemes were deliberately designed to take a large throughflow of cases. This has enabled us to include in the evaluation approximately 840 restorative justice events, including conferencing, direct mediation, and indirect mediation, most of them involving adult offenders. We have observed some 285 conferences or direct mediations. Most of the conferences we observed were JRC conferences and so much of the empirical data referred to in this chapter comes from JRC work, but most findings were mirrored in direct mediations run by CONNECT and REMEDI.

Participation and the Allocation of Roles

Restorative justice is intended to be participative—"parties with a stake in a specific offence collectively resolve" (Marshall, 1999), so that all those who might have an interest in relation to that offense are invited. For JRC conferences, this meant victim(s) and offender(s) and their supporters. Braithwaite (1999) has termed this the *democratic element of restorative justice*. However,

JRC offenders and victims tended to invite mainly family members, close work colleagues, or friends (Shapland et al., 2006a). Sometimes, an offender would invite a professional who was close to him or her, such as a probation officer. This is not surprising, given that these were usually serious offenses and offenders and victims would wish only to have those close to them present. However, it does mean that restorative justice, in our schemes, was not really involving the wider community in the conference. Restorative justice in relation to community mediation and mediation in housing also seems to have quite a small cast present at most mediations—normally only the tenant and housing association representatives, in the case of housing or affected neighbors in relation to neighbor disputes (Dignan, Sorsby, & Hibbert, 1996), rather than the whole community. There may be little difference between criminal and civil restorative justice in this respect, in terms of Western practice.

However, all three schemes were running restorative justice in parallel with criminal justice. It means that, in all cases, where the restorative justice process was linked to criminal justice decision making—and was intended to inform criminal justice decision-makers—then the wider community interest necessary for criminal justice would need to be provided outside the restorative justice process. Criminal justice decisions need to take account of this wider community interest, often expressed as "the public interest" in England and Wales (or *l'ordre publique* in France). We consider that it is not possible, in restorative justice intended to facilitate and encourage participants' communication, for facilitators themselves to take on the task of representing this public interest by introducing public interest elements into the restorative process or requiring them to be included in the outcome agreement. The facilitator's role is to facilitate communication between the parties, not to prescribe what should happen.

Hence, the criminal justice element of the consideration of what would be in the public interest needed to take place outside the restorative justice event itself. In the three schemes, where restorative justice was undertaken presentence, the outcome agreement would go to the sentencing judge or bench—and of course they are mandated to take such public interest considerations into account. A similar process occurs in statutory youth conferencing in Northern Ireland, whereby outcome agreements from conferences for court-ordered restorative justice are sent to the sentencing judge, while such agreements for prosecution-ordered conferencing go to the prosecutor (Campbell et al., 2006). This nesting of restorative justice within the criminal justice process seems to us to be an important element in any criminal justice-associated restorative justice that is not intended to be entirely diversionary. It is even more important for adult cases and serious offenses, where there may be more public concern. This is different from some civil mediation, where agreement by the participants themselves may end all justice processes.

Another key difference between restorative justice in the adult criminal justice context and other forms of restorative justice is that the main roles of victim and offender have already been set before the restorative justice process begins. As we indicated above, restorative justice in these three schemes only started after the offender had pleaded guilty, which means that the offender had already acknowledged that he or she had committed that offense (possibly with others) and also had acknowledged his or her responsibility for that offense. If the offender were to have completely denied responsibility for the offense in the restorative justice process, it would have been remitted back to the court or other referring authority.

Having the roles of victim and offender preset obviously affected the format of the conference or mediation, and there was usually no need to negotiate who was taking responsibility. However, pleading guilty to an offense does not always mean agreeing with every aspect of the case as set out by the prosecutor or as imagined by the victim. It was interesting that, although differences in the offender's story about the offense from that of the "official" version might sometimes occur, particularly in respect of the actions of co-offenders, these only caused difficulty during the restorative process if the victim did not agree (Shapland et al., 2006a, 2007).

Sometimes both victim and offender were quite happy to agree during the conference that "the police had got that bit wrong" and then proceeded to continue to discuss from that base. However, on the relatively rare occasions when offender and victim disagreed about what had happened during the offense (e.g., that the offender denied taking all the property missing, or said that he did not do certain elements, but a nonapprehended co-offender had done that), this could cause serious disruption to the restorative justice process and result in major dissatisfaction. Overall, both victim and offender levels of satisfaction with JRC conferencing (and other schemes' mediation) were very high, with 80% of offenders and 85% of victims being very or quite satisfied with JRC conferences (Shapland et al., 2007). Only six offenders (of 152 interviewed) and six victims (of 216 interviewed) were dissatisfied overall with JRC conferencing—but the key reason for those 12 people being dissatisfied was disagreement between victim and offender about the role played in the offense.

Communication

In interviews with victims and offenders, the major element they valued about restorative justice was the communication it allowed between victim and offender. In conferencing and direct mediation, this was direct, two-way communication, involving question and answer and discussion, as well as expression of views, attitudes, and emotions. Communication in restorative justice in these cases involving adult offenders and serious offenses often included emotion, not surprisingly, given the long-term and serious effects that offenses of violence can have (Shapland & Hall, 2007). Harris, Walgrave, and Braithwaite (2004), in their evaluation of restorative conferencing in Australia, found similar forms of communication.

This discursive context for discussion of the offense and its effects can be present within youth court and youth justice processes. However, it is far from the traditional process between conviction and sentence for adult offenders' cases at court, which tends to be a fairly constrained and coded exchange between professionals (Shapland, 1981). In adult criminal cases in England and Wales, the defendant will normally only speak during conviction and sentence if he or she has no legal representative. Legal representatives will produce speeches in mitigation, in which the defendant is put in the role of a spectator to his or her own apology and plans. Victims are normally not allowed to address the court orally at all, although they may be cross-examined in evidence taken where there may be a dispute about the amount of losses etc. A victim's personal statement, if present at all, is a written document, often one written by a police officer and not in the victim's own words (Graham, Woodfield, Tibble, & Kitchen, 2004).

The restorative justice process, whether conferencing or mediation, is a much freer one. Participants can ask questions, link what they are asking to other events or experiences outside the frame of the instant offense, and change the time frame from before the offense to the future or back to what they see as having contributed to offending in the past. The language used during direct meetings and in letters written in indirect mediation was the participants' own words, rarely prompted by facilitators. Some of the main reasons why participants wanted to undertake restorative justice related to these communication aspects: 66% of victims and 91% of offenders interviewed preconference said that it was very or quite important to them in wishing to participate in JRC conferences that they would be able to express their feelings and speak directly to the other person (Shapland et al., 2006a). Looking back at the process from interviews conducted several months afterward, 77% of victims and 80% of offenders said it was very or quite important to them (Shapland et al., 2007).

The importance of communication in the participants' own words is also underlined by the fact that, from our observations and interviews, the second reason why conferences might, very occasionally, break down and create dissatisfaction was where participants felt they were not able to communicate (Shapland et al., 2006a, 2007) because of particular circumstances or disabilities of one or more participants. Overall, there was an expectation of free, but respectful, communication.

As we have argued elsewhere, participants expected procedural fairness (Shapland et al., 2006b), by which they meant that each participant should have his or her turn to speak on each relevant matter, while the facilitator ensured that people had said all they wanted but did not monopolize the conversation or conference. Providing it did not touch on taking ultimate responsibility for the offense, participants expected some potential disagreement and possibly different views from others (a phenomenon also noted when victims give evidence at criminal trials; Shapland et al., 1985). Often they were surprised at just how similar others' views were.

Both victims and offenders in general felt that communication had been achieved. So,

81% of victims and 85% of offenders felt they had been listened to carefully in JRC conferences;
93% of victims and 84% of offenders felt they had the opportunity to express their point of view;
89% of victims and 82% of offenders felt they had the opportunity to explain the consequences of the offense;
90% of victims and 80% of offenders thought all sides had a fair chance to bring out what happened (Shapland et al., 2007).

It was these very high ratings for achieving communication that linked to the very high overall satisfaction expressed by victims and offenders about JRC conferencing. There were few cases run by the other two schemes that resulted in direct mediation and so were comparable to conferences as experiences of communication, and here again, most participants were generally very satisfied, for similar reasons. Indirect mediation, however, does not provide the same opportunities for communication between victim and offender. Each message from one to the other has to be conveyed by the mediator—and will necessarily tend to be said in the mediator's own words. Although most victims and offenders were satisfied with this experience, some felt they spent some time waiting for the next stage of communication or were not sure whether they were always really being told everything. There was no doubt that direct face-to-face communication was found to be more beneficial—but of course those experiencing indirect mediation were those who did not feel able, for whatever reason, to undertake a direct meeting.

Ensuring Procedural Justice

Procedural justice theories (Lind & Tyler, 1988; Tyler & Huo, 2002; Tyler, Sherman, Strang, Barnes, & Woods, 2007) "argue that experiencing fair procedures leads offenders to view the law and legal authorities as legitimate, leading to enhanced commitment to obey the law" (Tyler et al., 2007). They are seen as one of the psychological ways in which restorative justice may lead to decreased offending and indeed as a way in which restorative justice may be superior to victims' and offenders' experiences with traditional criminal justice. Tyler et al. (2007) found that the procedural justice and reintegrative shaming experienced during a restorative conference linked to perceived legitimacy of the law. Their conferences were held in relation to offenses of drunk driving, which may have less automatic presumption of the legitimacy of the law than, for example, burglary or robbery. So it mattered whether offenders' views of the law were essentially being reinforced during the conference, through the procedures being operated being seen as fair.

The four aspects of communication we refer to above for our own evaluation—being listened to carefully, being able to express one's point of view, having the opportunity to explain one's point of view, and everyone having a fair chance to bring out what happened—are also aspects of procedural justice: of procedures being seen as fair. A further two aspects of procedural justice were also measured in our study and seen to be occurring (Shapland et al., 2007):

> 66% of victims and 80% of offenders felt the outcome of the conference was very fair, reasonably fair, or okay in terms of the amount the offender had to do, compared to the harm caused;
> 93% of victims and 88% of offenders felt the facilitator let everyone have their say.

Clearly, experiencing procedural justice was very important for both victims and offenders. We would argue, however, that all these aspects of procedural justice depend on certain circumstances being present during the conference. If people are to be able to have their say—all of them—then those conferences need to be well controlled and people need to feel safe to talk freely, even about aspects that have affected them deeply or that are very important to them. In other words, the conference needs to feel a safe experience, and the power dynamics of the conference need to be carefully considered.

It was this potential concern about power dynamics that originally led to the exclusion from all three schemes of offenses of spousal abuse and of sexual assault. The schemes felt they could not adequately deal with the potential imbalance between victim and offender, in terms of power, for all these offenses. In fact, as facilitators gained confidence and experience, they came to the view in all three schemes that it was not necessarily sensible to have such clear categories of offenses that should be excluded (Shapland et al., 2004). They felt that restorative justice could take place within some of these previously excluded categories and that it would depend on the exact circumstances of the case.

The facilitators were reflecting, on the basis of their experience, what are, in many cases involving adult offenders, considerably changing power dynamics among offender, victim, and system as the case proceeds through the criminal justice system. The situation is different again for young offenders.

We have argued elsewhere that the original power balance at the time of the offense, in which the offender has clearly exerted power over the victim, changes when the criminal justice system becomes involved (Shapland et al., 2006b). Victims have long been complaining that they remain relatively powerless when it comes to police and prosecutorial action, not even necessarily being given information about what is happening to the case (Allen, Edmonds, Patterson, & Smith, 2006; Shapland et al., 1985). It becomes the criminal justice system's decisions that prevail about charging, prosecution, and the conduct of the case. In most cases, however, victims' complaints are not about their lack of power to decide but about their lack of power to have any input or know what is happening. Indeed, they may feel that the quality of information the criminal justice system has about their victimization and its effects is so poor that it is difficult to see how just decisions can be made. If so, then victims are doubting the legitimacy of criminal justice. Restorative justice, through allowing that input and communication, may be restoring the sense of procedural justice that the relatively impoverished systems of traditional criminal justice have ceased to foster.

In England and Wales, similar disempowering factors impinge on the offender as well when the criminal justice system becomes involved. Clearly, the offender is now under the power of the system, which takes to itself decisions about how and where the offender is to live and what punishment will be inflicted. Yet offenders often have legal representation—and so would seemingly have considerable possibilities to make an input. However, it is the legal representative, rather than the offender himself or herself, who can decide on and make that input. Many offenders are "managed" by their legal representatives (McConville, Hodgson, Bridges, & Pavlovic, 1994), often in the direction of discouraging offender input. Defense input is also often restricted by courts to the circumstances of the offense. During the sentencing process, defense input may not be encouraged as to the offender's potential in the future and how offenders may themselves turn their lives around. In contrast, restorative justice allows offenders the opportunity to talk about their own possible futures and the ways in which they themselves might wish to take agency over their lifestyles and change them.

We would argue, therefore, that both offenders and victims may find themselves perceiving a lack of procedural justice in traditional criminal justice, in the ways in which it is currently being operated in England and Wales (and probably in other countries as well). If criminal justice is actually intending to try to reduce reoffending, then it is in fact difficult to see how it can operate without much participation by or input from offenders and victims.

Yet restorative justice will not be able to correct any perceived lack of procedural justice or legitimacy unless it can provide a place and space whereby fair communication can be encouraged. We think it is not an accident that the very positive ratings for communication and fairness that we have described above were accompanied by similar high ratings of the perceived safety of the process (Shapland et al., 2007):

> 88% of victims and 84% of offenders felt the facilitator was in control of the conference (but not too much in control);
> 99% of victims and 96% of offenders felt very safe, safe, or okay at the conference.

It is important to consider what mechanisms may be necessary, particularly for serious offenses and adult offenders, to create these feelings of safety that permit communication and perceptions of procedural justice. As we have argued elsewhere, although informality is often seen as a key component of restorative justice, too much informality may be deleterious in criminal justice-related conferences (Shapland et al., 2006b). For young offenders (or young victims), as Daly (2003) has pointed out, it is important that the atmosphere is sufficiently relaxed and not intimidating such that the young person feels able to contribute. For older offenders and serious offenses, the point is not to make the atmosphere in the conference more formal but to ensure it is a safe space. A room of sufficient size, the presence of two facilitators (where necessary either for safety, for conducting participants to the venue, or to record notes), having security staff (prison officers, etc.) on call if necessary, and the use of time out (and somewhere to go without leaving the building) if things get heated may all be helpful. We have argued that the presence of supporters can also be helpful.

It is also crucial that the facilitator is seen as a neutral, helpful figure who is in control of the situation but is not taking on the embodiment of the authority of criminal justice. It would not be procedural justice if the facilitator—who is there primarily to aid communication between the participants—becomes a judge, social worker, prosecutor, or arbitrator who starts to impose ideas, probe or interrogate regarding unrelated matters, or pass judgment on what others have said. Some restorative justice schemes have seen the facilitator adopt just one point of view (e.g., a police standpoint; Daly, 2003; Hoyle, Young, & Hill, 2002). Clearly, the participants in the schemes we were evaluating valued the much more neutral style adopted by all the mediators and facilitators, which occurred whatever their professional background.* Overall, we would argue that adopting standards that facilitate

---

* Facilitators for JRC included police officers, probation officers, prison officers, people with a background in Victim Support, and community mediators. Mediators for CONNECT and REMEDI sometimes had criminal justice backgrounds but were not serving personnel from criminal justice agencies.

procedural justice, including the provision of a safe space for the discussions, creates means to balance at that point what may have been very unequal power relationships previously.

The Work Being Done by an Apology

If, in our everyday lives, we bump into someone in the street inadvertently, the normal reaction is to apologize. The apology is clearly dyadic: from the aggressor to the victim, with the victim needing to acknowledge the apology has been made (Bottoms, 2003)—although the victim may not go so far as accepting the apology (Tavuchis, 1991). When the offense is more serious and results in a criminal prosecution, then offenders may also apologize in court: it is common for young or unrepresented offenders, in particular, to mutter "sorry" (Shapland, 1981). In this court situation, it is not very clear to whom the apology is directed or who hears it. The victim, for example, is very rarely present (Shapland et al., 2006a; Strang, 2002). Only 15% of the JRC conference victims in our evaluation had any contact at all with a court; only 6% gave evidence. Very few indeed had heard any apology in court from the offender. Clearly, the apology muttered by the offender in court cannot normally be directed to an immediately present victim.

So to whom are apologies in court directed? I have argued that they are triadic: toward the judge as the embodiment of society and reflecting the breach of the criminal law and through the judge, toward the (absent) victim (Shapland, 1981). Where the offender is legally represented, the position becomes even more complicated—someone representing the offender is saying sorry on their behalf to several audiences. It becomes reminiscent of the dance of international diplomacy. In restorative justice conferences and direct mediations, the victim is present. Restorative justice theorists have therefore concentrated on this and stressed the difference in audience for apologies—in restorative justice, the victim can hear an apology directly; in criminal justice, any apology that is made will normally only reach the victim through press reporting or through a judge's comments (Strang, 2002). This is a very proper stress, in our opinion. Offering an apology directly can bring an element of closure for offenders. It can help victims. It can lead on to a discussion of the future.

In cases involving young offenders, quite often, the apology is the main or a substantial element of the outcome agreement or even the sentence, with few other elements being required or being present (Holdaway et al., 2001; Shapland et al., 2004). However, for adult offenders and more serious offenses, just offering an apology is unlikely to be seen, by offender or victim, as enough. It is even possible that victims who feel that the offender is just trying to offer an apology may come to think that the offender may be insincere or be trying to "get away with just an apology."

Partly, we think this lack of sufficiency of pure verbal apologies with serious offenses is because of the triadic nature of criminal justice-related apologies. If the offender is addressing society/the judge as well as the victim, then it is clear, for a serious offense causing harm, that words alone cannot suffice. In our initial example, a similar situation might be that instead of just bumping into someone, the bump causes the person to drop their shopping and some things were broken. In addition to offering an apology, we would be likely to offer to pay for the ruined shopping.

However, in the criminal justice context, for serious offenses, we have found that compensation is not the immediate wish of victims. In our evaluation in England, although offenders came into restorative justice wishing not only to offer an apology, but restitution or compensation as well, victims were far less keen on either monetary payment or direct reparative work as an outcome (Shapland et al., 2004, 2006a). Very similar results occurred in Northern Ireland youth conferencing (Campbell et al., 2006).

Instead of compensation, for adult offenders and serious offenses, we think that the need to offer more than an apology links to the criminal justice outcomes and the triadic nature of apologies. An apology by itself is not sufficient for the victim, but it will also not be seen as sufficient by criminal justice. One element of this is that both offender and victim were very aware in some sites that the case would be going back before the sentencer or other criminal justice decision maker. For presentence restorative justice in our evaluation, in some sites, this meant that everyone knew that the offender was likely to receive a prison sentence. Outcome agreements were framed with this in mind, considering what options might be available at which prisons, and taking advice on this if necessary (Shapland et al., 2004).

A second element was that the symbolic reparation of changing one's life and following rehabilitative programs seemed to replace direct reparation or compensation as an additional element to the apology.

Changing One's Life as Symbolic Reparation

One key difference between adult and youth cases may then be that in adult cases, apologies are important but not sufficient. A young offender's apology, even for a moderately serious offense, may be taken by the victim (and society) as a sign that they have learned their lesson, appreciated the harm done, and deserve credit for having made the apology. We are more cynical about adult offenders. In a sense, both victims and society seem to want more evidence of possible or potential change.

Those restorative justice events that had a future-oriented phase, where all present started thinking what should happen now, not just about what had happened in the past and what effects it had had, focused in this future-oriented phase on how the offender was going to change. This may appear a very offender-oriented focus. Was restorative justice merely replicating the tendencies of criminal justice to focus on the offender and ignore the victim? Given the focus of the evaluation on victim needs and victim views, we looked very closely at who participated in these elements of the restorative justice event and who seemed to be leading the discussion. It became clear that this focus on what the offender might do was not ignoring victim views and needs. After having their own questions answered and after explaining the effect of the offense on themselves, victims wished to focus on what would prevent reoffending rather than on compensation to themselves, and what all the participants in the event clearly felt would best prevent reoffending was to concentrate on what kinds of problems or events had led to the offending, how much they were still present in the offender's life, and, if so, how this might change.

Both victims and offender supporters strongly emphasized and reinforced any expressed desires of the offender to tackle any offending-related problems or circumstances that had led to offending or to find ways of creating a nonoffending life (or at least a less offending life—everyone tended to be rather realistic). So the kinds of elements that were emphasized were tackling substance abuse problems (alcohol or drugs), improving skills to obtain legitimate employment, tackling family or relationship problems, encouraging more care and support, and so on (Shapland et al., 2004). All of these essentially involve statements by offenders that they wish to lead a rather different life—a less offending or more desisting life. We have argued elsewhere that restorative justice events can be seen as providing platforms in which offenders can rehearse and try to put in place plans for desistance (Robinson & Shapland, 2008; Shapland, in press). Here, the important point is that victims, victim supporters, offender supporters, and offenders themselves were all stressing and supporting offenders to turn their lives around. Observing the conferences, it was clear that this was not only to prevent reoffending but also because it added emphasis to apology. Saying "sorry" was important and was a start. Saying sorry and doing something about one's life to minimize such a thing happening again emphasized the change implicit in apology.

Changing one's life has previously been seen in penology as embodying the penal philosophies of reform or rehabilitation. Often, however, rehabilitation has been an other-imposed process, where offenders have been "persuaded" to undertake activities that will rehabilitate them. Here we are indicating that offenders offering to change their lives can also be seen as symbolic reparation to victims. It is a way of offering to pay back that does not involve direct monetary or work payment but that in many ways may be far more costly than direct reparation. Indeed, in some ways, it is much closer to the philosophy of reform rather than rehabilitation because it is the offender indicating that he or she has different ideas about offending.

We need to note that talking about possibilities for the offender in the future is also potentially empowering and democratizing decision making—if reports arising from the restorative justice process reach criminal justice decision makers. This was a characteristic of JRC's and CONNECT's presentence conferences. Modern Western criminal justice decision making has tended to be concentrated within a small group of professionals, with lay people—even the offender—rarely being consulted about what should be done. Criminal justice decision making itself, at least for adult offenders and serious offenses, needs to be undertaken by duly appointed criminal justice personnel. So, for example, sentencing, to be seen as legitimate by the public and to reflect the public interest, needs to be decided by judges.

However, decision makers cannot make good decisions unless informed by relevant, up-to-date information. The perceived need for more victim input and hence better information on the effects on victims has driven the adoption of victim impact statements in Australia and the United States (Erez & Rogers, 1999) and the adoption of victim personal statements in England and Wales (Morgan & Sanders, 1999). The deliberations of restorative justice events, including both victim and offender, would clearly be an additional and helpful aid. They have been found to be such in the statutory youth conferencing now used routinely in Northern Ireland (Campbell et al., 2006).

Erez and Rogers (1999) and Erez and Tontodonato (1990) have argued that in practice, criminal justice decision makers rarely take notice of victim impact statements, with only the unusual case being noteworthy. However, outcome agreements from restorative justice events may spark different views. Such agreements, if they have both met victims' needs (in as far as this is possible at this point) and pointed to directions that may promote reduction in reoffending, all of which have been agreed by all participants, are potentially providing far more help to criminal justice decision makers than even the best presentence reports from probation officers. Such seemed to be the experience in Northern Ireland (Campbell et al., 2006).

There needs, however, to be one caveat to this rosy view. Restorative justice events are shaped by their participants. By definition, restorative justice has to be participative and democratic. We have argued that it is hence driven by the participants' own values of what is important in justice and what needs to be achieved: what we have called participants' "justice values" (Shapland et al., 2006b). Participants bring these values (which in our evaluation included inclusiveness, procedural justice, answering others' questions, reducing reoffending, etc.) to the restorative justice event. Justice values, though, are culturally created and enabled. English participants' values may not be identical to those in France, in the United States, or in other countries.

If participants' justice values are in tune with those of criminal justice in that place and at that time, then the two can help each other. Restorative justice outcome agreements will be helpful in informing sentencing and sentencers. If, however, the public's (and so victims' and offenders') justice values have grown apart from criminal justice values, then there may be conflict. Sentencers may find what is being proposed in outcome agreements unhelpful and reject them. If this happens, restorative justice participants will feel snubbed. Victims will feel ignored. Offenders will feel that the system is not trying to help them stop offending and desist from crime. Yet this should only occur if either public views have grown far away from criminal justice sentencing views or maverick sentencers are determined to do their own thing and are not reined in. Both, we would argue, would be very bad news for the legitimacy of sentencing and the legitimacy of the criminal justice system itself. Indeed, having the information from restorative justice events available to criminal justice decision makers may prevent such growing apart.

Restoring Security?

The theory behind restorative justice initiatives has primarily been developed when key ideas behind dealing with crime and offending were essentially correctional and penological. Restorative justice has been compared with other means of dealing with offending through the criminal justice system (see Dignan, 2005). Restorative justice schemes have primarily been developed to provide means of dealing with young offenders, knowing that such offending often ceases after the adolescent years and, if checked by a penal or even a diversionary sanction, may cease very quickly.

More recently, the language of dealing with offending has changed dramatically. Dealing with offending has been described, not in terms of justice, or penal/correctional solutions, but in relation to the crime problems it creates for ordinary people (Loader & Walker, 2007). "Fear of crime" has become a major political issue in Europe. Politicians have responded to what they feel is public alarm by talking about a "war on crime."* Locally, this has led to multiagency action, particularly in Europe, to consider and then respond to "local crime profiles" (Crawford, 2002; van Swaaningen, 2008).

---

* This is not the place to consider whether the "war on crime" can easily be waged or is able to succeed. It is important to note, however, as Christie (2004) has pointed out, that other "wars," like the "war on drugs," have often had rather vaguely defined other protagonists as the "enemy," who, nonetheless, are seen as highly threatening. The war on crime is peopled by just as scary "criminals," normally portrayed as adults or persistent offenders, rather than the youngsters in nearby residential areas.

Very recently, it has become apparent that even "crime problems" are no longer seen as the major threat. At a recent criminology conference (European Society of Criminology Conference, Tubingen, August 2006), there was no doubt that one word was dominant in all the plenary sessions. The word was *security*. The way in which it was used by different speakers brought in all sorts of connotations—security checks; terrorism; the speed of change of lifestyles; globalization and cross-national chains of criminality—but above all, it seemed to relate to ordinary people's feelings of unease. People did not feel secure. People did not feel safe. As Hans Boutellier (2006) commented, in Dutch, the words for *security* and *safety* are the same.

The difficulty for politicians, criminal justice practitioners, and the general public is that these fundamental worries seem disassociated from the total amount of crime committed. Total crime has decreased in all Western countries over the last few years (International Crime Victimisation Survey, van Dijk, 2006). However, people still say they are afraid and insecure, and victims, of course, feel even more insecure when a crime has been committed—victimization punctures the cocoon we build up around ourselves to lead our daily lives. It makes us question the habitual accommodations and routines we have developed.* This loss of trust is particularly evident for more serious victimization. We also know that in England and Wales, those who have been victimized tend to rate their local police more negatively than those who have not been victims (Nicholas et al., 2007), and that experience of victimization, either personally or among family, neighbors, or friends, significantly affects perceptions of how good a job the criminal justice system does (Skogan, 1994).

Could the experience of participating in restorative justice impact on these feelings of insecurity, particularly for victims? Could it reduce the additional insecurity brought on by victimization, and does it affect perceptions of the effectiveness and legitimacy of criminal justice? There are some pointers that it might, in cases involving adult offenders. Victims in our own evaluation of JRC said that participating in restorative justice had helped in relation to the effects of the offense (62% said it had made them feel better, 30% said it had had no effect, while just 2% said it made them feel worse: Shapland et al., 2007). As Strang and Sherman (2006, with Angel et al.) have also commented, most victims in other studies have felt restorative justice

---

* This is a routine observation for victim assistance workers and has been noted in the literature on the effects of crime on victims from the earliest studies (Shapland et al., 1985). The shock of victimization produces feelings of dislocation from the local community and distrust of who might have committed the offence—victims commonly feel that the world is not as they thought it was. It is one of the prime reasons why victim assistance in many European countries, such as the United Kingdom, has deliberately sought to remain a locally based service, so that volunteers from the local community are those delivering support to local victims (Victim Support, 2008).

helped, but there were a few who were not helped. In addition, for JRC, the victims in the restorative justice group who experienced a conference had significantly more satisfaction in what the criminal justice system had done with their case than those in the control group who only had the preparation phase and were then randomized out and so did not experience a conference (Shapland et al., 2007). We would suggest that two factors may be underpinning this increased satisfaction: the procedural justice they had experienced during restorative justice procedures (see above) and the opportunity for fears to be quelled about the actual offender, what motivated the offense, and their own likelihood of revictimization.

Similar factors are evident in a very different field of research. Liebling (2006) and Liebling and Arnold (2004) have undertaken very substantial pieces of research on the cultures of different prisons in England and Wales. She found that what matters to prisoners in terms of how safe they feel is, first, respect (in relationships within the prison with staff and the ways in which they are supported and trusted as people), and, second, fairness (being able to say things about the regime and what is happening, procedural justice). Her analysis indicates that respect may lead through to perceptions of fairness that then leads through to perceptions of security and safety.

Research on what is underpinning the development of feelings of security and insecurity is still very much in its infancy. However, it is clear that whenever threats are amorphous, may impinge suddenly on people's lives, and come from unknown directions, insecurity will tend to rise. It is a theoretically big leap to move from that to consider the effects of restorative justice. However, crime is known to lead to increased insecurity not only for victims but also for offenders. Restorative justice, at its best, provides conditions in which offenders and victims can communicate about what has happened and what the future might be in a safe setting. If victims and offenders are given the license to do that, then maybe that will lead to a greater feeling of security for those who have participated.

Restorative Justice within Criminal Justice with Adult Offenders

We have discussed three major themes that become, we consider, more important when restorative justice is used with adult offenders within criminal justice, particularly for serious offenses:

- Ensuring procedural justice so that communication can take place between the participants safely and with accountability to criminal justice.

- Future-oriented problem solving to look at the problems behind the offender's offending and its role as symbolic reparation for victims.
- The potential that restorative justice may have in restoring victims' sense of security and, through this, quieting insecurity in local areas.

If these elements of restorative justice are particularly important in relation to criminal cases involving adult offenders, particularly serious offenses, then they have a number of consequences.

First, considerable attention needs to be paid, both in the preparation phase and in the arrangements for the restorative justice event itself, to ensure that all participants are aware of the need for procedural justice (everyone can speak, people must let others have their say). The physical space to be used for restorative justice events needs to be suitable. Many such events may need to take place in prison, either presentence or prerelease. Prisons often do not have the flexible and secure space for meetings that restorative justice events require, particularly space that will allow refreshments to be served afterward to participants in an informal way. Other criminal justice buildings can be even more cramped, particularly when offices (with their attendant IT paraphernalia) have to be pressed into use.

Second, it takes time and considerable negotiation to ensure that there is the right kind of accountability to criminal justice decision makers after the event: that events remain relatively private in terms of the details of matters disclosed (by victims and supporters, as well as offenders) but that decision makers are confident that any agreement was made voluntarily and with the agreement of all participants. For human rights reasons, we have argued else-where that there may also be a need to record events to counter potential power imbalances (Dignan et al., 2007).

Third, the type of restorative justice that is undertaken needs to permit, even encourage, future-oriented discussion between the participants at the restorative justice event. This would seem to be facilitated by direct meetings and seems to be more prevalent in conferences than in mediation (where there are no supporters present) (Shapland et al., 2006). Both victim and offender will need to be encouraged to bring supporters.

Fourth, the participants will almost certainly need information about the practical possibilities that are available in relevant locations, to formulate an outcome agreement that is specific and able to be achieved.

Fifth, it is important to check after the restorative justice event that par-ticipants are happy with how it went and that they do not have continuing worries and problems. If they do, then facilitators need to be able to "signpost" them or refer them (with their agreement) to relevant agencies, such as victim assistance agencies, criminal justice authorities, or schemes that help people to tackle offending-related behavior.

Sixth, restorative justice is still a relatively unknown form of procedure for many people in Western countries. Knowledge about it, what it can do and what it cannot achieve, will need to improve very considerably for us to get to a position where it is possible for victims and offenders not just to agree to participate but proactively to have considered such a possibility and to nudge criminal justice to provide it.

Although the schemes that we have evaluated have clearly shown that it is possible to undertake restorative justice, within criminal justice, for cases involving adult offenders and serious offenses—and that both victims and offenders find it helpful—there are still many practical and organizational elements to sort out to work out what is best practice in these cases and to be able to deliver it routinely to all who wish it.

References

Allen, J., Edmonds, S., Patterson, A., & Smith, D. (2006). *Policing and the criminal justice system—Public confidence and perceptions: Findings from the 2004/05 British Crime Survey* (Home Office Online Report 07/06). London: Home Office.

Bottoms, A. E. (2003). Some sociological reflections on restorative justice. In A. von Hirsch, J. Roberts, A.E. Bottoms, K. Roach, & M. Schiff (Eds.), *Restorative justice and criminal justice: Competing or reconcilable paradigms?* (pp. 79–114). Oxford: Hart.

Boutellier, H. (2006). *From criminal justice to governing security.* Paper presented at the European Society of Criminology conference, Tubingen, 29 August 2006.

Braithwaite, J. (1999). Restorative justice: Assessing optimistic and pessimistic accounts. *Crime and Justice: A Review of Research, 25,* 1–127.

Campbell, C., Devlin, R., O'Mahony, D., et al. (2006). *Evaluation of the Northern Ireland Youth Conferencing Service* (NIO Research and Statistical Series Report No. 12). Belfast: NIO. Retrieved 21 March 2008 from http://www.nio.gov.uk/evaluation_of_the_northern_ireland_youth_conference_service.pdf.

Carlen, P. (1976). *Magistrates' justice.* London: Martin Robertson.

Christie, N. (2004). *A suitable amount of crime.* London: Routledge.

Council of Europe. (1999). *Mediation in penal matters* (Recommendation R(99)19, adopted 15 September 1999).

Crawford, A. (Ed.). (2002). *Crime and insecurity: The governance of safety in Europe.* Cullompton: Willan.

Daly, K. (2001). Conferencing in Australia and New Zealand: Variations, research findings and prospects. In A. Morris & G. Maxwell (Eds.), *Restoring justice for juveniles: Conferencing, mediation and circles.* (pp. 59–84). Oxford: Hart.

Daly, K. (2003). Mind the gap: Restorative justice in theory and practice. In A. von Hirsch, J. Roberts, A. E. Bottoms, K. Roach, & M. Schiff (Eds.), *Restorative justice and criminal justice: Competing or reconcilable paradigms?* (pp. 219–236). Oxford: Hart.

Daly, K. (2004). A tale of two studies: Restorative justice from a victim's perspective. In E. Elliott & R. Gordon (Eds.), *Restorative justice: Emerging issues in practice and evaluation.* Cullompton: Willan.

Dignan, J. (2005). *Understanding victims and restorative justice.* Maidenhead: Open University Press.

Dignan, J., Atkinson, A., Atkinson, H., et al. (2007). Staging restorative justice encounters against a criminal justice backdrop: A dramaturgical analysis. *Criminology and Criminal Justice, 7,* 5–32.

Dignan, J., Sorsby, A., & Hibbert, J. (1996). *Neighbour disputes: Comparing the cost-effectiveness of mediation and alternative approaches.* Sheffield: Centre for Criminological and Legal Research, University of Sheffield.

Erez, R., & Rogers, L. (1999). The effects of victim impact statements on criminal justice outcomes and processes: The perspectives of legal professionals. *British Journal of Criminology, 39,* 216–239.

Erez, E., & Tontodonato, P. (1990). The effect of victim participation in sentencing on sentence outcome. *Criminology, 28,* 451–474.

European Union. (2001). *Council Framework Decision 2001/220/JHA of 15 March 2001 on the standing of victims in criminal proceedings.* Brussels: Council of the European Union.

Garland, D. (2001). *The culture of control: Crime and social order in contemporary society.* Oxford: Oxford University Press.

Graham, J., Woodfield, K., Tibble, M., & Kitchen, S. (2004). *Testaments of harm: A qualitative evaluation of the Victim Personal Statements scheme.* London: Home Office.

Harris, N., Walgrave, L., & Braithwaite, J. (2004). Emotional dynamics in restorative conferences. *Theoretical Criminology, 8,* 191–210.

Holdaway, S., Davison, N., Dignan, J., Hammersley, R., Hine, J., & Marsh, P. (2001). *New strategies to address youth offending: The national evaluation of the pilot youth offending teams* (Home Office Occasional Paper). London: Home Office.

Home Office. (2003). *Restorative justice: The government's strategy. A consultation document on the government's strategy on restorative justice.* London: Home Office.

Hoyle, C., Young, R., & Hill, R. (2002). *Proceed with caution: An Evaluation of the Thames Valley Police initiative in restorative justice.* York: York Publishing Services for the Joseph Rowntree Foundation.

Liebling, A. (2006). *Moral climate in prisons and prison performance: Important effects of imprisoning offenders.* Paper presented at the European Society of Criminology conference, Tubingen, 28 August 2006.

Liebling, A., & Arnold, H. (2004). *Prisons and their moral performance: A study of values, quality and prison life.* Oxford: Oxford University Press.

Lind, E. A., & Tyler, T. (1988). *The social psychology of procedural justice.* New York: Plenum.

Loader, I., & Walker, N. (2007). *Civilizing security.* Cambridge: Cambridge University Press.

Marshall, T. (1999). *Restorative justice: An overview* (Occasional Paper). London: Home Office. Available from the Home Office Web site, http://www.homeoffice.gov.uk/rds/pdfs/occ-resjus.pdf

McConville, M., Hodgson, J., Bridges, L., & Pavlovic, A. (1994). *Standing accused: The organisation and practice of criminal defence lawyers in Britain*. Oxford: Clarendon Press.

Morgan, R., & Sanders, A. (1999). *The uses of victim statements* (Home Office Occasional Paper). London: Home Office.

Morris, A., & Maxwell, G. (2001). Implementing restorative justice: What works? In A. Morris & G. Maxwell (Eds.), *Restorative justice for juveniles: Conferencing, mediation and circles*. (pp. 267–282). Oxford: Hart.

Nicholas, S., Kershaw, C., & Walker, A. (2007). *Crime in England and Wales 2006/07* (Home Office Statistical Bulletin 11/07). London: Home Office.

Robinson, G., & Shapland, J. (2008). Reducing recidivism: A task for restorative justice? *British Journal of Criminology*, doi: 10.1093/bjc/azn002.

Shapland, J. (1981). *Between conviction and sentence: The process of mitigation*. London: Routledge.

Shapland, J. (in press). Desistance from crime and the potential role of restorative justice, In F. Losel, A. Liebling, & J. Shapland (Eds.), *What is criminology?: Celebrating the work of A.E. Bottoms*. Cullompten: Willan.

Shapland, J., Atkinson, A., Atkinson, H., Chapman, B., Colledge, E., Dignan, J., et al. (2006a). *Restorative justice in practice: The second report from the evaluation of three schemes* (The University of Sheffield Centre for Criminological Research Occasional Paper 2). Sheffield: Faculty of Law. Available at the University of Sheffield Centre for Criminological Research Web site, http://www.shef.ac.uk/law/research/ccr/occasional

Shapland, J., Atkinson, A., Atkinson, H., Chapman, B., Colledge, E., Dignan, J. et al. (2006b). Situating restorative justice within criminal justice. *Theoretical Criminology, 10*, 505–532.

Shapland, J., Atkinson, A., Atkinson, H., Chapman, B., Dignan, J., Howes, M., et al. (2007). *Restorative justice: The views of victims and offenders* (Ministry of Justice Research Series 3/07). London: Ministry of Justice. Available at the Ministry of Justice Web site, http://www.justice.gov.uk/docs/Restorative-Justice.pdf

Shapland, J., Atkinson, A., Colledge, E., Dignan, J., Howes, M., Johnson, J. et al. (2004). *Implementing restorative justice schemes (Crime Reduction Programme): A report on the first year* (Home Office Online Report 32/04). London: Home Office. Available at the Home Office Web site, http://www.homeoffice.gov.uk/rds/pdfs04/rdsolr3204.pdf

Shapland, J., & Hall, M. (2007). What do we know about the effects of crime on victims? *International Review of Victimology, 13*, 175–218.

Shapland, J., Willmore, J., & Duff, P. (1985). *Victims in the criminal justice system*. Aldershot: Gower.

Sherman, L., Braithwaite, J., Strang, H., Barnes, G., Christie-Johnston, J., Smith, S. et al. (1997). *Experiments in restorative policing. Reintegrative shaming of violence, drink driving and property crime: A randomised controlled trial*. Canberra: Australian National University and The Australian Federal Police.

Sherman, L., & Strang, H. (2007). Restorative justice: The evidence. A report to the Smith Institute. *University of Pennsylvania Jerry Lee Center of Criminology and the Esmee Fairburn Foundation*.

Skogan, W. (1994). *Contacts between police and public: Findings from the 1992 British Crime Survey* (Home Office Research Study 134). London: HMSO.

Strang, H. (2002). *Repair or revenge: Victims and restorative justice.* Oxford: Clarendon Press.

Strang, H., & Sherman, L. (with C. Angel et al.). (2006). Victim evaluations of face-to-face restorative justice conferences: A quasi-experimental analysis. *Journal of Social Issues, 62,* 281–306.

Sudnow, D. (1965). Normal crimes: Sociological features of the penal code. *Social Problems, 12,* 255–276.

Tavuchis, N. (1991). *Mea culpa: A sociology of apology and reconciliation.* Stanford, CA: Stanford University Press.

Tyler, T., & Huo, Y. (2002). *Trust in the law: Encouraging public cooperation with the police and courts.* New York: Russell Sage Foundation.

Tyler, T., Sherman, L., Strang, H., Barnes, G., & Woods, D. (2007). Reintegrative shaming, procedural justice, and recidivism: The engagement of offenders' psychological mechanisms in the Canberra RISE Drinking-and-Driving experiment. *Law and Society Review, 41,* 553–585.

Van Dijk, J. (2006). *Crime prevention, policing and trends in crime: Results of the ICVS.* Paper presented at the European Society of Criminology meeting, Tubingen, 27 August 2006.

Van Ness, D. (2003). Proposed basic principles on the use of restorative justice: Recognising the aims and limits of restorative justice. In A. von Hirsch, J. Roberts, A. E. Bottoms, K. Roach, & M. Schiff (Eds.), *Restorative justice and criminal justice: Competing or reconcilable paradigms?* (pp. 157–176). Oxford: Hart.

Van Swaaningen, R. (2008). Sweeping the street: Civil society and community safety in Rotterdam. In J. Shapland (Ed.), *Justice, community and civil society: A contested terrain.* Cullompten: Willan.

Victim Support. (2008). *Webpage: Help for victims.* Retrieved March 20, 2008, from http://www.victimsupport.org.uk/vs_england_wales/services/victim_services.php

Wozniakowska, D. (2007). Restorative justice in Poland. In D. Miers (Ed.), *International co-operation on the implementation of restorative justice in Poland and Great Britain. Report to the British Academy.*

State, Community, and Transition: Restorative Youth Conferencing in Northern Ireland

7

JONATHAN DOAK
DAVID O'MAHONY

Contents

Introduction

In recent years, restorative justice principles have come to feature prominently in transitional processes within divided societies. The truth commissions of South Africa and Latin America, as well as the Gacaca courts of Rwanda, have all adopted methods or processes that might be described as "restorative" in a broad sense in the hope that they may assist efforts in fostering reconciliation and social cohesion in the aftermath of violent conflict (Aldana-Pindell, 2004; Ironside, 2002; Parmentier, 2001). The extent to which restorative principles have come to feature in transitional justice should not surprise us. There is, after all, a considerable paradigmatic overlap between the two concepts, with both espousing similar themes and values such as accountability, reparation, reconciliation, conflict resolution, and democratic participation. As such, both restorative justice and transitional justice can be viewed as nonpunitive methods of reconstructing the truth of past events and making amends for wrongdoing.

Despite widespread acceptance that restorative and transitional models of justice may mutually reinforce and cross-fertilize each other, there has been relatively little discussion as to how restorative justice might be used as a mechanism to legitimize the mainstream criminal justice system in these divided societies. This is despite the fact that, in countries marred by political conflict, the machinery of the criminal justice system is often perceived to suffer from a legitimacy deficit, with a sizeable proportion of the population suspicious of state agencies and institutions. The quest for legitimacy in the criminal justice system, as the cornerstone of the rule of law, is thus always fundamental to any democratic settlement; but reform in this area is often difficult to effectuate in practice (Tolbert & Soloman, 2006). In South Africa, for example, proposals for a relatively modest form of restorative justice for juveniles contained in the Child Justice Bill have seemingly been halted in their tracks since 2002. However, in nontransitional states, such as New Zealand, Canada, and the United States, there has, by contrast, been a much higher level of interest in integrating restorative principles within existing criminal justice structures.

One notable exception to the above is Northern Ireland. Following the Belfast Agreement in 1998, a major review of the criminal justice system was instituted. One of its guiding objectives was the need to make the system of justice more accountable and acceptable to the community as a whole and to encourage community involvement and be responsive to the community's concerns (Criminal Justice Review Group, 2000). The Review, which was published in July 2000, contained a total of 294 recommendations, one of the most radical of which proposed the adoption of a mainstreamed restorative response to juvenile offenders. Among the various models of restorative justice considered, the Criminal Justice Review Group opted for one known as "youth conferencing," which was to be based in statute and become the primary response for offending involving all young persons (10- to 17-year-olds). Drawing on a major evaluation of the scheme (Campbell et al., 2006), this chapter describes the operation of the scheme to date and explores the extent to which the scheme enhances both victim and offender satisfaction with criminal justice. We then proceed to ask whether the new arrangements might hold the potential to fulfill the objective of the Criminal Justice Review in contributing to the overall legitimacy of the criminal justice system in the eyes of the community.

Background

The model of youth conferencing proposed for Northern Ireland was similar to the New Zealand family group conference, although the Northern Ireland model placed much more emphasis on the role of victims and sought to locate them at the center of the process. Although it was recognized that the New Zealand system had been the basis for many restorative justice schemes worldwide, it was acknowledged by the Criminal Justice Review that the local context and background of Northern Ireland was very different, and therefore, it was not appropriate to simply transplant it.

Unlike New Zealand, Northern Ireland was just emerging from three decades of violent political conflict. Within nationalist, and to a lesser extent, loyalist communities, there was deeply rooted suspicion of the police, criminal justice system, and state institutions generally. In the 1990s, despite the worst years of the conflict having passed, this sense of hostility continued to prevail and resulted in the development of informal and community-based schemes to deal with low-level crime and antisocial behavior (McEvoy & Mika, 2002). Although these initiatives were promoted as a form of restorative justice, they operated entirely independently of the criminal justice system and had little interaction with the police or any other state agency. Concerns were expressed in some quarters that, without state oversight, such schemes might not be fully accountable in terms of human rights and might expose young people to the risk of "double jeopardy" (Dignan & Lowey, 2000).

By contrast, the conferencing model proposed by the Criminal Justice Review would be enshrined in legislation, which would fully integrate it into the formal criminal justice system. Conferencing was to become the primary means of responding to youth offending, and unlike the youth panels that had been recently adopted in England and Wales, it would not be limited to first-time offenders or low-level crime. Moreover, it was considerably more victim-focused in nature and sought to actively promote victim involvement and reparation in every case of juvenile offending.

However, in contrast to other transitional societies, one factor that made restorative justice particularly attractive was that it would amount to a normative reorientation of youth justice, whereby crime was reconstructed as an offense against individuals and communities as opposed to simply an offense against the state (McCold, 1996; Zehr, 2005). In adopting structures that would reflect these norms, it was hoped that the impact of this lingering suspicion over the role of the "state" would help make the new system more legitimate in the eyes of all sections of the community.

The scheme was introduced under the Justice (Northern Ireland) Act 2002, which provided for the establishment of an independent Youth Conferencing Service to organize and facilitate conferences. Two forms of conferences were provided for in the legislation: "diversionary" conferences and "court-ordered" conferences. "Diversionary" conferences are convened after a referral from the prosecutor in all those cases where court proceedings would otherwise have been instituted. These referrals cover all forms of crime, including serious and repeat offenders. Those who commit minor criminal acts are dealt with by the police and are usually given an informed warning with a "restorative theme" or a restorative caution (O'Mahony & Doak, 2004). By contrast, diversionary conferences are often initiated as a "follow-up" intervention to curb offending, particularly where there has been previous contact with the criminal justice system. For the diversionary conference to take place, two conditions must be fulfilled: the young person must admit to the offense and he or she must consent to involvement in the restorative process. If either of these conditions is not met, the case will be referred back to the Public Prosecution Service, which may then decide to proceed with a court-based prosecution in the conventional manner.

In regard to court-ordered conferences, the young person is referred to the Youth Conferencing Service through the court. Again, it is essential that the young person admit to the offense and consent to the conferencing process; otherwise, a conventional court hearing is instituted. This will obviously occur in all those cases where the accused contests guilt. If he or she is then found guilty, the legislation stipulates that the court *must* refer a young person to a youth conference, provided he or she consents. This stipulation, contained in Section 59 of the act, highlights the intended centrality of conferencing to the youth justice system. Only offenses with a penalty of life imprisonment are ineligible for conferencing; those that can be tried under indictment only and scheduled offenses (those that are terrorist-related) may be referred to conferencing at the discretion of the court. Therefore, young persons convicted of very serious offenses, such as rape or grievous bodily harm, can be referred for conferencing.

In practice, the conferencing process is resource-intensive and typically involves a lengthy and thorough preparation process. A trained conference coordinator from the Youth Conferencing Service will contact both victim and offender to organize the conference and ensure that the potential for any heated conflict is minimized. The victim is encouraged to attend, although the principle of voluntariness is preserved and no pressure is exerted. Even in cases where the victim chooses not to attend, the conference will proceed, and a "surrogate" victim may instead be asked to provide input.

The conference coordinator facilitates the conference, during which the main stakeholders are usually seated in a circle. They typically include the offender plus a parent or guardian, the victim and a support person, and a police officer plus the facilitator. Others who may intend include community representatives, social/probation workers, and a solicitor. During the conference, the young person is asked to reflect on the factors that led to his or her offending behavior. The victim is then given the opportunity to explain the impact of the offense to give the offender an understanding of the victim's perspective. The group will then have to come up with a conference plan that will address the needs of the victim (such as some form of reparation) and address the offending behavior of the young person. The conference plan takes the form of a negotiated contract, which will be monitored and enforced by the Youth Conference Service. This will usually require the offender to complete some act of reparation to the victim or community, although in common with all other stages of the process, entering into the agreement is voluntary and subject to the consent of the young person.

The Research

The conferencing arrangements were subject to a major evaluation from 2003 to 2005 in which the proceedings of 185 conferences were observed and personal interviews were completed with 171 young people and 125 victims who participated in conferences (Campbell et al., 2006). Overall, the findings were generally positive insofar as they seemed to enhance the experience of both victims and offenders within the criminal justice system. Logistically, conferences were generally well organized, proceeded smoothly, and conformed to international standards of best practice and accepted human rights safeguards.

The Experience of Victims

Although victims of the offense are entitled to attend, when they choose to not attend in person, they can still contribute to the conference process indirectly. This may be through a telephone link, a written statement, letter, or tape recording in which victims can express the impact of the crime to the offender. One of the most striking findings of the research was that more than two thirds of conferences (69%) had a victim in attendance, which contrasts favorably with other restorative programs (cf. Maxwell & Morris, 2002; Newburn et al., 2002; O'Mahony & Doak, 2004). Of these, it should be underlined that 40% were personal victims and 60% were victim representatives. The latter group of victim representatives were drawn mostly from groups of retail managers or from victim support organizations. They tended to participate in cases where there was damage to public property or where there was no directly identifiable victim. This enabled offenders to gain an insight into the consequences of their actions from a "victim's perspective," thus boosting the overall potential for reintegrative shaming and restoration to occur (Braithwaite, 1989, 2002).

Interviews carried out immediately after the conferences revealed that 79% of victims said they were actually "keen" to participate, and an overwhelming majority (91%) reported that the decision to take part was their own and not a result of pressure to attend. One of the more surprising findings was that victims' motives for participating often appeared to be benevolent. In contrast to some of the literature that tends to portray victims as vengeful or unpredictable (e.g., Ashworth, 2001; Buruma, 2004; Coen, 2006), few victims were motivated through retribution or a desire for punishment (Doak & O'Mahony, 2006). More than three quarters (79%) of victims reported that they attended "to help the young person," and many victims said they wanted to hear the young person's side of the story or simply wanted to ask "Why me?" Others identified a social responsibility in seeing the conference as an attempt to deter the young person from future offending, as one victim noted: "I was encouraged to attend. I did not want to go at first, and was sold on the idea. I was forced by guilt…. I had to take my own responsibility."

A substantial majority of victims (88%) attended to hear what the young person had to say, and 86% wanted the young person to know how the crime had affected them. Just more than half (55%) said they attended the conference to hear the offender apologize. These findings, which go some way to debunking the myth of the vengeful victim, largely correlate with the desires of victims recorded in other recent studies (Hoyle et al., 2002; Newburn et al., 2002; Shapland et al., 2004, 2006; Strang, 2002).

There was also a clear desire among victims to participate in a forum that would enable them to express themselves and explain the impact of the crime to the offender in person. This opportunity for victims to give their account of past events in their own words and in their own time contrasts sharply with the treatment of victims in the conventional criminal justice system. Over the course of the past three decades, a considerable body of research has documented how victims often find themselves excluded and alienated within the criminal justice system (Angle, Malam, & Carey, 2003; Rock, 1993; Shapland, Willmore, & Duff, 1985; Victim Support, 1996), or simply used as "evidentiary cannon fodder" for the prosecution (Braithwaite & Daly, 1998). In conferencing, the opportunity for free narrative was clearly valued: 92% said they had said everything they wanted to during the conference. The research also found 81% of victims preferred conferencing as opposed to going to court. The reasons provided for favoring the conference included the opportunity presented to express a personal view, to meet the young person face to face, and to help achieve closure.

Overall, victims were enthusiastic within the conference and engaged well with the process and discussions: 83% of victims were rated as "very engaged" and almost all (98%) were rated as "talkative." To some measure, their readiness to participate was evidently attributable to the preconference preparation that had been invested by the conference service facilitator. Only a fifth (20%) of victims were observed to be visibly nervous at the beginning of the conference in contrast to 71% of offenders. However, in the case of victims, nervousness seemed to subside as the conference proceeded, and for victims in particular, nearly all reported that they were more relaxed once the conference was under way.

Although many of the victims (71%) showed some degree of frustration toward the young offender at some point in the conference, most listened to and seemed to accept the young person's version of the offense either "a lot" (69%) or "a bit" (25%), and three quarters of victims expressed a degree of empathy toward the offender. It should be underlined, however, that despite the inevitable underlying apprehension, an overwhelming majority (93%) of victims displayed no signs of hostility toward the offender at the conference.

At the end of the conference, nearly all victims (91%) received at least an apology and 85% said they were happy with that apology. Most of the victims were happy with the conference plan, and only 9% of victims indicated any degree of dissatisfaction with it. This was despite the fact that material reparation in the form of pecuniary recompense occurred in only one third of cases and that 73% of conference plans had contained no element that could be classed as "punitive." This reflects the finding that the majority of victims did not actually expect, nor want, compensation from the young person. The fact that symbolic forms of reparation, provided they are genuine, tend to be prioritized by victims over and above pecuniary recompense reflects findings in other studies (Braithwaite, 2002; Shapland et al., 2004, 2006; Strang, 2002). A genuine gesture, which may take the form of a handshake, an apology, or a form of community work, may be a very difficult and highly emotive experience for an offender, which tends to debunk the idea the restorative processes are somehow an "easy option."

Overall then, victims appeared to be satisfied with both processes and outcomes and to be genuinely glad that they had the opportunity to meet the young person and explain the impact of the offense on them. Rather than seeking an outlet through which to vent their anger, many victims were more interested in "moving on" or putting the incident behind them and "seeing something positive come out of it." When victims were asked what they felt were the best and worst aspects of their experience, the best features appeared to be related to three issues: helping offenders in some way, helping prevent offenders from committing an offense again, and holding them (offenders) to account for their actions. The most positive aspects of the conferencing were clearly nonpunitive in nature for victims; most seem to appreciate that the conferences represented a means of moving forward for both parties, rather than gaining any sense of satisfaction that the offender would have to endure some form of harsh punishment in direct retribution for the offense.

The Experience of Offenders

It was evident that the conferencing process held offenders to account for their actions. In all cases, they were required to explain to the conference why they had committed the offense in question. A clear majority also stated that they had wanted to attend. Although the desire to avoid court was an important factor in this decision, most young people felt that meeting the victim would provide them with the opportunity to take responsibility for their actions, seek forgiveness, and put the offense behind them. They gave reasons such as wanting to "make good" for what they had done or wanting to apologize to the victim and seek forgiveness. One commented that, "it gives you a chance to say what you want to do and what you are comfortable with; victims have a say in what you do too." Only 28% of offenders said they were initially "not keen" to attend. Indeed, many offenders seemed to genuinely appreciate the opportunity to interact with the victim and wanted to make amends for the harm they had caused.

As suggested above, conferencing was by no means an undemanding alternative to court, and most young people found the prospect of confronting their victim extremely challenging. Almost three quarters (71%) of offenders displayed nervousness at the beginning of the conference, and only 28% appeared to be "not at all" nervous. However, despite their clear anxiety, offenders were observed to engage constructively in conference discussions, with nearly all (98%) being able to talk about the offense and the overwhelming majority (97%) accepting responsibility for what they had done.

Just as the conference experience contrasts favorably with court in terms of victim participation, it also provides similar benefits to the young people in giving them an opportunity to explain their actions. One of the major criticisms of juvenile courts in adversarial systems is that they fail to give the young persons adequate opportunity to participate in proceedings against them. Such proceedings thus appear to fall well short of conforming fully to international benchmarks, most notably the decision of the European Court of Human Rights in *T and V v. United Kingdom* (1999) 30 EHRR 121, where it was held that children must be able to participate effectively in criminal proceedings brought against them. Typically, the Northern Irish youth court is lawyer-dominated, with offenders exercising a very passive role. Generally, they do not even speak other than to confirm their name, plea, and understanding of the charges. Legal counsel will generally advocate on their behalf.

Foremost among the aspects of the conferencing process that the young offenders found particularly difficult was the prospect of coming face to face with the victims. They were often observed, through their posture and body language at the beginning of the conference, as being visibly nervous. On many occasions, they would avoid eye contact, fidget, or shake. Yet despite this nervousness, most were able to give a full and frank account of the offense, speaking directly to the victim, maintaining good eye contact, and appearing ashamed. As one offender said, "I feel stupid, I shouldn't have done it, I'm sorry." Another offender had brought notes along with him to the conference and referred to them in giving a full and frank account of what he had done.

The process of participation for offenders went beyond simply having to respond to questions; it was an active process that involved them in a dialogue, both holding them to account and engaging them so there was clear "ownership" of the dispute by all the parties. On the whole, young people felt engaged in the process, and nearly all of them (98%) felt that the other participants had listened to what they had to say. Most young people were also attentive to the accounts of victims, particularly regarding the impact of the offense. This was apparent through much of their body language, such as direct eye contact, nodding, and confirming what the victim was saying. Moreover, 97% of the offenders accepted responsibility for their actions. As one young person said, "We all take responsibility for our actions. Nobody can say we didn't do it, because we did."

The act of apologizing is a central feature of any restorative process in that it symbolizes remorse and a desire to seek forgiveness. Moreover, it may be viewed as an intentional, although intangible, form of reparation in itself. Nine of 10 victims who attended a conference received some sort of apology from the young person. It was often a spontaneous act and some of the young people apologized on a number of occasions during the conference. For offenders, the apology was a particularly important aspect of the process, and most said they felt it had made both the victim and themselves feel better. Most victims also accepted the young person's apology, and most (81%) even expressed forgiveness toward the young person.

As far the conference plans were concerned, most young people played a proactive role in agreeing with the plan and thought it was both fair and proportionate. In contrast to the punitive sanctions imposed by the Youth Court, the plans tended generally not to focus on punishment, but, in line with the victims' desires, on ways to address the young person's offending behavior. As such, many plans contained positive elements that constructively looked at ways to deal with factors contributing to the young person's behavior, the most common being substance misuse, peer pressure, and family difficulties.

The Community

Ironically, the conflict-ridden history of Northern Ireland has meant that society has been less exposed to the globalized erosion of "community," and certain community values have even been preserved or developed as a form of "social cement" (O'Mahony, Geary, McEvoy, & Morison, 2000). As such, Northern Ireland has a strong history of proactive civil society and highly mobilized political communities. The community sector has performed a wider role in terms of both service provision and policy development than its counterparts in Great Britain or North America (McEvoy & Mika, 2002). All these would suggest that if the new youth conferencing arrangements were to gain the trust of community activists from those areas that have traditionally felt alienated from the state, Northern Ireland should be a fertile ground for restorative-based initiatives to flourish.

The task of determining the extent of community participation is considerably more difficult to measure than examining the process from the perspective of the victim or offender. This problem primarily arises because the very concept of "community" is vague and contested, and there is little consensus among commentators in relation to what constitutes a "community" (O'Mahony & Doak, 2007). The term means very different things to different people, but a common theme appears to be that it can be used to describe a form of social network where individual lives converge (Braithwaite, 1989) through diverse media including work, neighborhood, family, friends, leisure, religion, or politics. Pavlich (2005) perhaps best sums this up in writing of "an ephemeral quality of identification through connection with others." Within restorative justice discourse, the term tends to be used in a slightly more specific sense. The concepts of "microcommunities" or "communities of care" are frequently used to refer to the range of stakeholders that have emerged from the circumstances surrounding the offense and have developed to encourage, help, and support those directly involved. Such communities are constructed out of the events in question and reflected in the "supporters" of victims and offenders and may include schools, churches, youth organizations, or family and friends (Braithwaite, 2002; McCold, 2000).

By adopting this fairly specific idea of what constitutes a "community," some degree of certainty is imported into restorative processes insofar as specific individuals may be more readily identified and included within conferencing arrangements. The involvement of such individuals is widely regarded as a sine qua non of the restorative paradigm, and three major benefits are commonly cited. First, community involvement assists with localized problem-solving efforts in terms of contributing toward public safety and crime prevention (Braithwaite, 2002; Zehr, 2005). Second, community input provides a framework for the restoration of harm and reintegration of the offender. Through offering a forum for the symbolic acknowledgment that harm has occurred, community involvement may be said to have a denunciatory function (Sullivan & Tift, 2001). Third, such participation may help boost legitimacy of criminal justice through laying down norms of acceptable and unacceptable conduct (Olson & Dzur, 2004; Weisberg, 2003). In turn, this can help foster a sense of civic ownership of disputes.

Although the extent of community involvement in any process is difficult to measure, the Northern Ireland arrangements appear to have been relatively successful in engaging community stakeholders. Section 57 of the Justice (Northern Ireland) Act 2002 stipulates that the young person, the conference coordinator, a police officer, and an appropriate adult must attend a conference, thereby immediately widening the circle of participants. The young person is entitled to have legal representation at the conference, but solicitors may attend only in an advisory capacity and cannot speak for the young person. In addition, the coordinator may also include anyone else they believe may be "of value" to the process, such as a community worker or someone who is likely to help either the young person or the victim, either during the conference or as part of the conference plan. Thus, all conferences during the period of the research received inputs from parents or guardians, and it was not unusual for them to include other supporters, such as social workers or probation officers, who had been working with the young person. These individuals were encouraged to support the young person, and observations showed that 77% of supporters were engaged to at least some extent when discussing the crime. At the invitation of the coordinator, many of these participants made a positive contribution by describing positive aspects of the offender's life, and several supporters intervened to assist where young people experienced difficulties in articulating themselves. In addition, the use of surrogate victims, described above, meant that representatives of local businesses or community centers were able to participate as vicarious stakeholders, thereby injecting an additional community perspective.

Beyond the various stakeholders and their supporters, a range of service providers, including voluntary and community organizations, also contributed to the successful operation of the conferencing arrangements. Although these organizations only occasionally participated in the conference itself, they played a key role in assisting with the operation of the conference plans through the provision of various services, including one-to-one mentoring, drug and alcohol counseling, voluntary and community-based work programs, victim awareness sessions, peer education, and other diversionary programs. The reliance on the voluntary and community sector was significant, and 83% of conference plans included activities or programs that were provided through the community and voluntary sector. Without the cooperation of these organizations, it would be doubtful whether conference plans could be effectively implemented or monitored.

One of the more negative findings at the time of the research, however, was that there was very little evidence of cooperation with the community-led restorative schemes that were well established in certain areas of Belfast long before the Belfast Agreement or Criminal Justice Review came into being. Therefore, some form of engagement with them is clearly important if conferencing is to be viewed as a legitimate and fair response to youth offending, especially within communities that have traditionally been detached from state-led initiatives and criminal justice institutions. Interviews conducted with representatives from the two main community-based restorative projects revealed that they both felt excluded from the formulation and rollout of the conferencing arrangements. Although there were a few isolated cases where there was some limited contact with the Youth Conferencing Service, this was the exception rather than the norm. Both the statutory and community schemes were adopting a similar approach to juvenile offenders, with presumably the same restorative-based goals in mind, and it was thus unfortunate that there was little active consultation or exchange between them.

For their part, leaders of the community schemes were also skeptical of the rollout of conferencing, and some saw it as an attempt by the state to monopolize or claim ownership of juvenile offending. It may thus appear that the modus operandum of community schemes was under threat by the introduction of a statutory state-led system, which had already secured a substantial investment of resources. However, this cynicism cut both ways. At the time the research was conducted, the Northern Ireland Office was advising the Youth Conferencing Service not to engage with the community-based programs because they were not accountable to the police or the courts. Certainly, this situation was particularly unfortunate for some young people. Interviewees from the community organizations recalled at least two incidences of double jeopardy, whereby a young person had gone through two separate restorative processes for the same offense. Clearly, this was highly undesirable; it is not only a breach of the young person's human rights, but it also has the potential to thwart the reintegrative purpose of the process.

Discussion

The research in Northern Ireland examining the youth conferencing process was overwhelmingly positive. The conferencing arrangements were well resourced and were managed by a team of highly professional and well-trained facilitators. The researchers did report some teething problems relating to attitudinal resistance on the part of a small number of criminal justice practitioners and magistrates, but these did not generally impede on the overall effectiveness of the scheme. Certainly, in relation to other programs, the findings compare extremely favorably, particularly as far as victim participation and victim–offender interactions are concerned. Recent research findings assessing the impact of the scheme on recidivism rates show those given restorative conferences had a lower one-year reconviction rate than those given community disposals or custody (Lyness, 2008). Indeed, research into recidivism rates following restorative measures elsewhere has shown them to be better than other interventions, though not by a very wide margin (Sherman and Strang, 2007). Nevertheless, it may be overly simplistic to measure the success of the arrangements against this one particular benchmark. It could be that, for example, where young people feel they have been treated fairly by the criminal justice system, they are more likely to respect and obey the law in future (Tyler, 1990). If this were the case, it would need to be measured over a considerable stretch of time; any impact might not be immediately apparent from data concerning recidivism. Furthermore, it can be argued that the process itself seems to have inherent value, given the high rates of satisfaction and perceptions of fairness indicated by victims and young people. Certainly, in contrast with the orthodox court process, the opportunity for victims, offenders, and the community to actively participate is something that should be embraced, irrespective of any short-term impacts on recidivism.

In summary, four major factors can be said to have contributed to the overall success of the youth conferencing arrangements. First, and most important, the scheme is mainstreamed. Unlike many other restorative programs, the conferencing arrangements have been placed on a statutory footing at the center of the criminal justice system. As such, the conventional system of prosecutions was entirely sidelined, and the new scheme was well resourced and financed by government. In practice, this has meant that prosecutors, defense lawyers, and magistrates received training on how the new system would operate, while the Youth Conferencing Service itself was overseen by experienced managers and staffed by well-trained facilitators.

The second factor, related to the first, is that the arrangements are mandatory in nature. Together, the Public Prosecution Service and the courts have a duty to refer most cases to conferencing. Thus, even where magistrates or prosecutors believe that a particular case is unsuitable for conferencing, there is little discretion to interfere with statutory stipulations. Previous studies have shown that attitudinal resistance can act as a major obstacle to restorative justice initiatives (Edgar & Newell 2006; Mestitz & Ghetti 2004), thereby producing a chasm between law in the books and law in practice. The potential for this gap to expand is clearly exacerbated where decision makers are given maximum scope to maneuver; this is clearly not the case with restorative youth conferencing in Northern Ireland.

Third, the scheme is victim-centered. In practice, this has meant that considerable time and energy have been invested by the Youth Conferencing Service through staff meetings, advising, and reassuring victims about the process. It is well documented that criminal justice reforms designed to enhance the experience of victims are often undermined by the fact that their expectations are not properly managed (Erez & Tontodonato, 1992; Sanders, Hoyle, Morgan, & Cape, 2001). Here, close contact with the Youth Conferencing Service clearly helped to ensure that the expectations of victims were realistic, which meant that most victims stated that they were satisfied with the process and glad they had participated. Furthermore, although few of the plans provided for any material reparation, virtually all contained some form of symbolic recompense. Thus, in the eyes of victims, not only were they given the opportunity to tell their story and have their feelings acknowledged, but they were also able to get something back with the offenders having made some form of amends.

The fourth factor contributing to the success of the conferencing arrangements relates to the transitional context in which they were introduced. As noted previously, Northern Ireland is a society with a long history of vibrant community activism. Moreover, postconflict societies tend to lend favorable conditions to promote restorative justice because, at their core, transitional justice and restorative justice are both fundamentally transformative discourses that have much in common (Skelton, 2002). The fact that the scheme had been devised around the recommendations of the Criminal Justice Review Group meant that the reforms to the youth justice system were systemically interlinked with the peace process and the transition from armed conflict. Having invested so heavily in developing a new criminal justice system that sought support from all sections of the community, it would have been unthinkable that the government would not have invested a considerable amount of effort and resources in ensuring that all 294 of the recommendations of the group were fully implemented.

The positive tenor of the findings should not, however, paint an overly optimistic picture of criminal justice reform in Northern Ireland. It is a welcome fact that, after decades of conflict and suspicion, a state-led process seems to be working well in practice. There was no evidence from the research of any form of bias or discriminatory practice on the part of the Youth Conference Service or indeed of the police officers who participated in the conferences. Moreover, these key actors were *perceived* by victims and offenders to act impartially; in all 165 conferences observed and all the interviews that were carried out, no allegations of sectarian bias or prejudice were made by the participants. This is a remarkable achievement: although the physical conflict may be drawing to an end, Northern Ireland is still a society where sectarian tensions and mistrust play a major role in politics and public life.

The arrangements have clearly made a significant contribution to the stated objective of the Criminal Justice Review of "enhancing community involvement and support for the criminal justice system." It is evident that they have been effective in broadening participation beyond individual victims and offenders and have engaged with community and voluntary organizations that have not traditionally worked in close partnership with criminal justice agencies. The lack of interaction between the Youth Conference Service and the community-led restorative programs, evident at the time of the research, posed a risk that youth conferencing might not be viewed as being fully legitimate in some republican and loyalist communities, particularly in Greater Belfast. However, in looking to the future, it may be that we can now afford to be considerably more optimistic in that regard.

When the research was carried out, the future of criminal justice reform in Northern Ireland remained uncertain. Devolved government had been suspended since October 2002, and deep rifts concerning policing and demilitarization seemed to preclude any progress in the short term. However, as political negotiations on devolution gathered momentum, the Northern Ireland Office issued new protocols in July 2006 that stated that, in return for government recognition and funding, the community schemes had to accept vetting by the police and be prepared to work with the Youth Conferencing Service. Following Sinn Fein's acceptance of the policing arrangements and a commitment from the Democratic Unionist Party to work towards the devolution of criminal justice matters from London, the state has apparently acknowledged that the community restorative justice projects have a valuable role to play in dealing with low-level criminality in Northern Ireland. Following agreement of protocols between the Northern Ireland Office and the community schemes, government funding and a promise of mutual cooperation has recently (August 2008) been announced which should mean that the community and state-led schemes will find it easier to engage with each other and cross-fertilize aspects of best practice.

Conclusions

The introduction of restorative youth conferencing in Northern Ireland has clearly had an impact beyond providing an alternative form of justice for victims, offenders, and the community. The restorative philosophy has contributed to the very process of transition away from conflict toward stability and "normalization." Assuming that the public and political will continues, there is every possibility that most obstacles can be overcome in time, and there is every reason to expect that public confidence will grow in both the community- and the state-led schemes. Over time, it can be assumed that a broader range of actors from former conflict-ridden communities will have some degree of interaction with the conferencing process, be that as victim, offender, supporter, or service provider. As the process of normalizing policing continues, it is also suggested that the presence and the involvement of the police within the conferencing arrangements may foster a great sense of respect for the law and the police. This was one of the findings of the evaluation by Sherman et al. (1998) on police-led conferencing in Australia. In this way, restorative youth conferencing can act as both a vehicle for and beneficiary of further community building and thus may have a modest role to play in boosting the overall legitimacy of the Northern Ireland criminal justice system.

On a final note, the success of the youth conferencing arrangements also highlights the importance of building any process of criminal justice reform around a set of certain core values and standards. Before its peace process, Northern Ireland was a society in which secrecy, suspicion, and mistrust interacted to undermine public confidence in the criminal justice system. However, the Belfast Agreement, along with the Criminal Justice Review and devolution of power that followed, served to establish fresh normative themes and values such as reconciliation, inclusivity, accountability, and healing, similar to the communitarian values as espoused in restorative justice theory and practice. It is these same themes and values that, it is hoped, will continue to influence governance, criminal justice reform, and political transition for many years to come.

References

Aldana-Pindell, R. (2004). An emerging universality of justiciable victims' rights in the criminal process to curtail impunity for state-sponsored crimes. *Human Rights Quarterly, 26,* 605.

Angle, H., Malam, S., & Carey, C. (2003). *Witness satisfaction: Findings from the witness satisfaction survey 2002.* London: Home Office.

Ashworth, A. (2001). Is restorative justice the way forward for criminal justice? *Current Legal Problems, 54,* 347–376.

Braithwaite, J. (1989). *Crime, shame and reintegration.* Cambridge: Cambridge University Press.

Braithwaite, J. (2002). *Restorative justice and responsive regulation.* Oxford: Oxford University Press.

Braithwaite, J., & Daly, K. (1998). Masculinities, violence, and communitarian control. In S. L. Miller (Ed.), *Crime control and women: Feminist implications of criminal justice policy* (pp. 151–172). Newbury Park, CA: Sage.

Buruma, Y. (2004). Doubts on the upsurge of the victim's role in criminal law. In H. Kaptein & M. Malsch (Eds.), *Crime, victims, and justice: Essays on principles and practice.* Aldershot: Ashgate.

Campbell, C., Devlin, R., O'Mahony, D., Doak, J., Jackson, J., Corrigan, T., et al. (2006). *Evaluation of the Northern Ireland youth conference service* (NIO Research and Statistics Series Report 12). Belfast: Northern Ireland Office.

Coen, R. (2006). The rise of the victim—A path to punitiveness? *Irish Criminal Law Journal, 16,* 10–13.

Criminal Justice Review Group. (2000). *Review of the criminal justice system.* Belfast: HMSO.

Dignan, J., & Lowey, K. (2000). *Restorative justice options for Northern Ireland: A comparative review.* Belfast: Criminal Justice Review Group, HMSO.

Doak, J., & O'Mahony, D. (2006). The vengeful victim? Assessing the attitudes of victims participating in restorative youth conferencing. *International Review of Victimology, 13,* 157–177.

Edgar, K., & Newell, T. (2006). *Restorative justice in prisons—A guide to making it happen.* Hampshire: Waterside Press.

Erez, E., & Tontodonato, P. (1990). The effect of victim participation in sentencing on sentence outcome. *Criminology, 228,* 451–474.

Hoyle, C., Young, R., & Hill, R. (2002). *Proceed with caution: An evaluation of the Thamas Valley police initiative in restorative cautioning.* York: Rowntree.

Lyness, D. (2008). Northern Ireland youth re-offending: results from the 2005 cohort. *Research and Statistical Bulletin 7/2008.* Belfast: Northern Ireland Office.

Maxwell, G., & Morris, A. (2002). Restorative justice and reconviction. *Contemporary Justice Review, 5,* 133–146.

McCold, P. (1996). Restorative justice and the role of community. In B. Galaway & J. Hudson (Eds.), *Restorative justice: International perspectives* (pp. 85–102). Kluwer: Amsterdam.

McCold, P. (2000). Towards a holistic vision of restorative juvenile justice: A reply to the Maximalist model. *Contemporary Justice Review, 3,* 357–414.

McEvoy, K., & Mika, H. (2002). Restorative justice and the critique of informalism in Northern Ireland. *British Journal of Criminology, 42,* 534–562.

Mestitz, A., & Ghetti, S. (2004). *What do prosecutors and judges think about victim-offender mediation with juvenile offenders?* Paper presented at the Third Conference of the European Forum for Victim-Offender Mediation and Restorative Justice, Budapest, Hungary, 14–16 October.

Morris, A. (2002). Critiquing the critics: A brief response to the critics of restorative justice. *British Journal of Criminology, 42,* 595–615.

Newburn, T., Crawford, A., Earle, R., Goldie, S., Hale, C., Hallam, A., et al. (2002). *The introduction of referral orders into the youth justice system: Final report* (HORS 242). London: Home Office.

Olson, S., & Dzur, A. (2004). Revisiting informal justice: Restorative justice and democratic professionalism. *Law and Society Review, 38,* 139–176.

Parmentier, S. (2001). The South African truth and reconciliation commission: Towards restorative justice in the field of human rights. In E. Fattah & S. Parmentier (Eds.), *Victim policies and criminal justice on the road to restorative justice: Essays in honour of Tony Peters* (pp. 401–428). Leuven: Leuven University Press.

O'Mahony, D., & Doak, J. (2004). Restorative justice: Is more better? *Howard Journal, 43,* 484–505.

O'Mahony, D., & Doak, J. (2007). The enigma of community and the exigency of engagement: Restorative youth conferencing in Northern Ireland. *British Journal of Community Justice, 4,* 9–24.

O'Mahony, D., Geary, R., McEvoy, K., & Morison, J. (2000). *Crime, community and locale: The Northern Ireland communities crime survey.* Aldershot: Ashgate.

Pavlich, G. (2005). *The governing paradoxes of restorative justice.* London: Glasshouse Press.

Roche, D. (2002). Restorative justice and the regulatory state in South African townships. *British Journal of Criminology, 42,* 514–533.

Rock, P. (1993). *The social world of an English Crown Court: Witnesses and professionals in the Crown Court Centre at Wood Green.* Oxford: Clarendon Press.

Sanders, A., Hoyle, C., Morgan, R., & Cape, E. (2001). Victim impact statements: Don't work, can't work. *Criminal Law Review,* 447–458.

Shapland, J., Atkinson, A., Atkinson, H., Chapman, B., Colledge, E., Dignan, J., et al. (2006). *Restorative justice in practice—Findings from the second phase of the evaluation of three schemes* (Home Office Research Findings 274). London: Home Office.

Shapland, J., Atkinson, A., Colledge, E., Dignan, J., Howes, M., Johnstone, J., et al. (2004). *Implementing restorative justice schemes—A report on the first year* (Home Office Online Report 32/04). London: Home Office.

Shapland, J., Willmore, J., & Duff, P. 1985. *Victims and the criminal justice system.* Aldershot: Gower.

Sherman, L., & Strang, H. (2007). *Restorative justice: The evidence.* London: Smith Institute.

Sherman, L., Strang, H., Barnes, J., Braithwaite, J., Inkpen, N., & Teh, M. (1998). *Experiments in restorative policing: A progress report on the Canberra reintegrative shaming experiments (RISE)*. Canberra: Australian Institute of Criminology.

Skelton, A. (2002). Justice as a framework for juvenile justice reform: A South African perspective. *British Journal of Criminology* 42:496–513.

Strang, H. (2002) *Repair or revenge? Victims and restorative justice*. Oxford: Oxford University Press.

Sullivan, D., & Tift, L. (2001). *Restorative justice: Healing the foundations of everyday lives*. Monsey, NY: Willowtree Press.

Weisberg, R. (2003). The practice of restorative justice: Restorative justice and the danger of community. *Utah Law Review, 42*, 343–374.

Tolbert, D., & Solomon, A. (2006). United Nations reform and supporting the rule of law in post-conflict societies. *Harvard Human Rights Journal, 19*, 29–62.

Tyler, T. (1990). *Why people obey the law*. New Haven, CT: Yale University Press.

Zehr, H. (2005). *Changing lenses*. Scottdale, PA: Herald Press.

Restorative Justice and Antisocial Behavior Interventions as Contractual Governance: Constructing the Citizen Consumer

8

ADAM CRAWFORD

Contents

Introduction

In recent years, the emergence of a number of new "social technologies of control" in the United Kingdom concerned with responding to and regulating (primarily low-level) crime and disorder has been witnessed. These have emerged as partial critiques of the acknowledged limitations and ineffectiveness of traditional criminal justice processes and sanctions. As such, they stand in awkward relation to established modes of crime control. In the discussions that follow, my interest is with a cluster of innovations that coalesce around two interconnected conceptual and policy developments: those that have been advanced in the name of restorative justice, on the one hand, and

167

those that have emerged under the banner of tackling antisocial behavior, on the other hand. Despite their apparent commonalities, at present, these developments are likely to be analyzed separately.

In one corner of the crime control field, restorative justice values and principles have informed a series of practices, including family group conferencing, restorative cautioning, youth offender panels, reparation orders, reparative boards, and sentencing circles. These and allied restorative practices have come to prominence in various countries around the world in dealing with interpersonal disputes and in the resolution of collective political struggles,* as well as international conflicts. According to some commentators, restorative justice became the social movement for criminal justice reform at the turn of the new millennium (Braithwaite, 1998). Restorative practices are now used at diverse stages of the criminal process as supplements and/or alternatives to criminal justice, although most frequently they are used with juveniles in relation to minor offenses (Dignan, 2006). Importantly for our purposes, restorative practices are also to be found outside criminal justice, informing noncriminal decision making in contexts such as child protection, school discipline, and neighborhood disputes.

Elsewhere in the field of crime control, the extensive array of new powers introduced as part of the "antisocial behavior agenda" (and subsequent "Respect" program) in the United Kingdom variously include acceptable behaviour contracts, antisocial behavior orders (ASBOs), parenting contracts and orders, tenancy demotion orders, antisocial behavior housing injunctions, dispersal orders, and penalty notices for disorder (PNDs), as well as the latest proposals for premise closure orders and "deferred" PNDs.† More broadly, since the Housing Act 1996, the regulation of antisocial behavior has become a central feature of tenancy contracts in social housing.‡ This reflects the manner in which antisocial behavior regulation has its genesis in the management of social housing. Although the control of access and tenants' conduct have been ever-present features of social landlordism since the late Victorian era (Burney, 1999), social housing management embracing a more central position in crime control and the regulation of behavior has been seen in recent years (Cowan, Pantazis, & Gilroy, 2001). The new technologies that

---

* Such as South Africa's Truth and Reconciliation Commission.
† As outlined in the Criminal Justice and Immigration Act 2007. The former will allow for the temporary closure of premises regardless of tenure type. The latter will extend and formalize the use of acceptable behavior contracts by deferring the imposition of a PND where the individual agrees to and complies with such a contract.
‡ Most prominent is the power of local authorities and Registered Social Landlords to apply to court for a demoted tenancy on the basis of antisocial behavior. If granted, tenants' rights under their secure or assured tenancy are terminated and replaced with more limited rights under the demoted tenancy. This lasts for up to a year during which noncompliance may lead to possession proceedings, resulting in eviction. In addition, antisocial behavior is itself grounds for a civil injunction and eviction.

have emerged have done so as constituted by, and implicated in, the conflu-ence of housing management, policing, and community safety. This has seen the realignment of professional interests and working assumptions among housing officers, police, and council staff.

Restorative practices have largely been invested with a benevolent logic, interpreted as inclusionary and nonpunitive. They have often been con-trasted to the punitive and exclusionary tendencies of established crimi-nal justice and identified as a countervailing trend in the context of wider contemporary shift in "populist punitiveness" (Bottoms, 1995). Daly notes: "What started out in North America and the United Kingdom in the 1970s as a way for individual offenders and victims to meet each other has morphed into a *global justice metaphor* for a kindler, gentler, more reasonable, hopeful and negotiated justice: a 'good' justice" (2004, emphasis in original). Astute commentators, however, have long noted a considerable dissonance between restorative rhetoric and practices (Daly, 2003; Matthews, 1988).

The reception accorded to restorative practices stands in marked contrast to the more critical appraisal provoked by the introduction of the host of new antisocial behavior interventions, at least from within the academic commu-nity (Burney, 2005; von Hirsch & Simester, 2006). Thus far, however, much of the critical commentary has focused almost exclusively on the ASBO and has largely been "directed at the rhetoric rather than on evidence of what the impacts of the new policies have actually been" (Smith, 2003). This empirical "knowledge gap" has been exacerbated both by the frenetic pace of change and the fact that the British government has explicitly preferred not to fund significant or detailed evaluations. Instead, oversight has been restricted to the collection of limited data on the use of powers via annual surveys and the monitoring of crude measurements of public perceptions. This dearth of evaluation contrasts strikingly with the growing abundance of research into restorative justice interventions (see Crawford & Newburn, 2003; Shapland et al., 2006; Sherman & Strang, 2007).

Collectively, these new technologies of control share a number of salient features. Most conspicuously, they:

- appeal to forms of "contextual" or "responsive" regulation that are more closely tailored to the interests, capacities, and needs of, or risks presented by, the parties;
- seek to regulate future behavior and conduct by imposing or agreeing conditions aimed at preventing or avoiding potential consequences and risks;
- enlist active compliance and promote "self-regulation";
- seek to operate through informal social bonds, rendering families, and communities more responsible;

- are informed by communitarian-influenced preoccupations with recalibrating rights and responsibilities in favor of the latter;
- cede considerable discretion and quasi-judicial decision making authority to nonjudicial officers—including police, council and housing staff, youth justice workers, and a panoply of para-professionals and "expert" facilitators/mediators;
- refigure and (con)fuse civil and criminal processes and principles; and
- muddy relations between formal and informal responses.

In this chapter, I will explore the manner in which these commonalities find expression in a contractualization of control and might be understood as reflecting forms of contractual governance of behavior (Crawford, 2003). This contractualism is also to be found informing wider welfare reform, most notably welfare-to-work programs in the form of "jobseekers agreements" that render benefits conditional on actively seeking work as set out in personalized contracts (Beem & Mead, 2005; White, 2003). However, this chapter is restricted to an overview of the conceptual parameters offered by such an insight with regard to crime and disorder.* The chapter critically situates and analyzes the use of contract-type regulatory instruments in relation to young people's behavior. It considers the implications of regulating through contractual forms of control for conceptions of youth, the construction of the citizen-consumer, and debates about compliance.

In contrast to dominant (humanist) interpretations that seek to explain the emergence of restorative justice either as a good idea whose time had come or a reversion to ancient forms of justice (Weitekamp, 2002; Zehr, 1990), my argument is that restorative justice runs with the grain of wider shifts in technologies of control to be found within, but crucially also beyond, formal systems of criminal justice. At its core, restorative justice constitutes a form of contractual governance. This is most evident in the youth offender contract that is the outcome of a referral order in England and Wales (Crawford & Burden, 2005) but also finds expression in analogous restorative "agreements" and "resolutions" secured through family group conferences, restorative cautioning, victim–offender mediation, and the like. It is worth stressing that many of these technologies are not rarely used or marginal developments (as some restorative justice interventions have frequently remained) but are both central to the operations of control and extensively deployed. For example, in England and Wales, the referral order constituted approximately one quarter of all court sentences imposed on juveniles—28,394 in 2005/2006 (Youth Justice Board, 2007)—and that approximately 14,500 acceptable behavior contracts and more than 3,300 parenting contracts were recorded

---

* For a more detailed account of the diverse new technologies of control, their genesis and implications, see Crawford (forthcoming).

as agreed in the 2 years (2004–2006), most likely significant underrepresentations of the actual figures (Home Office, 2007a). Home Office guidance explicitly links the use of acceptable behavior contracts with restorative justice interventions more generally (Home Office, 2007b).

Both collectively and individually, many of the new technologies of regulation represent a shifting orientation toward forms of governance and behavioral control that focus less on knowing and accounting for past incidences than disrupting, reordering, and steering possible futures. They are part of a wider shift to a preventive mentality that seeks to govern future conduct. In so doing, they attempt to regulate crime and disorder through their consequences for, and interconnections with, broader social problems. They reflect a move toward a more calculative and formalized approach to social regulation that mimics forms of control derived from modes of consumption and commerce. Through contract-type arrangements, a "sense of choice," an allusion to reciprocity, an appeal to active responsibility, and a conscious awareness of the future are fostered in ways that conceive the subjects of regulation as rational and competent actors. They are deemed capable of knowing and articulating their preferences, as well as adhering to the conditions agreed, regarding future conduct, and upon which they are subsequently to be judged.

This is not to deny fundamental differences between the diverse technologies of control in their implications, implementation, and the manner in which they are experienced. Most obviously they differ in the extent to which:

- coercion and the threat of sanctions are apparent;
- individual autonomy can be exercised through an adequacy of options and a minimum bargaining capacity;
- procedural justice is ensured in that the parties are treated fairly and with respect, and authority is appropriately exercised;
- a degree of reciprocity and mutuality is a genuine aspect of exchange relations;
- outcomes are imposed upon, or actively shaped by, the parties;
- oversight and the contestability of unfair terms are guaranteed; and
- the parties are supported in fulfilling the terms of the resultant agreement.

These are crucial litmus tests of how well practices conform to ideal norms of restorative justice and relational contracts (Macneil, 1980). In this sense, interventions that most closely approximate to restorative justice ideals and values lie at one end of a continuum of contractual governance.

Contrary to some recent contributions that seek coherence through broad rationalities of rule (Rose, 2000) in interpreting contemporary crime control policies, it is not my intention to suggest that all criminal justice developments can be understood as emanating from, or the outcome of, a prevailing logic. Nor should we seek explanatory values through the same conceptual lens. Given the emotive and affective, as well as managerial and instrumental, dimensions embedded in forms of control, policy coherence would be surprising to say the least. Rather, as commentators have noted, contradiction, ambivalence, and volatility are often the outcomes of contemporary policies (Crawford, 2001; Garland, 1996; O'Malley 1999). In contrast, my intention is merely to draw out one strand influencing diverse contemporary trends, albeit in ways that find ambiguous and unpredictable expressions, and to highlight the shape of certain prevailing dynamics within the changing contemporary face of control.

New Technologies as Adaptations

The new modes of control constitute what Garland (2001) refers to as "adaptations" to the contemporary "crisis of penal modernism" that disrupted many of the taken-for-granted assumptions of correctionalist criminology. As Garland notes:

> For the first time since the formation of the modern criminal justice state, governments have begun to acknowledge a basic sociological truth: that the most important processes producing order and conformity are mainstream social processes, located within institutions of civil society, not the uncertain threat of legal sanctions (2001, p. 126)

Recognition of this "sociological truth" has caused policy makers to look to pragmatic ways of influencing decision making through a revival of classicist notions of deterrence combined with an emphasis on informal mechanisms of control (Wilson, 1975). It is with some irony that this acknowledgment coincides historically with the gradual fragmentation of bonds of informal control (Putnam, 2000), the reordering of gender and family relations (Williams, 2004), the breakdown of traditional forms of authority and deference, and the decline of secondary agencies of social control (Jones & Newburn, 2002). Garland goes on to suggest:

> The state's new strategy is not to command and control but rather to persuade and align, to organise, to ensure that other actors play their part. Property owners, residents, retailers, manufacturers, town planners, school authorities, transport managers, employers, parents, individual citizens...the list is endless...must all be made to recognise that they have a responsibility in this regard. They must be persuaded to exert their informal powers of social control, and if necessary, to modify their usual practices, in order to help reduce criminal opportunities and enhance crime control. Government authorities are, in this

field of policy as in several others, operating across and upon the boundaries that used to separate the private from the public realm, seeking to renegotiate the question of what is properly a state function and what is not. In doing so, they are also beginning to challenge the central assumption of penal modernism, which took it for granted that crime control was a specialist task, best concentrated within a differentiated state institution (2001, p. 126).

In this renegotiation of responsibilities, the archetypical neoclassical instrument of regulation—the contract—has been a prominent container in which the terms and conditions of social organization, as well as expectations about conduct in parochial relations, have increasingly come to supplement the wider (implicit) social contract.

As important as Garland's insights are, they also highlight a number of shortcomings apparent within much criminological analysis. The story of contemporary "adaptations" is largely written as if it were something imposed by governments on businesses, organizations, authorities, and the citizenry through programs of "responsibilization" (Garland, 1996), emanating outward/downward from the center, and evidenced by key policy initiatives and governmental strategies. Problematically, this largely underplays the crucial role that institutions—in civil society and the marketplace—have played and were already playing as agents of social control in the regulation of both deviant and conformist behaviors. It accepts, too readily, the idea of the myth of state sovereignty that is now deemed to be exposed as having been more real than fictitious. It fails to connect sufficiently with wider developments and shifts in informal control and regulation outside the narrow field of crime. Braithwaite (2003) reminds us that there is a very different history of policing to be derived from the business regulatory field as distinct from the "police-prisons" arena. One of the principal historical lessons drawn from the diverse body of regulatory agencies established in the 19th century is the manner in which they prioritized nonpunitive modes of enforcement, preferring strategies rooted in persuasion through market-based disciplines and mentalities.

By contrast, much of the credit for the contemporary rise in preventive thinking and regulatory innovation should properly be attributed to small-scale, local, and pragmatic developments often outside the orbit of the state, within civil society and the business sector.* In reality, both criminology and government policy were relative latecomers to a preventive way of thinking. Insurers, for example, have acted as key "agents of prevention," helping to spread actuarial logics, technologies of prediction, and regulation through contract, as well as fostering networks with state agencies that have

---

* The genesis of "acceptable behavior contracts" is an excellent example of this practice-led regulatory innovation (Crawford, forthcoming).

been instrumental in the wider ascendancy of crime prevention (Ericson, Doyle, & Barry, 2003; O'Malley & Hutchinson, 2007).

Furthermore, there is a tendency in much criminology to operate within an insular understanding of crime control, one that often underplays both informal mechanisms and the influence of modes of regulation in other areas of social life. Criminologists tend to focus on spectacular displays of coercion and sovereign rule rather than mundane, routine, and ordinary operations of control. As Rose notes, "the criminal justice system itself plays a minor role in control practices" (2000). He outlines a need to "relocate the problem of crime and its control within a broader field of rationalities and technologies for the conduct of conduct" (ibid.). In many senses, as Garland (1997) notes, this observation is hardly new. However, it is true to say that significantly less criminological (rather than sociological) attention has been accorded to the ways in which systems and modalities of formal (crime) control are molded, influenced, and supported by other forms of regulation. Important exceptions include Cohen's (1985) incisive study of the blurring and inter-meshing of forms of behavioral control and Shearing and Stenning's (1983, 1987) path-breaking studies of the connections between forms of public and private policing.

Recently, much recent scholarship has drawn attention to the cross-fertilization and penetration of instrumental mentalities of prevention and control in the field of crime and policing (Johnston & Shearing, 2003; O'Malley, 1992), a domain traditionally associated with expressive and punitive senti-ments, censure, moral reform, and disapprobation. These more instrumental approaches are allied with what Garland (1996) aptly refers to as the "new criminologies of everyday life." However, in outlining the novelty of these adaptations, less attention has been given to the manner in which they are informed by and ape existing forms of regulation outside the field of crime control. For, as Jones and Newburn (2002) states, intimate, current shifts and developments in crime control and policing may represent a "formalization of social control" or a transformation in its presentation, more so than a funda-mental rupture with the past—as subtly implied in Cohen's and Shearing and Stenning's theses. In advancing this line of argument, I suggest that contem-porary trends in the regulation of low-level criminal and antisocial behavior not only reflect a formalization of social control but also express the growing penetration of consumerist and commercial values and modalities of control, as ways of structuring human associations and relations. In many senses, this is unsurprising given the contemporary dominance of consumerist values (Bauman, 1998) and the "marketisation of everyday life" (Clarke, Newman, Smith, Vidler, & Westmarland, 2007). As Collins notes, "the shift towards contractualisation in social life is perhaps one of the most potent symbols of political and business culture at the close of the twentieth century" (1999), and, we might add, beyond.

The Politics of Behavior

One of the most prescient and powerful British political voices that has championed the "antisocial behaviour agenda" as an urgent focus of governmental attention has been Frank Field, Labour MP, for Birkenhead and former Minister for Welfare Reform in the first Blair government. In his book *Neighbours from Hell: The Politics of Behaviour,* Field (2003) argues that the foremost issue facing government is the collapse in social virtues and common decencies. Politics, he contends, needs to reconnect with questions about "the kinds of people we want as citizens." For Field, the "politics of behavior" has replaced the historic "politics of class" that structured traditional political divisions and was instrumental in molding respectability and decency in Britain during the 19th and 20th centuries. He claims, "the drive for respectability has not only been thwarted but has gone into reverse" (2003).

Crucial to Field's analysis is the belief that the type of antisocial behavior that blights social relations is novel. Hence, it demands new modes of response: "because it is new, effective means of dealing with it have generally still to be devised" (ibid.). For Field, a distinctive characteristic of antisocial behavior is that each incident, by itself, does not warrant legal response, but in its regularity and repetitiveness, antisocial behavior "wields its destructive force" (ibid.). A further distinguishing feature is the focus on "public space" and local order. He is keen to stress that intervention should not encroach on the private sphere. However, once private opinions and the "values that determine conduct" operate in the public domain "they cease to be a private concern only, and become part of the stuff of politics" (ibid.). In sum, he continues: "If the new politics can be said to be about anything, it is on how best to challenge the private views and values which are impacting so adversely on public conduct" (ibid.).

Field places the blame for the decline in standards of civility on the absence of self-imposed rules of behavior and consideration for others due to the confluence of factors including:

- the demise of authority wherein "respect is no longer awarded, or even conceded, simply because a person holds a position";
- the decline of religiosity;
- the loss of people's ability to think over the long term and the contemporary cultural emphasis on the "here and now";
- dysfunctional families failing to teach their children common standards of decency and respect for others;

- the unconditionality of much welfare that has served to sever the connection between individuals' actions and acceptance of the consequences;
- the ineffectiveness of formal legal processes and sanctions in dealing with bad behavior.

According to Field, in the absence of a framework of rules, the egocentric side of human nature prevails. Bad behavior is not, therefore, seen as a response to injustice, deprivation, or inequality but simply the product of people's base instincts coming to the fore in a normative vacuum.

Field's analysis is pertinent, not only because his diagnosis of contemporary problems of behavior chimes with (and has informed) much government thinking but also because of the solutions that he proffers. He articulates the need for a new politics that seeks to rebuild "a shared sense of common decencies":

> the best way of doing this is to begin forging a series of contracts which cover the behaviour of all of us as we negotiate the public realm….These contracts need to cater for each key stage in our life, at birth, at school, in work, in drawing welfare and at retirement. If the tide is to be turned and anti-social behaviour put to flight, the task is nothing less than the forging of a series of public contracts on behaviour…to help shape behaviour these contracts have to be built up, taught and enforced" (ibid., p. 82).

For Field, contracts are crucial in reminding individuals of the reciprocal relationship between rights and responsibilities and reinforcing the message that something received demands something given. They also allow people to participate directly in their construction, to acknowledge the norms they set down through signing ceremonies, and to be held to account for their actions. From this perspective, microsocial contracts constitute a lived experience of active engagement with normative value systems—of civility and decency—relations of mutual obligations and accountability for conduct. The spread of behavioral contracts across all walks of social life, extending from the cradle to the grave, in effect, is intended to establish "a social highway code" (2003), providing clear parameters to guide conduct. In short, through the process of active contracting, young people can become, in Field's terms, "the kinds of people we want as citizens."

Contractual Governance

Contract is a specific instrument of social regulation and a legal form but also a way of conceiving social relations, commitments, and obligations. As a mentality, contract constructs specific ways of thinking about the possibilities of social ordering, responsibility, and discipline. When people enter contractual relations, or those that ape contractual forms, not only do they take on the obligations set down in the agreed terms, but they also enter a particular frame of reference that constructs the way they relate to others. Contracts speak to the subjects of regulation in a manner that regard them as individual agents capable of taking control of their own risks and life trajectories. Contracts communicate a language of self-determination, choice, and the active construction of one's own future possibilities, in a manner that is simultaneously calculative and formal. Contracts engage people as "active and free citizens, as informed and responsible consumers, as members of self-managing communities and organizations, as actors in democratizing social movements, and as agents capable of taking control of our own risks" (Dean, 1999). As such, contract as a mentality and mode of governance is consistent with "institutionalised individualism" (Beck & Beck-Gernsheim, 2001), whereby human personhood and identity are increasingly transformed from a fixed "given" into a malleable "task." A defining feature of contemporary living is the need to construct and invent one's own self and actively shape one's future. Individuals are progressively charged with responsibility for self-determination: for consciously making choices, for performing the associated tasks, and for the consequences and implications of their accomplishment. "Individualization" highlights the manner in which individuals are invited, encouraged, cajoled, and even compelled to construct their personal biographies through their own actions and conscious decisions. Life trajectories in "an age of individualization" have become "elective," comprising "do-it-yourself" biographies (Bauman, 2001). Compulsory and obligatory self-determination becomes a prevailing narrative. As Beck and Beck-Gernsheim contend: "Life, death, gender, corporeality, identity, religion, marriage, parenthood, social ties—all becoming decidable down to the small print; once fragmented into options, everything must be decided" (2001). To this list we might add crime, deviance, antisocial behavior, and, by implication, social exclusion. Contract as a technology of social control both manifests and advances institutionalized individualism.

Collins usefully highlights the manner in which contracts establish "a discrete communication system between individuals" in which "the contract 'thinks' about the relation between people in a particular way" (1999). Contract transforms diffuse expectations about the future into new, more specific and concrete obligations. In this, contracts bestow a quality of "explicitness." However, contracts also confine expectations and separate them from wider social commitments, pressures, norms, or practices that are indeterminate and extensive. As such, contracts are delimited and exhibit a quality of "boundedness." They encircle particular facets of a relationship, sheltering wider aspects of human interactions from view, thus reducing the complexity of human relations to specified essentials and pathways that have significance within the contractual arrangement. Those aspects of conduct deemed worthy of specification are bestowed with a greater salience and become measurable. This is what Collins refers to as the "valuation of conduct" (ibid.). In this sense, contracts are myopic. By bracketing off wider obligations and relations (in the name of reducing complexity), they accord heightened value to narrowly delimited and exclusive points of reference. The fact that a young person "contractually" agrees regularly to attend school, to apologize for previous bad behavior, to look actively for work, to not disturb the neighbors, or to not associate with certain peers, for example, accords to those forms of conduct additional significance. Conversely, for the purpose of the contract other things become less important.

This myopic quality of contract also means that only those commitments and obligations specified in the contract can be expected to be mobilized in support of the contractual goals. This is particularly problematic where the capacity to realize contract goals lies beyond responsibilities or competencies of the parties. For example, where a contract is agreed between a young person and a housing officer, it may necessitate ignoring the range of implications and possible inputs from other services, such as education or health precisely because the relevant agencies were not party to the contract and therefore could not be mobilized directly. In theory, multidisciplinary and interagency governance structures, such as youth offending services, may be better placed to avoid such shortcoming. In practice, however, contracts are likely to restrict any reciprocal support available to those services most readily available to the contracting parties.

As Marx (1954) noted, contracts reduce commitments to commodities that are the subject of exchange. Enduring social relations and diffuse social commitments that cannot be so commodified—exchanged—are devalued. Relations are viewed through a lens of exchange. In Collins' view, this dimension to contractual thinking endows "social relations with a *currency of exchange* which is quantifiable and measurable" (1999, emphasis in original). Contractual relations think in terms of "what can I get for what?" Maximizing benefit to oneself is the credo of the contract. Consequently, contracting can encourage an instrumental logic that displaces or marginalizes normative commitments as the basis of mutual obligations and reciprocity. It may foster a culture in which rational economic behavior dominates as nobler motives of moral worth are eclipsed by baser instincts of personal gain. This produces what some commentators have noted as an "irony of contracting"—that while effective contracting springs from and presupposes environments of trust, the introduction of contract may foster the breakdown of trust (Neu, 1991). This perverse effect may arise precisely because contracts appear to discount the value of wider social relations by thinking of relationships purely in terms of autonomous unsituated obligations. The contractualization of social life is important, not because it strips social relations of meaning, as Marx's theory of commodification suggests, but rather because it attributes specific meaning to, and directs, the flow of social relations: "In short, if a social relation is conceived of as contractual, then people tend to exhibit contractual behavior within it and towards it" (Collins 1999).

Furthermore, contracts presuppose a conscious awareness of the future and a desire to control uncertainty by regulating its excesses. Thus, the logic of contract connects with wider discourses of prudent risk management and "actuarial justice" (Feeley & Simon, 1994). It assumes future-oriented and preventive thinking. Contracts necessitate what Macneil (1980) refers to as "presentiation": the bringing of the future into the present. Governing the future, paradoxically, requires both planning and flexibility. Planning seeks to know the future on the basis of the present but confronts the demand for flexibility in the face of ever-changing circumstances. As such, contracting allows for the specification of objectives and goals, as well as how these are to be measured and monitored. In looking to the future, contracts require the use of foresight in planning.

Crucially, contracts assume a "sense of choice." They presuppose an acceptance on behalf of the parties of the terms agreed. However, a concept of contract does not require that choice be real, only that the parties act as if it were. As in most commercial contracts, the reality frequently is that the terms are preordained by the more powerful party and imposed on the other party. Choice is invariably reduced to a "take it or leave it" relation, as reflected in the routine and extensive use of standard form contracts in consumer affairs. Nevertheless, it is the acceptance of imposed obligations that provides the essential quality of contracts. This is what Macneil refers to as the norm of "effectuation of consent": "Contractual exercises of choice have not only the usual effect of sacrificing other opportunities, but a very special characteristic of their own: the power in someone else to restrain one's future choices" (1980). The potency of this quality may frequently be reinforced through the symbolic signing of agreements. The contract here is a formal representation that parties have enlisted themselves to certain obligations. This constitutes a key adhesive in the "bindingness of obligations" with implications for compliance.

Freedom's Children?

In contrast to Field's analysis, Beck and Beck-Gernsheim assert that "the talk of a 'decline of values' contains something else, namely the fear of freedom, including the fear of freedom's children, who must struggle with new and different types of problems raised by *internalised* freedom" (2001, emphasis in original). "Individualization" exhibits both a positive face and a dark side. "Creating the self" generates self-determination with democratic potential, whereby individuals can escape from fate and play a greater part in public life, particularly evident in the increased range of choices and wider public participation available to girls. However, the flip side of the obligation to actively shape one's future destiny is personal blame for failure. How one lives becomes a "biographical solution to systemic contradictions" (Beck, 1992). Risks and contradictions continue to be socially produced, but it is the responsibility and the necessity of coping with them that have become increasingly individualized. Binding traditions and long-term commitments have been replaced by institutional guidance regarding how one's life is to be organized. This guidance focuses more evidently on influencing people's choice rather than the circumstance in which choices are made or people's capacities to realize their preferences. As a consequence, individualization produces vastly different effects where there are institutional resources (welfare, education, health, human rights, etc.) that people can draw upon in coping with the contradictions of modern personal biographies. Failure is internalized as the product of one's own doings. Causes are detached from wider structural or societal dynamics and become fastened to individual responsibility. Social problems are recast as personal faults, individual deficits, and psychological deficiencies—the result of (bad) choices as well as the incapacity of individuals to respond to opportunities and shape events.

Ultimately, public issues are redefined as private and personal troubles. From this perspective, we can see how the skills and competencies associated with contracting have, and continue to, become increasingly fundamental for young people in shaping their futures, negotiating their transitions into adulthood and attaining their status as consumer-citizens. Preparations and training for adulthood are thus associated with "learning to contract."* As a development in schooling, "learning to contract" is implicitly being implemented in the shift toward "personalized education" and "individual learning promises" (Arnot, 2008; Barber, 1996), as well as explicitly reproduced in the use of contracts and home-school agreements, both within and in relation to the school.† Thus, the skills of contracting are promoted and cultivated through experience. In the contemporary jargon, the "soft skills" or "noncognitions" of negotiation, decision making, motivation, the ability to plan for the future, and self-control have grown in salience. According to research by the Institute for Public Policy Research (IPPR) comparing the strength of the link between

---

* In a deliberate, if oblique, reference to Willis' (1977) ground-breaking study *Learning to Labour*, I am intimating, here, that in a consumer society the production of contractually competent individuals is becoming a contemporary function of education alongside the production of skilled and disciplined laborers.
† Home–school agreements were introduced for all maintained schools and city technology colleges by the School Standards and Framework Act 1998 (Section 110). They require the negotiation and publication of expectations and responsibilities on behalf of the school, parents, and pupils.

noncognitions and social mobility in the 12 years between those children born in 1970 and 1958, personal and social skills or "capabilities" became "33 times more important in determining relative life chances" (Margo & Dixon, with Pearce & Reed, 2006). However, the data do not suggest that this reflects greater social mobility. On the contrary, parental income increasingly determined people's noncognitive development. The findings show that "the rising association between parental income and background, children's personal and social skills and attributes, and subsequent achievement explains 22 per cent of the rise in *social immobility* between the 1958 and 1970 cohorts" (ibid., emphasis added). This research prompts fundamental questions about the extent to which contractual capacity, itself, may be an increasingly defining attribute of social status and determining factor in young people's prospects. If so, this raises considerable implications not only for the negotiation of contracts with young people but also for the likely differential impact of contracting. Simply put, contracting may be another way of punishing the poor for being poor.

Contractual Governance and Young People

There are noteworthy ironies in contracting with young people. First, as far as the law is concerned, young people under 18 years cannot usually be held to a contract because they are deemed legally not to have attained full "contractual capacity." Yet, for the purposes of contemporary technologies of contractual governance, young people are to be treated as if they are "contractually competent." It was precisely the ascendancy of the view that child labor was not "free labor" because children did not have sufficient contractual capacity that prompted the introduction of the early Factory Acts in the 19th century to protect children from the tyrannies of contract. There could be little pretense that the labor–exchange relationship was freely entered into or that children had any equal bargaining position, a line of argument evident in the debates on the 1802 Factory Act.* This view of the child as "unfree" drew powerful inspiration from associated debates about the inequities of contract promoted by the antislavery movement that was reaching a crescendo at much the same time (Cunningham, 1991). As victims of an unconstrained economy, child laborers came to be compared with slaves, a comparison that underscored the notion that their condition was not one of "freedom." According to reformers, working children were to be restored to a "true" position of childhood which entailed protection and dependence. Children came to be viewed as having

---

* The Factory Act of 1833 represented a decisive first step in this direction as it sought to protect children younger than 9 years from the workplace and restricted hours for those younger than 13 years to 8 hours per day and 12 hours a day for those younger than 18 years.

insufficient capacity to be treated as autonomous individuals. They were thus explicitly excluded from the Social Contract. In the emerging 19th century conception of childhood, young people were to be conceived as "contractual nonpersons" (Cashmore, 1997). Children first needed to be trained in the prerequisites of thinking contractually. The expansion of universal compulsory education was to provide such training. Modern schooling, therefore, from its inception became the crucible in which a new relation of childhood–adulthood could be fashioned, by removing children from a wage-earning relationship (Aries, 1962; Postman, 1982).

Rather than effacing status, contractualism reconfigures individuals in a different kind of status, deriving from their capacity to contract. For, as Yeatman suggests, the contract as a means of organizing social affairs, rather than displacing status, relies on and embeds a specific understanding of status: "The contractual social order has its own distinctive status specification of what it means to be a person with contractual capacity" (1997). For people to be treated as contracting parties, they must be deemed to have acquired certain competencies, capable of knowing and articulating their preferences and acting upon them. Here, contractual capacity constitutes all the hall-marks of status, as fixed and as fundamental as property ownership, family background/class, gender, and race were to a feudal or precontractual social order. As commentators have noted (Mills, 1997; Pateman, 1988), at different times in history, these social divisions have themselves been determinants of contractual capacity—such that only white male property owners were at one time deemed capable of contracting. As Yeatman notes: "This idea of status as a supplement to contract begins to suggest that status and contract might not only co-exist, but mediate each other" (1997). Contracting with young people suggests that youth occupies a deeply ambivalent social status, at one moment rational and at the next moment incompetent.

Second, contract is understood as a radically different way of construct-ing social relations from, and in contrast to, family ties and parenting obli-gations (Maclean & Eekelaar, 1997). Nevertheless, through new modes of regulatory governance, we are witnessing the use of contract in structuring parenting commitments and family responsibilities, most explicitly in the form of "parenting contracts."* Within liberal contract theory, family ties and the social status that accrues to them are the antithesis of contractual relations (Maine, 1970). Yet not only does this dichotomy between contract

---

* Parenting contracts were first introduced by the Anti-Social Behaviour Act 2003 (Sections 19 and 25) and extended under the Education and Inspection Act 2006. These are volun-tary agreements between parents and a youth offending team, local authority, or regis-tered social landlord in relation to a child's crime and antisocial behavior or between parents and a school or education authority in relation to school indiscipline and truancy. Parenting contracts set out conditions that parents agree to comply with over a certain period and support arrangements. Failure to comply may result in a parenting order.

as choice and family/status as restraint or "nonfreedom" ignore the manner in which commercial contracting relies upon and presupposes noncontractual relations (Macaulay, 1963)—including the unpaid work of families and caregivers—but it also fails to attend to the nature of the "caring" relations that prevail in families. As Kittay notes, such relations are conceptually and normatively different: "The virtue of care, the asymmetrical, non-reciprocal and partial devotion to another's well-being, which requires that one makes oneself transparent to the other's needs, is a distinctive moral capacity" (2005). Dependency, from this vantage point, is not a pathological state but a fundamental human condition:

> The inevitable dependencies that arise in human life always serve to join us each to one another. We are connected through our own vulnerability when dependent and our vulnerability when caring for dependents, as well as through the potential of each of us to become dependent and to have the responsibility for a dependent (Kittay, 2001, p. 527).

In contrast to contractual relations, family relations are not conceived as voluntary—there is no pretense at equality and there is no clear notion of reciprocity. As Held notes:

> The relative powerlessness of the child is largely irrelevant to most of the project of growing up. When the child is physically weakest, as in infancy and illness, the child can "command" the greatest amount of attention and care from the mothering person because of the seriousness of the child's needs (1987, p. 131).

This is not to neglect that care and caring relationships are often structured by inequalities. They can give rise to abuse of power and forms of unwanted dependency. It does, however, caution us to consider the extent to which an "ethos of contacting" may be in tension with, or serve to undermine, an "ethic of care." While the former emphasizes choice, autonomy, exchange, and the attainment of instrumental goals, the latter centers on interdependency, acknowledges vulnerability, and encourages normative commitments and trust. Whether the absence of care can be rectified by contracting (as implied in parenting contracts) remains a moot point.

One of the principal lines of objection to the social use of contracting put forward by legal commentators has been to highlight the "counterfeit" nature of the contract "as a sham" (Wonnacott, 1999). Commentators correctly highlight not only the legal and moral obstacles to contracting with young people but also that the reality is often one of limited choice, a lack of real options, and a weak bargaining position on the part of the young person. Triggered by antisocial or criminal conduct and in the shadow of the coercive criminal justice apparatus, restorative practices and antisocial behavior agreements are invariable contaminated by an imbalance of power relations. The only option available may be nonparticipation and the resultant coercive and/or punitive sanctions that await. Choice, central to the ideal liberal contract, is all but absent or heavily constrained. Nor does the young person have significant "resources" or "tools" with which to challenge the norms, values, and procedures of the regulatory system. For a child in a room full of adults, negotiation may mean little. What levers can he or she deploy to advance his/her position? In reality, the "contract" is not a product of a fair negotiation between two equal parties but the outcome of an imbalanced relation between state power on the one hand and an individual young person and his or her parent/carer on the other hand. However, the extent to which the experience of contracting conforms to ideal contract norms is ultimately an empirical one that is likely to vary both between different technologies of control and in their implementation.

The nonreciprocal nature of much contractual governance initiated through the "antisocial behaviour agenda" was acknowledged by one of its principal architects, David Blunkett, in an interview:

> I think there was a desire to see building blocks which would entitle you to be able to dig your way out of a problem and to require that society also recognised that there might be something it needed to do as well. And we haven't been as good on that latter bit as we have on the others. My regret is we didn't ever really get properly engaged…in saying what do we do on the positive side of helping people themselves to get out of this, rather than merely the threat that if you don't comply, you'll be in trouble (personal interview, January 2007).

The policy preoccupation with enforcement is evidenced through the lagged development of institutionalized support programs to assist people who are the subject of specific orders to overcome personal difficulties that might impede their compliance. For example, it was 5 years after ASBOs were first introduced that individual support orders (ISOs) became available, to assist young people given an ASBO.* Despite the fact that when a juvenile receives an ASBO, the court is required to consider making an ISO, during 2004/2005, merely 1% of ASBOs had an ISO attached.

Young People, Rights, and Responsibilities

The use of contracting with young people reflects a wider paradox regarding the status of youth. Although the period of preadulthood has been extended in recent years in most fields of public policy, it has contracted in relation

---

* ISOs are available for 10- to 17-year-olds and provide support and "positive obligations" to address the causes of behavior and assist compliance with the terms of the ASBO which can only impose "negative obligations."

to criminalization and the "politics of behavior." On the one hand, we have witnessed the stretching of youth beyond the teenage years both de facto and de jure. Entry into the workplace is postponed for many as education extends into the mid-twenties and the average age at which women first have a child continues to rise. The government's intention to raise the minimum school leaving age from 16 to 18 by 2013 is further evidence of this wider trend. So too, the raising of the age at which young people can buy tobacco from 16 years to 18 years in 2007 reflects not only greater knowledge about the harms of tobacco but also the perception that young people need to be protected from their own "bad choices."

On the other hand, we have seen the adulteration of young people in relation to criminal wrongdoing and antisocial behavior. Children and young people are increasingly treated like adults for the purpose of rendering them responsible for their conduct. This adulteration is particularly marked in the jurisdictions of the United Kingdom as compared with other European countries (Muncie & Goldson, 2006) and reflects a deeper cultural malaise engendered by the "fear of freedom's children" that echoes throughout the contemporary "politics of behavior." In the realm of criminal justice, the countervailing logic of adulteration is evidenced not only by the abolition of *doli incapax* and the concomitant lowering of criminal responsibility to children as young as 10 (under the Crime and Disorder Act 1998) but also the more general erosion of "special procedural protections" once deemed essential to safeguard young people from the stigma and formality of the adult criminal justice process. Children are increasingly being treated "like adults" for criminal justice purposes as changes to the youth court, youth sentences, and custodial regimes have eroded the distinctiveness of the youth justice system. The significant use of ASBOs in relation to juveniles, for example, has hastened an erosion of the right to anonymity in civil and criminal proceedings (Cobb, 2007).* Home Office guidance explicitly advocates the identification of people given an ASBO, including young individuals, as integral to enforcement (Home Office, 2005).† Furthermore, because they are informal, acceptable behavior contracts can be, and are being, used with children younger than 10 years. Here also, official guidance promotes the use of publicity (Home Office, 2007b).

Despite the government's insistence on the correlativity of responsibility and rights in the so-called "something for something" society lauded in the *Respect and Responsibility* white paper (Home Office, 2003) that preceded the

---

* More than 40% of all ASBOs issued up to the end of 2005 in England and Wales were for young people aged 10–17 years.

† Furthermore, section 49(4A) of the Crime (Sentences) Act 1997 provides the Youth Court with the power to set aside the presumption in favor of anonymity if it is judged to be "in the public interest."

AntiSocial Behaviour Act 2003, this appears to be singularly lacking in relation to children and young people. Although criminal responsibility attaches
to children as young as 10 years, it is less clear what rights accrue them from
this age. Just as there are dangers of underprotection as well as overprotec-
tion, there are pitfalls of too much as well as too little responsibility. One
of the protections of childhood has traditionally taken the form of young
people not being burdened with inappropriate responsibilities or compelled
to take decisions that they are not competent to take. Children may be doubly
vulnerable—first by being denied participation rights they may be unable to
control the experiences which they are subject to because of their status as
child and, second, they may be burdened with excessive responsibility beyond
their capabilities. There are clear dangers of inappropriately overburdening
young people through forms of contractual governance that presuppose the
capacity to formulate and articulate preferences, weigh risks, compare opportunities and costs, choose from options presented, and comply with decisions
made. Exercising "voice" in deliberative negotiations and restorative forums
demands certain attributes and competencies that may not be available to all
young individuals. Some young people may be better capable of exercising
their voice than others.

One response to the dilemma of young people's engagement in forms
of contractual governance might be to remove decision making out of the
context of criminalization and the shadow of criminal justice altogether.
Although this would avert much of the stigma, blame allocation, and punishment traditionally associated with criminal justice proceedings, it would
not necessarily evade other punitive sanctions that may come into play in
the regulation of young individuals. One of the evident insights provided
by antisocial behavior interventions is that noncriminal sanctions can be as
punitive as, if not more punitive, than criminal punishments. For example,
the threat of eviction from social housing often serves as a greater incentive to engage in acceptable behavior contracts than criminal prosecution.
Similarly, exclusion or expulsion from school may have a greater impact on a
young person than a fine or criminal record.

Compliance

Like all interventions that seek to change behavior, forms of contractual governance rest on certain assumptions and theories about human motivations,
values, and personal capacities. These are rarely rendered explicit either in
general policy debates or in instances of individual decision making. Yet,
the various new technologies of control embody a variety of (sometimes
confused) assumptions about compliance, as a result of which young people
may be being set up to fail. To what extent are motivations understood as

either instrumental or moral and/or are young people conceived as capable of knowing their interests and articulating their preferences? To highlight the complex mix of both motivations and capacities among young people, it is useful to specify five broad ideal types that revolve around two axes informing compliance: the first (Points 1 and 2) relates to questions of motivation and the second concerns different levels of capacity or agency along a continuum (Points 3–5):*

1. Normative compliance: whereby motivation is triggered by normative commitments, beliefs, attachments, and perceptions of legitimacy—a moral agent capable of virtuous acts.
2. Instrumental compliance: whereby motivation is premised on maximizing self-interest and stimulated by sanctions and rewards—a rational choice actor.
3. Unassisted compliance: whereby the individual is deemed fully competent and able to exercise self-determination and personal agency—an active agent capable of independent action.
4. Enabled compliance: whereby the individual is deemed not fully competent but dependent and with limited capacity for independent action, self-determination, and personal agency—a needy individual requiring empowerment and assistance.
5. Imposed compliance: whereby the individual is a passive victim of circumstance, unable or unwilling to assert sufficient agency due to his or her limited scope of action—an incompetent, dependent, or vulnerable individual.

These can be represented diagrammatically as follows (Figure 8.1).

Reality is more fluid than such bald typologies might suggest. However, they usefully accentuate the different, and potentially competing, assumptions that underlie and inform specific regimes of regulation. They highlight how technologies of control that assume those to whom they are targeted are moral agents will have very different effects if most are in fact self-interested actors. Likewise, regimes of control that assume people to be self-interested actors will have distorted effects if they serve to erode normative commitments and motivations. Similarly, policies that treat people as lacking in agency may patronize and demotivate. Finally, where policies treat people as wholly active agents, they may give them too much scope such that they may make mistakes that damage their own or others' welfare. With regard to young people in particular, the typologies prompt consideration of the extent to which and how young people are to be assisted and enabled to make

---

* This typology draws inspiration from, and is influenced by, the work of Le Grand (2003) and Bottoms (2001).

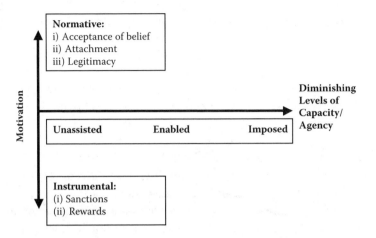

Figure 8.1 Types of compliance.

agreements and comply with them. As already suggested, contractual governance implies notions of exchange and instrumental reasoning. It holds out "sticks and carrots"—the apt title of the Scottish guidance on the use of acceptable behavior contracts (Scottish Executive, 2005)—as levers of motivation and behavioral change. This prompts concerns about the extent to which moral judgments and normative commitments are eclipsed by baser instincts of personal gain and individual benefit. Despite its instrumental discourse, however, contractualism also embodies values and virtues (Freedland & King, 2003).

Frequently, "sticks and carrots" are accompanied and supplemented by "sermons" in which notions of responsible agency are conceived in highly moralistic tones that accord privilege to individual autonomy and choice. As Jayasuriya contends, the new contractualism embodies a "rather distinctive moral sociology which seeks to lay out proper modes of social conduct" (2002). This gives rise to a paradox of liberal intent producing illiberal outcomes—a neoliberal instrument (the contract) hosting a neoconservative moral content. This clash of values has distinct implications for compliance.

In reality, young people are liable to be motivated by diverse levers, dependent on the particular situation in which a decision is made. The crucial question, then, is whether different assumptions about motivation can coexist without adverse implications for compliance. This raises issues regarding possible interaction effects, both between the various types of compliance and between compliance mechanisms and different groups of individuals (Bottoms, 2001). These may serve to reinforce pressures toward compliance, pull in different directions potentially undermining each other, or compound pressures against compliance.

Bottoms astutely observes that: "Those who seek to induce compliance in others very often think they know what it will be like to be on the receiving end of the measures that they administer. But…people in power frequently misjudge their audiences" (2001). The implications of this insight are likely to be particularly apposite with regard to regulatory systems designed by adults and imposed on young people. Yet we know very little about the manner in which young people interpret and react to attempts to alter their behavior through diverse forms of normative and instrumental inducements. We also know little about how the interaction of competing logics is understood and experienced by young people. What are the implications of treating a young person as capable one moment and incompetent the next, as a rational actor one day and a moral agent the next? Young people, as we have seen, are subject to diverse, inconsistent messages as to their competencies as they proceed through their transition to adulthood. More profoundly, young people may experience being treated as fully competent—as an adult—as liberating or constraining, or even perhaps both simultaneously. Denying their youthful status, their dependencies and limitations may impose obligations and responsibilities on young people that they are not well equipped to deal with.

Conclusion

In drawing connections between regulatory innovations in the field of antisocial behavior and restorative justice practices, it has not been my intention to suggest that these social technologies of justice are the same in their origins, values, or impact. Nor is it my intention to imply that restorative justice is doomed to a fate of illiberal outcomes akin to those prompted by the "antisocial behaviour agenda" (Burney 2005). Rather, I have sought to highlight how we might understand restorative practice not as some counterfactual to "bad" or "retributive" justice that runs against the grain of the contemporary culture of control (as some commentators would have us believe) but as sharing certain core features with a shift to a more individualized, calculative, future-oriented, and "responsibilizing" form of control that reproduces dominant features of regulation derived from the fields of commercial and consumer relations. As with the various technologies spawned to tackle antisocial behavior, restorative justice expresses a contractualization in which a particular form of responsible agency is extolled, one that sits awkwardly with the lived realities of evolving competencies among children and young people. Furthermore, as I have sought to show, contractualism as a way of structuring interpersonal relations has ambivalent implications for an ethic of care that informs relations with young people.

Importantly, these social technologies encourage a questioning of many of the assumptions of traditional criminal justice, most notably with regard to changing behavior and compliance. As awkward as the insertion of contractual modes of regulation are in regulating youthful conduct, it opens up an important debate about the social status of young people, their developing competencies, and the manner in which they should be involved in decisions about their futures, as well as the conditions under which their agency and voice might be enhanced and maximized. The implications of these insights have been insufficiently grasped or addressed in practice.

In this chapter I have largely sought to advance the explanatory and analytical value of contractual governance as a way of seeing and describing a cluster of regulatory developments as well as highlighting potential implications. However, contractual governance also raises a host of normative concerns about the appropriateness and ethics of certain types of regulation. One implication of seeing regulatory reform through the lens of contractualization is to question the extent to which given arrangements live up to the (ideal) norms of contract and to seek to render practices more adequately contractual. To do so, consideration would need to be given to "the building and resourcing of effective contractual capacity of all individuals; and the requirement that not just the points of exit and entry to relationships become accountable to contractualist norms, but that the internal conduct of these relationships are accountable to contractualist norms" (Yeatman, 1997). This might entail maximizing the conditions under which individual autonomy can be exercised both in terms of a minimum adequacy of options (to enhance substantive autonomy) and a minimum bargaining capacity (to guarantee procedural autonomy); ensuring a sufficient degree of reciprocity and mutuality on the part of the parties; minimizing coercion and the threat of sanctions; and guaranteeing reviewability, democratic oversight, and the contestability of unfair terms. In many instances, there is an evident need to subject contractual governance to constitutional rules of democratic participation and procedural standards of fairness. In essence, there is a need for the control of control. The challenge is to ensure against dangers regarding the arbitrary and inequitable use of contracting with its potential to micromanage individual behavior in ways that are more intrusive and illiberal and to render accountable the significant discretion accorded negotiators.

The introduction of contractual language has brought with it an allusion to, and illusion of, "choice" on the part of young people (and their parents). Restorative interventions and acceptable behavior and parenting contracts, in particular, are premised on the idea that agreements have been consented to— symbolically reinforced by signing ceremonies. In the process, the regulated have become the architects of their own regime of regulation in which they are actively enlisted to comply with the terms. Subsequent failure becomes a double failure. Individuals both transgress the social norms and their own commitments. In being treated as responsible and capable agents, thus they are to be judged. The extent to which this narrative truly reflects young people's experiences of behavioral regulation is questionable. How their failure is interpreted by others, notably legal authorities, is paramount. The concern is that more punitive futures await those unable to comply. Punitive outcomes become more easily justified where individuals have been given the opportunity to participate in and choose their destiny, despite the fact that, ultimately, they may have little scope to assert their agency or control the wider pressures that influence their lives. An unpalatable conclusion—notably for proponents of restorative justice—may be that the new social technologies of regulation extend rather than undermine the place of punishment at the apex of regulation. In this manner, contractualization is in danger of redefining the problems confronting people as no longer the product of social or structural forces but rather as a result of personal decisions. Failure to comply becomes symptomatic of poor choices made by uninformed, unmotivated, incompetent, or irresponsible individuals. The plight of those who fail the appropriate standards of conduct of the new citizen-consumer is reconstituted as an outcome of their own personal choices rather than a compelling symbol of the need for a politics of social solidarity and care. They are the architects of their own predicament.

Acknowledgment

I gratefully acknowledge the generous support of a Leverhulme Trust Major Research Fellowship that facilitated much of the research that informs this chapter.

References

Ariès, P. Y. (1962). *Centuries of childhood: A social history of family life*. London: Jonathan Cape.

Arnot, M. (2008). *Educating the gendered citizen*. London: Routledge.

Barber, M. (1996). *The learning game. Arguments for an education revolution*. London: Victor Gollancz.

Bauman, Z. (1998). *Work, consumerism and the new poor*. Buckingham: Open University Press.

Bauman, Z. (2001). *The individualised society*. Oxford: Polity Press.

Beck, U. (1992). *Risk society: Towards a new modernity*. London: Sage.

Beck, U., & Beck-Gernsheim, E. (2001). *Individualization*. London: Sage.

Beem, C., & Mead, L. (Eds.). (2005). *Welfare reform and political theory*. New York: Russell Sage Foundation.

Bottoms, A. E. (1995). The philosophy and politics of punishment and sentencing. In C. Clarkson & R. Morgan (Eds.), *The politics of sentencing reform* (pp. 17–49). Oxford: Clarendon Press.

Bottoms, A. E. (2001). Compliance and community penalties. In A. E. Bottoms, L. Gelsthorpe, & S. Rex (Eds.), *Community penalties: Change and challenge* (pp. 87–116). Cullompton: Willan.

Braithwaite, J. (1998). Restorative justice. In M. Tonry (Ed.), *Handbook of crime and punishment* (pp. 323–344). New York: Oxford University Press.

Braithwaite, J. (2003). What's wrong with the sociology of punishment? *Theoretical Criminology, 7,* 5–28.

Burney, E. (1999). *Crime and banishment: Nuisance and exclusion in social housing.* Winchester: Waterside Press.

Burney, E. (2005). *Making people behave: Anti-social behaviour, politics and policy.* Cullompton: Willan.

Cashmore, J. (1997). Children: Contractual non-persons? In G. Davis, B. Sullivan, & A. Yeatman (Eds.), *The new contractualism?* (pp. 57–70). Melbourne: Macmillan.

Clarke, J., Newman, J., Smith, N., Vidler, E., & Westmarland, L. (2007). *Creating citizen-consumers: Changing publics and changing public services.* London: Sage.

Cobb, N. (2007). Governance through publicity: ASBOs, young people, and the problematization of the right to anonymity. *Journal of Law and Society, 34,* 342–373.

Cohen, S. (1985). *Visions of social control.* Cambridge: Polity.

Collins, H. (1999). *Regulating contracts.* Oxford: Oxford University Press.

Cowan, D., Pantazis, C., & Gilroy, R. (2001). Social housing as crime control. *Social and Legal Studies, 10,* 435–457.

Crawford, A. (2001). Joined-up but fragmented: Contradiction, ambiguity and ambivalence at the heart of Labour's "Third Way". In R. Matthews & J. Pitts (Eds.), *Crime, disorder and community safety* (pp. 54–80). London, Routledge.

Crawford, A. (2003). Contractual governance of deviant behaviour. *Journal of Law and Society, 30,* 479–505.

Crawford, A. (forthcoming). *Governing the future: The contractual governance of anti-social behaviour.* Cambridge: Cambridge University Press.

Crawford, A., & Burden, T. (2005). *Integrating victims in restorative youth justice.* Bristol: Policy Press.

Crawford, A., & Newburn, T. (2003). *Youth offending and restorative justice.* Cullompton: Willan.

Cunningham, H. (1991). *Children of the poor: Representations of childhood since the seventeenth century.* Oxford: Blackwell.

Daly, K. (2003). Mind the gap: Restorative justice in theory and practice. In A. von Hirsch, J. Roberts, A. E. Bottoms, K. Roach, & M. Schiff (Eds.), *Restorative justice and criminal justice* (pp. 219–236). Oxford: Hart.

Daly, K. (2004). Pile it on: More texts on RJ. *Theoretical Criminology, 8,* 499–507.

Dean, M. (1999). *Governmentality: Power and rule in modern society.* London: Sage.

Dignan, J. (2006). Juvenile justice, criminal courts and restorative justice. In G. Johnstone & D. van Ness (Eds.), *Handbook of restorative justice* (pp. 269–291). Cullompton: Willan.

Ericson, R., Doyle, A., & Barry, D. (2003). *Insurance as governance.* Toronto: University of Toronto Press.

Feeley, M., & Simon, J. (1994). Actuarial justice: The emerging new criminal law. In D. Nelken (Ed.), *The futures of criminology* (pp. 173–201). London: Sage.

Field, F. (2003). *Neighbours from hell: The politics of behaviour.* London: Politico's.

Freedland, M., & King, D. (2003). Contractual governance and illiberal contracts: Some problems of contractualism as an instrument of behaviour management by agencies of government. *Cambridge Journal of Economics, 27,* 465–477.

Garland, D. (1996). The limits of the sovereign state: Strategies of crime control in contemporary society. *British Journal of Criminology, 36*, 445–471.

Garland, D. (1997). "Governmentality" and the problem of crime: Foucault, criminology, sociology. *Theoretical Criminology, 1*, 173–214.

Garland, D. (2001). *The culture of control.* Oxford: Oxford University Press.

Held, V. (1987). Non-contractual society: A feminist view. *Canadian Journal of Philosophy, 13*(suppl.), 111–137.

Home Office. (2003). *Respect and responsibility—Taking a stand against anti-social behaviour* (Cm 5778). London: Home Office.

Home Office. (2005). *Guidance on publicising anti-social behaviour orders.* London: Home Office.

Home Office. (2007a). *Tools and powers to tackle anti-social behaviour.* London: Home Office.

Home Office. (2007b). *Acceptable behaviour contracts and agreements.* London: Home Office.

Johnston, L., & Shearing, C. (2003). *Governing security.* London: Routledge.

Jones, T., & Newburn, T. (2002). The transformation of policing. *British Journal of Criminology, 42*, 129–146.

Kittay, E. F. (2001, April). A feminist public ethic of care meets the new communitarian family policy. *Ethics, 111*:523–547.

Kittay, E. F. (2005). Equality, dignity and disability. In M. A. Lyons & F. Waldron (Eds.), *Perspectives on equality: The Second Seamus Heaney Lectures* (pp. 93–119). Dublin: Liffey Press.

Jayasuriya, K. (2002). The new contractualism: Neo-liberal or democratic? *Political Quarterly,* 309–320.

Le Grand, J. (2003). *Motivation, agency and public policy.* Oxford: Oxford University Press.

Macaulay, S. (1963). Non-contractual relations in business: A preliminary study. *American Sociological Review, 28*, 55–67.

Macneil, I. (1980). *The new social contract.* New Haven: Yale University Press.

Maclean, M., & Eekelaar, J. (1997). *The parenting obligation.* Oxford: Hart.

Maine, H. S. (1970). *Ancient law: Its connections with the early history of society and its relation to modern ideas.* London: John Murray.

Margo, J., & Dixon, M. (with Pearce, N., & Reed, H.). (2006). *Freedom's orphans: Raising youth in a changing world.* London: IRRP.

Marx, K. (1954). *Capital, volume one.* London: Lawrence & Wishart.

Matthews, R. (Ed.). (1988). *Informal justice?* London: Sage.

Mills, C. (1997). *The racial contract.* Ithaca, NY: Cornell University Press.

Muncie, J., & Goldson, B. (2006). States of transition: Convergence and diversity in international youth justice. In J. Muncie & B. Goldson (Eds.), *Comparative youth justice* (pp. 196–218). London: Sage.

Neu, D. (1991). Trust, contracting and the prospectus process. *Accounting, Organizations and Society, 16*, 243–256.

O'Malley, P. (1992). Risk, power and crime prevention. *Economy and Society, 21*, 252–275.

O'Malley, P. (1999). Volatile and contradictory punishment. *Theoretical Criminology, 3*, 175–196.

O'Malley, P., & Hutchinson, S. (2007). Reinventing prevention: Why did "crime prevention" develop so late? *British Journal of Criminology, 47*, 373–389.

Pateman, C. (1988). *The sexual contract.* Cambridge: Polity Press.

Postman, N. (1982). *The disappearance of childhood.* New York: Delacorte Press.

Putnam, R. (2000). *Bowling alone: The collapse and revival of American community.* New York: Simon and Schuster.

Rose, N. (2000). Government and control. *British Journal of Criminology, 40*, 321–339.

Scottish Executive. (2005). *"Sticks and carrots": Guidance on acceptable behaviour contracts.* Edinburgh: Scottish Executive.

Shapland, J., Atkinson, A., Atkinson, H., Chapman, B., Colledge, E., Dignan, J., Howes, M., Johnstone, J., Robinson, G., & Sorsby, A. (2006). *Restorative justice in practice: Findings from the second stage of the evaluation of three schemes,* Research Findings 274. London: Home Office.

Shearing, C., & Stenning, P. (1983). Private security: Implications for social control. *Social Problems, 30*, 493–506.

Shearing, C., & Stenning, P. (1987). Say "cheese"!: The Disney order that is not so Mickey Mouse. In C. Shearing & P. Stenning (Eds.), *Private Policing* (pp. 317–323). London: Sage.

Sherman, L., & Strang, H. (2007). *Restorative justice: The evidence.* London: Smith Institute.

Smith, D. (2003). New Labour and youth justice. *Children & Society, 17*, 226–235.

Von Hirsch, A., & Simester, A. P. (Eds.). (2006). *Incivilities: Regulating offensive behaviour.* Oxford: Hart.

Weitekamp, E. G. M. (2002). Restorative justice: Present prospects and future directions. In E. G. M. Weitekamp & H.-J. Kerner (Eds.), *Restorative justice: Theoretical foundations* (pp. 322–338). Cullompton: Willan.

White, S. (2003). *The civic minimum.* Oxford: Oxford University Press.

Williams, F. (2004). *Rethinking families.* London: Calouste Gulbenkian Foundation.

Willis, P. (1977). *Learning to labour.* Farnborough, Hants: Saxon House.

Wilson, J. Q. (1975). *Thinking about crime.* New York: Vintage.

Wonnacott, C. (1999). The counterfeit contract—Reform, pretence and muddled principles in the new referral order. *Child and Family Law Quarterly, 11*, 271–287.

Yeatman, A. (1997). Contract, status and personhood. In G. Davis, B. Sullivan, & A. Yeatman (Eds.), *The new contractualism?* (pp. 39–56). Melbourne: Macmillan.

Youth Justice Board. (2007). *Youth Justice Annual Statistics 2005/06.* London: Youth Justice Board.

Zehr, H. (1990). *Changing lenses.* Scottdale, PA: Herald Press.

Restorative Justice: Five Dangers Ahead

9

NILS CHRISTIE*

Contents

Introduction

It is good to be back in Sheffield. It has taken some time—30 years, I understand. Then as now, the topic is conflicts. The question then was who owns the conflicts (Christie, 1977). Now, the question is: Are there dangers ahead?

During this period, restorative justice has been quite a remarkable growth area. The time was clearly ripe for it. Measured by the number of articles, books, small and large conferences, and most of all, in concrete initiatives, not much can compete with restorative justice among other fields of penal policy. Obviously, it has been a great success. However, nothing might fail like success. There are dangers ahead. These dangers will be my major theme in what follows, but first, I would like to provide some short remarks on why there has been this surge in interest for restorative justice— why the time was ripe.†

---

* He gave the foundation lecture of the then Centre for Criminological Studies at the University of Sheffield, United Kingdom, on March 31, 1976 (Christie 1977).
† See Christie (2007) for a more thorough discussion of these points.

Factors behind the Growth in Restorative Justice

First among the growth factors for interest in restorative justice has been that highly industrialized societies have been increasingly interested in and aware of their roots, examples being the Maoris in New Zealand, North American Indians, or Eskimos or Inuits in the far north. The culture of the original inhabitants has attracted more and more attention. Maybe there was after all something of value there? One of their values increasingly deemed useful for modernity has been seen to be their ways of solving internal conflicts, with the emphasis on creating peace rather than civil war.

Another factor behind the growth of restorative justice has to do with the demise of participation in local neighborhoods and their affairs. Informal types of social control are seen to be failing, with more people receiving various forms of formal punishments. The criminal courts have in this situation become machines of mass production.

To me, a third factor has been of particular importance for my interest in mediation. This is our loss of arenas for participation in modern life. We are less involved in each other's lives and also in each other's deaths, our own included, and only to a limited extent part of networks that have binding importance for us. If we want to preserve civil societies, it is essential to prevent the loss of all tasks of importance. Conflicts can function as gasoline for social life. It is therefore important to keep them as a driving force inside local communities.

I am not alone in these views. Therefore, there has been easy acceptance of some of such ideas about increasing participation in handling conflicts. Fine. But also not so fine. There are dangers ahead. These dangers will be my theme in what follows.

The Potential Dangers Ahead for Restorative Justice

Mediative Imperialism

One danger in the surge of interest and enthusiasm for restorative justice might simply be exaggerated expectations as to what can be accomplished, followed by what I would like to call mediative imperialism.

Central to this imperialism are claims that mediation can lead to the *abolition of penal law.* However, this is an impossible idea. Mediation or various forms of restorative justice can relieve the pressure on the criminal courts and sentencing but not abolish these courts. On the contrary, well-functioning penal courts are essential to protect some of the basic principles of mediation, particularly its noncompulsory nature. Sometimes it is impossible to get the parties to meet. Some potential participants would not dare to meet those they might have harmed. Some harmed people would not accept meeting those who are supposed to have done it. And some might insist in continuing what society in general saw as harmful behavior. Mediation cannot take place in such cases.

However, it cannot be denied that some participants in mediation are under considerable pressure to attend mediation meetings. If they were to decide not to participate, they might come to realize that a criminal prosecution will follow. But also a young person below the age of criminal responsibility might feel pressured to meet for mediation and may agree to repair or pay for damaged property. Yet, if they were first offenders below the age of criminal responsibility and the damage was not enormous, the case would in my country most probably just have been shelved by the prosecution rather than being prosecuted. The danger here is what Stan Cohen has baptized as "net widening."

A related danger is where the hidden agenda of mediation is in the delivery of pain—camouflaged as mediation.* Mediation might end up analogous to what so often has happened with various offers of "treatment" or "education" in the penal system. Because the goals of those making these offers were benevolent, it was not seen as essential to control the unpleasant aspects of these offers. Seen as punishment, 3 months in a closed institution might be seen as suitable retribution. Seen as a health or educational matter, years might be spent in the same institution and seen as equally suitable—now it is not punishment but a rehabilitation measure, it is all in the best interests of the person affected.

This leads to a related topic—the attempts to merge mediation and criminal justice.

Unsuitable Partners

Attempts are sometimes made to combine punishment and mediation. Several interesting examples can be found in chapters of the work of von Hirsch, Ashworth, and Shearing (2003). Two of the chapters can be seen as attempts to combine "the best" from criminal justice and restorative justice. In my view, we get the worst from both from the merged product.

First, there is an article by Antony Duff (2003). He demands retribution as an integral part of restoration. Restoration, he claims, "is not only compatible with retribution, it *requires* retribution" (emphasis original). Later, he says: "What they deserve to suffer is not just 'pain or a burden', but the particular kind of painful burden which is integral to the recognition of guilt: they deserve to suffer that because it is an appropriate response to their wrongdoing; and criminal mediation aims precisely to impose or induce that kind of suffering."

---

* I am grateful to Jane Dullum and Cecilie Høigård who on several occasions have insisted that we have to be aware of this danger.

What is proposed here by Antony Duff is simply a reintroduction of the major purpose of the penal system: the intentional delivery of pain. But why?* Why should retribution be a basic premise in mediation or restorative justice? Jewish/Christian ideas of punishment and pain and retribution after wrong acts have an enormous influence in our culture. Criminal justice has model power. However, there are alternative models around, models *saying no to vengeance*. Mahatma Gandhi lived until 1948; some Christian ideas of forgiveness are still alive. The growth in mediation or restorative justice might to a large extent be related to its crystallization of nonpunitive values. As for those who have been harmed: They will often have a greater thirst for knowledge than for vengeance.

Many among us might feel pain and be filled with guilt by having committed acts for which we are blamed, and we also may be blaming ourselves. However, a meeting with those we might have hurt is not necessarily painful and does not need to be. On the contrary, such a meeting might be felt as a great relief. Participating in such a meeting is also a chance to explain, maybe even to be forgiven. Such a meeting might fill the person with deep relief, even joy. If the person supposed to have committed an unwanted act leaves such a meeting filled with joy, realizing he had done something wrong but now extraordinarily happy because he has done the right thing, should she or he then—according to the recipe of Antony Duff—be brought to suffer by the other participants in the mediation?

Mediation contains four basic ideas:

- Revealing what happened, and why, as the parties see it.
- Healing wounds for both parties by listening to what they see as their reasons for what happened (one example from South Africa from a white policeman: "I thought in those days that apartheid was the only possibility. I now understand how wrong I was").
- Reestablishing values ("I agree," the robber might say, "I should not have threatened you, but I was not aware that you became that scared").
- Then, at the very center of it all, the creation of peace, bringing the conflict to an end. That might be no more of a peace than creating the possibility of living with the other person in one's neighborhood— maybe giving him a nod when passing in the street. But it might also mean much more. We had a victim of torture visiting us at our institute in Oslo. He told his story at a seminar. After the seminar, another man from the same country (Uruguay under the former dictatorship) came up and said that he had acted as a torturer. It all ended with the tortured man inviting the torturer out for coffee.

* I am heavily influenced by Hedda Giertsen for the reasoning on this point.

Antony Duff is not alone in this demand for retribution. In the same volume, Andrew von Hirsch with Andrew Ashworth and Clifford Shearing build explicitly on Antony Duff by introducing what they call the "making amends model." This, they say, "involves a response negotiated between the offender and his victim, which involves (1) the implicit or explicit acknowledgement of fault and (2) an apologetic stance on the part of the offender, ordinarily conveyed through having him undertake a reparative task."

Before I comment on their proposals, I have to make clear that these authors have considerable reservations against the system they introduce. They say "we are not ourselves advocating this model here; rather we wish to make heuristic use of it, to suggest how RJ's aims and limits might be specified more clearly." And, as will be understood, the clarification makes it—at least to me—very clear that the "making amends model" cannot work. (In a recent discussion with Andrew von Hirsch, I understood him to be agreeing with this.) They have launched a model designed to be considered and discussed.

Andrew von Hirsch and his colleagues are highly aware that in the "making amends model," delivery of pain intended as pain is initiated and that protection is needed. As a consequence, we are told that there "should be some explicit principles suggesting what kind of dispositions might be appropriate, and what kind might not be....Calling for such guidance will mean that some rule generating process needs to provide it, and will mean that the guidance will need to be set forth in some useful and readily available form."

Adopting this viewpoint would simply be to destroy some of the basic elements in mediation. Mediators have no sword in hand. They have very little power. They can suggest, but not decide, particularly not decide, on the delivery of pain. They are therefore forced to come close to the parties, and also enabled to do so, and thereby see the conflicts as the parties see them. What is relevant in this process is what the parties see as relevant. It cannot be decided beforehand by those outside the conflict. There are of course limits also for mediators. This is one of the reasons for preserving the criminal courts as alternatives.

In this situation, it would be highly counterproductive to use the terminology from criminal justice, particularly to force the parties into categories such as *victim* and *offender*. Such terms contain a built-in conclusion. In contrast to this, it is central to mediation to emphasize "information as the parties see it," that is, to bring to the forefront the meaning the acts have for the participants and to obtain their stories in their own words. This process opens up new insights. So often, it is not the concrete acts that are disputed but the meaning of these acts, how they were intended, how they turned out, and how they later on were perceived.

For criminal justice, the situation is completely different. The legal system cannot create, and uphold, an image of equality that has a great number of elements to be compared. Lawyers are forced to limit the amount of information to be compared. With this small amount of information, they are able to construct what they see as equal cases—deserving equal suffering. Sentencing tables have grown out of the need for such reduction of information. Legal training is a systematic training in what is not to be accepted as arguments. The rules are decided from above: Moses against the people. In contrast, in mediation, it is the parties close to the events that should decide the relevance of arguments and the final result. Sentencing tables might prevent grave abuses in sentencing. However, they also prevent broad participatory discussions of moral questions. To lose the possibilities of such discussion, here exemplified in occasions for mediation or restorative justice, would mean a grave loss of arenas for moral clarification.

With modernity, we are in a situation where criminal justice systems are converted to systems for mass production. We need to stop this by bringing more social control back to ordinary people and thereby also strengthen civil society. However, if we do so, then the power to punish must be kept far away from the mediators. Intentional delivery of pain must be left to those specially trained to handle this task. To me, it seems as if Antony Duff and Andrew von Hirsch and his collaborators—if their models were to be realized—would reinvent the criminal courts. With models based on "retribution" or "making amends," the intended suffering becomes clear and so also the need for regulating the delivery of this pain.

My preliminary conclusion on this point would be: Give law what law can handle, but give ordinary people what ordinary people can handle; indeed, what they need to handle if our societies are not to be converted to nonsocieties, suffocated by experts.

Professionalization

A third danger for the future of restorative justice is increasing professionalization of the activity. Many want to join in with the increasing activity of restorative justice—the first professors in mediation are in post, and professional mediators are appearing in many countries. Professional standards are being developed. In 2006, I attended the Fourth Nordic Conference in Mediation and Conflict Management in Helsinki. A special session discussed guidelines for the practice of mediation. Educational requirements for mediators were raised, as well as potential quality control systems for mediation practice.

One driving force behind this professionalization is the recent explosion in higher education. An increasing part of the population is taking high school or university exams, often of an unspecified type. This means that they are highly educated for tasks not yet specified. Mediation is an obvious possibility for future jobs. It is a territory not yet occupied, except by lawyers. Handling conflicts is the new land of promise—entrepreneurs arrive, create training courses, establish firms—and little by little, a new profession of mediators comes into being. One more specialty. I warned against lawyers here in Sheffield 30 years ago and called them professional thieves (Christie, 1977). They still are but are now followed by a flock of well-educated generalists on the outlook for challenging tasks that it may be possible to convert into paid work.

If there were a considerable degree of professionalization of restorative justice, yet one more challenge would be removed from civil society. One more of those tasks that folks of all sorts could unite around would vanish. Ordinary people will hear that professional mediators know best, and abdicate. Soon there would be no tasks left in the neighborhood, and we can safely retreat to privacy and leave everything else to experts. They certainly know what is best. Mediation is only one example of a general development. With the explosion in higher education, a great number of activities are being taken away from ordinary people.

It might prove fruitful to think of three types of capital: money capital, social capital, and formal educational capital. Within all these sectors, there are great differences in how much of this capital a person perceives as being his own property. There are rich people within all forms, and there are also poor people. Mostly, those at the bottom in relation to one form are also at the bottom of the two others, with one exception: those with little money capital live sometimes in neighborhoods that make them rich on social capital. So rich that the money people may start moving in and taking over the area, as in lower Manhattan in New York and Chelsea in London. Most large cities have the same experience. Gentrification is the neutral name for the process whereby poor people lose their social capital. With the recent explosion in higher education, they lose out again. Those with little formal education often have a considerable amount of nonauthorized knowledge if they still live in reasonably stable neighborhoods. Maybe we could call it "life knowledge"— experience exchanged and elaborated over the kitchen table, in the streets, or in the pub. Bourdieu calls it "practical knowledge." However, with higher education being experienced by so many, and with neighborhoods emptied of tasks that can be undertaken there, the space for acquiring that sort of knowledge and for applying it is also lost. There are so many experts around. Why interfere when experts know better. They are certified to know better.

The Bookkeepers and Their Relatives

With growth, the bookkeepers and accountants also arrive. We need to know what is going on, and the bookkeepers need concepts that define what they are counting. I met this problem in the very first annual reports from our state system for mediation in Norway. The bookkeepers used concepts such as "offender" and "victims" and reported cases as being "solved" or "not solved." However, this terminology goes against the central ideas of mediation. At the core of a mediative process lies the intention to bring variations in meanings out in the open and thereby also open the possibility of changes to the meaning given to the acts by one or both parties. A theft is not always a theft—when the panorama of needs of participants is revealed.

Bookkeepers have relatives among social scientists. Discussing mediation, one is nearly always met with questions about efficiency. But, this is a narrowly conceived idea of efficiency. It asks: How many conflicts are solved? Or, if cases are diverted from police or prosecutors, as it is to some extent possible to do in Norway, questions are raised about recidivism rates. What happens later in these cases? How many "offenders" appear later in police registers of crimes; how many end up in prison? How does this compare with sanctions used in the criminal justice system?

These are legitimate questions, but they are dangerous if allowed to be the key indicators. As I have tried to describe above, mediation carried out by local people in local neighborhoods might represent a force to strengthen that particular neighborhood. In this situation, I am tempted to say that even with greater recidivism after mediation than after sentencing through the criminal justice system, mediation might be preferable. A gang war might have been prevented through mediation.

Equally, one might look to even broader questions. One might look at South Africa and ask: What would have been the alternative to peace and reconciliation? Some of the later critiques of the process have been justified; particularly the lack of compensation to the most suffering parties, but this has to be weighted against the potential horrors in a civil war. The effects of lack of mediation can be seen from some of the present horrors in Lebanon, Palestine, Iraq, and Afghanistan. From a perspective of mediation, September 11th might be seen as a case well suited to mediation, a case between New York and Kabul.

International Criminal Courts—A Setback for Peace Making

This leads me to the last danger threatening the very idea of mediation and peace making more recently. This is the expansion of international criminal courts.

Here, I will limit myself to an authoritarian provocation by claiming that the growth of international criminal courts represents a setback for the basic ideas of peace making and ideals of restorative justice. From the Nuremberg courts after World War II up to the present UN criminal courts for Yugoslavia and Rwanda, these courts have strengthened the idea that punishment is the only natural answer to atrocities, that impunity is unacceptable, and that some selected persons ought to receive a maximum of intended pain to make things right. International criminal courts prevent us from seeing the conflicts in a broader and politically relevant perspective. They may also prolong ongoing conflicts, as exemplified in Uganda where "Britain has been accused of hindering attempts to end the 20 years civil war in northern Uganda by insisting that leading rebels be arrested and tried for war crimes."* Similar problems appeared in conflicts inside the old Yugoslavia. International criminal courts are also in danger of blocking the way toward establishing commissions for peace and reconciliation. In the fight for human rights and decency, it is as if Amnesty International and other pressure groups willingly accept—and thereby give increased credibility to—those tools for the delivery of pain they usually detest. Their flat acceptance of international criminal courts is a setback for attempts to move conflicts from institutions for pain delivery to institutions for mediation.

References

Christie, N. (1977). Conflicts as property. *British Journal of Criminology, 17,* 1–15.

Christie, N. (2007). Restorative justice—Answers to deficits in modernity? In D. Downes, P. Rock, C. Chinkin, & C. Gearty (Eds.), *Crime, social control and human rights. From moral panics to states of denial. Essays in honour of Stanley Cohen* (pp. 368–378). Cullompton: Willan.

Duff, A. (2003). Restoration and retribution. In A. von Hirsch, J. Roberts, A.E. Bottoms, K. Roach, & M. Schiff (Eds.), *Restorative justice and criminal justice: Competing or reconcilable paradigms?* (pp. 44–59). Oxford: Hart.

von Hirsch, A., Ashworth, A., & Shearing, C. (2003). Specifying aims and limits for restorative justice. A 'making amends' model? In A. von Hirsch, J. Roberts, A. E. Bottoms, K. Roach, & M. Schiff (Eds.), *Restorative justice and criminal justice. Competing or reconcilable paradigms?* (pp. 21–41). Oxford: Hart.

* *Guardian Weekly* (2006, September 1–7, p. 7).

Index

A

Aas, Franko, xxiv, 107
Academic criminology
  business trade, xxvii
  knowledge for crime reduction, xxii
  media-based criminology, xix
Accountability, 143, 160
A certificate (public), 59, 61
Acquittals, 8, 12
Activist critics
  comics, 63–64
  film, 60–61
  video nasties, 68–69
Actuarial justice, 179
Adaptations, 172–174
Advertising Standards Authority, 66
Afghanistan, 202
Against Criminology, viii
Agger studies, 105
Aggression, media violence, 70
Agreements, restorative, 170
Ainsworth, William Harrison, 18
Aldana-Pindell studies, 149
Alexander II (Nikolaevich), Tsar, 87
Alien criminality, 91–94
Aliens Act (1905), 78, 93–94, 96
Aliens Branch and Criminal Record Office,
  81
Allaker and Shapland studies, xx
Allen, Edmonds, Patterson and Smith
  studies, 134
Alsatia, 2
Alton, David, 68
Amnesty International, 203
Anarchist criminality, 87–91
Anderson, Robert, 78, 83, 90–93
Anderson studies, 56, 84–85, 94
*An Enquiry into the Causes of the
  Late Increase of Robbers,* 4–5, 16

Angel studies, 141
Angle, Malam and Carey studies, 154
Anthropometric systems, 79–80
AntiSocial Behavior Act (2003), 186
Antisocial behavior interventions
  compliance, 186–189
  contractual governance, 176–179, 181–184
  fundamentals, 167–172, 189–191
  individualization, 179–181
  new technologies, 172–174
  politics of behavior, 175–176
  rights and responsibilities, 184–186
  young people, 181–186
Apologies, 136–137, 155
Arbeter Fraint, 88
Aries studies, 182
Armstrong, Gary, xii
Armstrong, Norris and, studies, 78
Arnold, Liebling and, studies, 142
Arnot studies, 180
Ashworth, Andrew, 199
Ashworth, Zedner and, studies, xvi
Ashworth and Shearing, Hirsch, studies, 197
Ashworth studies, 153
Asquith, Herbert, 85, 89
Attitudinal resistance, 161
Australia
  conferencing/direct mediation, 123
  Justice Research Consortium, 126
  longitudinal study, 40
  media-based criminology, xvii
  repeat victimization studies, 33
  restorative justice and practices, 124
  symbolic reparation, 139
  video nasties, 69
Austria-Hungary, 78
Automated sociotechnical system, 103
Autonomie Club, 88–89, 90n